OPUS REFORMATUM
OR, A
TREATISE
OF
ASTROLOGY.

IN WHICH

The Common Errors of that Art are Modestly Exposed and Rejected.

With an ESSAY towards the Reviving the True and Ancient Method laid down for our Direction by the GREAT PTOLOMY, and more agreeable to the Principles of Motion and Nature, than that commonly Practised and Taught.

In Two PARTS.

By JOHN PARTRIDGE, Physician to Her Present Majesty, and Student in Astrology.

Post Nubila Phœbus.

LONDON,
Printed for *Awnsham* and *John Churchill* at the *Black-Swan* in *Pater-Noster-Row.* MDCXCIII.

Kessinger Publishing's Rare Reprints
Thousands of Scarce and Hard-to-Find Books!

We kindly invite you to view our extensive catalog list at:
http://www.kessinger.net

Printing Statement:

Due to the very old age and scarcity of this book, many of the pages may be hard to read due to the blurring of the original text, possible missing pages, missing text and other issues beyond our control.

Because this is such an important and rare work, we believe it is best to reproduce this book regardless of its original condition.

Thank you for your understanding.

TO THE
READERS.

GENTLEMEN,

THO. I have here detected and discovered divers Errors in the Study and Practice of Astrology, especially in that Part of it that concerns Nativities; and also spoke slightly of some Authors who are much valued, and in great esteem among divers Practitioners; and likewise condemned their Writings, as being filled with little else but Errors and idle Innovations; which are indeed but the same thing, if rightly considered. Yet I would not be misunderstood in what I have here done; and thought (because I charge so many with Mistakes) that I think my self free from Faults, Errors, and Oversights, either in my Practice or Writings; or that I intend to direct and teach the Students in this Art to endeavour after such a Perfection: No, I know too well, that Over-sights and deceptio sensus, is too true, and too visible a Character of Human Nature; and to Err, is the known and common Calamity that Mankind is subject to; for besides the Infirmities of our Constitutions, the Depravity of our Wills and Affections, the Obscurity of our Understanding, and the Weakness of our Judgments; The Curse on our Original Parents for their Transgression at the beginning seems still to lye heavy on our Shoulders, and tells us plainly, That Sorrow and Sweat,

A 2   Thorns

To the Readers.

Thorns and Thistles, Life and Error, are inseperable. But yet there is a difference between the Errors of Nature, *contra voluntatem,* and the Errors of Practice, introduced by Custom and Discipline. And these are they that I contend against, and endeavour to reform, tho the other also ought not to be forgotten.

Nor would I have any one think, that I intend to destroy the Art of Astrology by what I have here done; no, I do assure you, that this is the least of my thoughts; nor would I impair any part of it that I judge useful and serviceable, either for its Support or Reputation. But my real Intent and Design is to excite the Lovers of this Contemptible Science, to refine it, and make it more coherent in its Principles, and more certain in its Use and Practice, than it is at present; and also to lay by those Idle Notions and Practices used therein, which have drawn the Objections of Learned Pens upon us. For tho I am not willing to swallow down those fulsom Errors with which it is clog'd and loaded; it doth not therefore follow, that I am an Enemy to its Truth and Excellence, and must be debarred my Inquiry towards its Perfection, and not permitted to approach the Spring of its Original Truth. I doubt not but you may find some Errors in this Treatise, which you may impute either to my Oversight, or want of Skill, which you please; yet I hope they may deserve your Excuse and Pardon, especially when you consider, that I have undertaken to turn the Torrent of a mighty Stream, and that with such little Assistance as I have received: I being indebted to no Man for any service or help therein, but to my Honoured Friend and Late Deceased Master, Dr. Francis Wright, by whose Instructions only, I own my self enabled to perform this, and what I have else at present under my Consideration for the Press. But for my Errors (if any shall think them

To the Readers.

so) laid down in Practice, by way of Rule, I desire no excuse for them, but refer them to your Consideration, and for that very purpose I have printed them here, and also hope, that those Gentlemen that think them so, will be pleased to inform my Understanding, and give me better Notions in print, with better Proofs for their Doctrine, than I have given for mine; and I do assure them, I will readily submit and cry Peccavi. And so I come to speak particularly.

First To the Book it self. In which thou hast the whole Mystery of Astrology relating to Nativities, according as I understand it; but it is dispersed here and there throughout the whole Book and Matter also, and will take thee some time and pains too, to collect and digest it into a method for Practice, which is no hard matter, if thou art but willing to take a little pains; and without pains, I can assure thee, thou wilt prove but a very ordinary Artist in thy Profession. I have there given thee the Nativity of Oliver Cromwell, with my Reasons for it's Correction, and also his Disease, by which he expired; with a Table of Directions from his Birth to his Death; with each Ark, its true Measure, and the Year of our Lord when it did begin to operate. I have also shewed the incoherence of those Rules laid down on several Occasions, not only in his Nativity, but in divers others; and the just Cause our Enemies have from thence to Cavil at, and ridicule the Art and its Professors. I have also throughout that Nativity, on my Judgment thereon, wholly dissented from the Common Method now practised; and where I have so done, I have also given you the Text of Ptolomy for my Justification to prevent my being question'd in print; that those who think my Method new, may examine that Author, and see whether I have done him and the Art

To the Readers.

it self Justice or not. I have also shew'd you the excellent use of the Hileg, and the vanity of their calling the Lord of the Eighth, the Anareta, and judging the Quality of Death from his Nature and Position. And indeed, I have been plain in every thing else useful in the Judgment of a Nativity, with my particular Opinion and Method, that I use in all Revolutional Figures, and also how to take them. And to tell you plainly, all other Methods are really Innovations, and new Projects without any ground from Authors of Authority.

In the Second Part, I have endeavoured to shew you, That the opinion of Cardinal Signs on Angles, according to Mr. Gadbury's Opinion in his Cardines Cœli, is vain and groundless; and the Arguments and Aphorisms he brings to prove it, are lug'd in by Head and Shoulders, and of no Validity to that purpose: and that the Nativities brought to that end, are also fictitious. In the Supplement I have given you several Nativities out of Heminga, that he brings as Arguments against Astrology, because he could find no Reasons directional for their Deaths, Sickness, and other things in his way of Astrology, which I have endeavoured here to shew was no hard thing to do, and in particular, in that Nativity of Cardan's Son, about which both he and Alexander de Angelis, do sufficiently abuse the Astrologers, and the Art, because there was no Direction found for his Death, either by his Father, Maginus, or Naibod, three Great Men in their Times. It was first printed by Placidus de Titis, in his Primum Mobile, which may admit of a Correction, as may be seen by that printed in this Book; and yet we both keep exactly to Cardan's estimate Time, as may be seen also by his own Figure in his Comment on Ptolomy, Lib. 3. Cap. 14. Aand indeed, I could have given you di-

vers

To the Readers.

vers more out of Heminga, *were I not certain that some of them are false, and sure he took them upon Trust. In the whole thing there is much Variety, both in the Matter and Method, and these founded on very good Principles which I shall deliver more methodically hereafter, according as I shall find this is received in the World. I do not pretend, that either the Matter or Method is either of them new, but only the old ones revived; and to say the truth, it is so old, that I can safely say, it is forgot, and the whole of it will seem strange to this Age. Which I humbly offer to the consideration of the Ingenious Students, and intreat every one to examine it seriously and deliberately before he gives a determinate Judgment, either in Approbation or Exprobation of what I have here done.*

Secondly, *To the Studious Lovers of* Astrology *in General. I hope Gentlemen, there will be no need to perswade you with Arguments, either to believe, or assert the Truth of Astrology; especially you that have already had a prospect of it from the Top of* Pisgah, *and have also a better opinion of its Truth and Excellence, than you are able to demonstrate to the Unbelievers; by Examples of your own; fair Predictions (I mean) of the Effects of any Direction before the Accidents happened, for it is that must give your Art a Reputation. And yet I judge it may not be wholly improper to perswade you to a greater diligence and labour in your several Methods of Practice in that Art; not so much for the discovery of New Whims and Notions, without either Ground or Reason, and some of them not at all understood by their Inventors and Teachers; But for improving those we have already in our Possession, and to try whether they will stand the Test of Examples and Examinations in several Nativities; not to spend*

time

To the Readers.

time in making a noise about a thing but little known, and perhaps less understood; but to work, and by the variety of Examples, to try and compare one with another; and at last, see how their Rules will agree in the general; for I can assure you, one hour spent that way, shall teach you more substantial Knowledge in these things, than a whole days praising. And to this end, it is not a rush matter what your Principles are, whether Geocentrick, Heliocentrick, or Selenocentrick; nor whether their Directions are Direct, Convers, Rapt, or Secondary, wrought in Mundo or Zodiaco, in the Crepusculine Circles, or the Obscure Arks, so you will but make your Doctrine all of a piece; and let your Directions do the same at one time, that they do at another, and not give something in one Nativity, and miss in Twenty others, when you try them again. And to this purpose, I do advise you not to rely on your Authors, nor take up their Rules in your Practice, without examining their Ability and Truth. For I can assure you, That all the Principal Authors of the last Century, and more (except two or three) have done very little for the Art of Astrology, unless it was to make it Ridiculous and Contemptible; so that those who are disposed to laugh at Astrology, need not read Heminga, Alexander de Angelis, Chambers, and the rest of them that have ridicul'd it in Print; but have recourse to our own Authors, and consider and compare them well, and they will find fooleries sufficient for their purpose and design that way, be it what it will. Our Rules in Judgment are so deficient, that they are generally not to be rely'd on; and what is more, one thwarts another, by which means the Young Students know not which to believe or follow. Our new-made Aphorisms are so false, that not one in ten of them will hold according to the Text given for our Direction and Guide. In the Effects

of

To the Readers.

of Directions they have followed Matchivel's Rule (Throw dirt enough, and some will stick); nam'd abundance of Accidents to attend each Direction, and the Devil's in't if some of them do not happen to take effect. But in the Directions assigned for all kind of Accidents, Death, &c. there they have out-done themselves; and so involv'd us into a Labyrinth of Confusion, that we are not able to understand them if we will make Reason our Guide, and compare one thing with another. Therefore pray Gentlemen, take it into your Consideration, and let something be done, that the next Age may be better inform'd by you, than we were by that which went before us. Let us have less Volumes, and more Truth; fewer Rules, and more to the purpose; plainer Directions how to work with fewer Contradictions; refine the Art, and reject those Fooleries it is loaded with; assert its Truths, and declaim its Errors, and then it will appear to be what we tell the World it is, and would have it thought to be. Nay, let us have all the New Inventions likewise that can be discovered, provided they are true. There is one thing more, Gentlemen, that I would say to you, and that is, Do not hug Innovations for no other Reason but because they are new; That trick hath been too often put upon us already, and even by those too, that knew very little of the matter; and had as little skill, as those that endeavoured to follow their Directions; by which means and ways our Erroneous Confusions were not a little increased. Nor would I advise you to be afraid of any thing that is new, because it is so; bring it to the Touchstone and try it; and that is to be done no otherways, but by Labour and Experience; for if the thing it self hath a good Bottom, and seems rational, it may prove worth your while to examine it. And by this way I intreat you to put what I have done to the tryal, and if it will not hold, and in the general stand

a the

the *Test*, I shall be ready to recant and beg your better *Information*.

Thirdly, To the Enemies of Astrology, to whom, tho I am not obliged either by *Kindness* or *Duty*, yet I have a few words to say, tho I do not expect to make one Convert by my so doing. It is the hard Fate of Astrology and Astrologers to undergo the severe Censure of you, Gentlemen, who never knew any thing of it, but its Name; and I am confident, some of you do not know one Character from another, nor did you ever yet arrive at that Skill to erect a Scheme of Heaven, which if you did, yet they are very small Abilities to entitle any man to be Judge of a thing he is so little acquainted with; as I am certain the Major part are, that pretend to ridicule this Study. For whatever the Common Professors pretend to, either by false Notions, or worse Practice, I own it, and study it no otherways than a Branch of Natural Philosophy, and do think it is no hard matter to give it a fair Foundation on very rational Principles, and those I think demonstrable too without any great Difficulty and Trouble; and they are Motion, Rays, and Influence; and these in that Part of Astrology that takes notice of Nativities in particular; which Part of it I have made most generally my Study; and for the other Parts of it, let those who have imploy'd themselves therein, take the same care to justify it both by Examples and Rules. And I do believe that this of Nativities being done, will give some Reputation to the other Parts of Astrology likewise; and this at present is fallen under my Consideration, tho I believe there are some far more able than my self to do it, if they were pleased to take the trouble of such a Work upon them.

And whatever your Assertions are of its being forbidden in Sacred Writ, they are really false, and do not any more

prohibit

To the Readers.

prohibit that, than the Command given to the Prophet Hosea to Marry a Whore, did justify Whoredom; for what is said there against it, doth only reprove the Pretenders abuse of it, and the Peoples superstitious dependance thereon; which every honest Artist will disown at this day, that believes the Power of an Eternal God.

Neither can it be an Enemy to Religion and Piety; for by how much the more every good Man knows the Mysteries of Nature in her various Ways and Operations, by so much the more it will bring him to admire and contemplate that undeniable Power of the Tremendus Deity that first gave it its Being and Order; and we see daily when the best of things fall into the Hands of Ill Men, what a Scandalous Account they give of them, and pervert their lawful Use. Hence there is no reason to believe, that the Abuse of Virtue, or any other useful thing, pleads its Prohibition, either by Law or Arguments; if so, farewell Food and Physick.

And besides, if we should allow (what some of you say) that there is no verity in it, yet that neither doth not proclaim it unlawful, but justly reprehends us for spending so much time in a thing void of truth, and would draw from good Men rather Pity than Scorn; but we desire neither, being able to justify its Truth, and that it is of more worth and use than some Studies that carry a greater Applause and Repute; concerning which, I hope something will be done hereafter.

But your great Objection that makes it Ridiculous and Scandalous, I must acknowledge is too true, That many of its Pretenders tell the World they can do things that are impossible, and under the pretence of *Astrology* act abundance of Villanies: And those, perhaps, ignorant of the Study, do not know to the contrary, but that such things are prescribed by its Rules and Rudiments. And seeing they

á 2

have

To the Readers.

have the Impudence to act such things, I hope it will be no Offence to the World to know some of them, nor to any honest Artist to hear it told; and therefore take these few, and judge by them what they are that use such Roguish Tricks.

There is a little Ruddy-fac'd Conjurer, who in my hearing had the Impudence (I being unknown to him) to tell the Company that he could do several things out of his Power; and at last said, That he could raise Spirits; and that if any of the Company would come to him one at a time, he would shew them a Spirit that should appear fairly on the Table. So I advised them to go, which they did, and always when they came, he put them off with a Roguish Excuse, till he had tired them, and so they went no more.

The same Man had a Woman came to him out of Southwark to ask him a Question; and that was, If her Misfortunes were all over, he told her, no, they were not, but he had an Art to make them go off quickly, which she desired: So having extorted a Fee for his Figure, told her, she must sit down and pare the Nails of her Fingers and Toes, and leave him six Shillings more to buy six Ounces of Aquafortis; and by setting them in a Sand-heat, as her Nails consum'd, so should her Misfortunes; all which the Woman did. Then he bid her remove from her House to another, and he would come and write something behind the Door that should make her fortunate. And a Month after, she sent a Friend to him, to know how it went on; so he went down Stairs pretending to see, and came up again and told her it went on very well; but the poor Woman is still as she was, poor and unhappy.

Mrs. B. in Holbourn took 3 l. of a Maid, to make her Sweet-heart Love and Marry her, who had then got a new Mistress, and left the former; the Maid finding her self cheated,

To the Readers.

cheated, *went to a Fellow about* White-Chappel, *who took* 10 s. *of her to make the other Cheat bring the* 3 l. *again: You may guess at the Consequence.*

There is one Ignorant Confident Fellow, that gives a Paper folded up and seal'd, for which he Bubbles some of 5, and some of 10 s a piece for them; and this is to make Men and Women love one another in order to Marriage, and to procure Lascivious Meetings, &c. and to make People fortunate. Thus he served a poor Maid in the Minories, and cheated her with them so long as she would find Money, and believe his Lies.

Others, and I could name them too, pretend to fetch People back that are absent or run away, and this by force of Magick as they call it; to take off Witch-craft from those they say are Bewitched; and also to promote or prevent Copulation, according to their Clients desire, either out of Love or Malice to those they intend it; with abundance more of such stuff, as I could relate, that is practised under the pretence of Astrology, by a Crew of Scandalous Cheats. Yet I hope, Gentlemen, you will not call this Astrology, but Cheating, Roguery, and Abuse, both on the Art; and the People, and therefore I would intreat you to consider what it is you would condemn, before you take the Seat of Justice, and pass the severe Sentence against that, which I am sure at present you do not understand.

Lastly, *Since these Sheets were printing, there is* a Treatise *come to my hand from* Padua, *written by one* Antonius Franciscus de Bonattis, *in which he gives us a new Method of Directions, but not by him (he says) invented, but by his Master* Confalonerius; *and because the thing is wholly New, and as yet strange to this Nation, there being no other of those Books in* England *but mine, I believe, and am partly sure; therefore I will give you one Operation in the Protector* Cromwell's *Nativity, according to his method, and it shall*

be

To the Readers.

be full as plain as those he hath given in his Book, without any Direction to understand them. And it is of the Sun to the Body of Saturn *at the time of his Death, in his Method and Operation, and to that end you must know that* Cromwell *lived* 59 *Years,* 4 *Months, and* 8 *Days.*

The Sem. Noct. Ark *of the* Radix, *is* 4162. *which gives the Suns distance from the Fifth House* 2045. *The* Sem. Noct. Ark *of the Direction, is* 3417. *hence it gives the distance of the Sun from the Fifth House,* 1679. *or* 27 d. 39 m. *which added to the place of the Direction, leaves the Cusp of the Fifth House in* 7 *degrees* 19 *minutes of* Leo, *as you may see by the following Figure and Direction together. For by a Figure he always explains and demonstrates his Directions; and indeed this Direction agrees to the time of* 59 *Years,* 4 *Months, and odd days.*

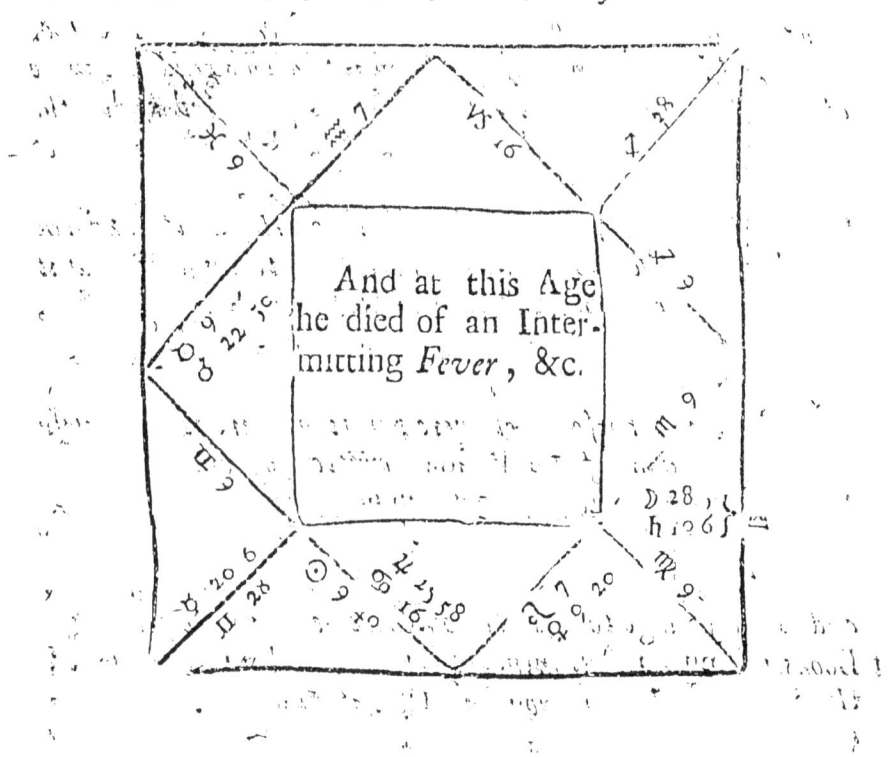

And at this Age he died of an Intermitting *Fever*, &c.

Thus,

To the Readers. xiii

Thus, Reader, I have given thee, with this Curiosity, a short Account of the Book, and desire thee to read it impartially, and consider the Matter and Design of it, to the end I have writ it. Correct the Errors that have slipt the Press, which are not many, yet perhaps there may be more than I have observed; Deal by me as you would have another do by you in the like Case. I beg no Pity, but Justice; use me genteelly, and it shall be a further Obligation

To your Friend,

JOHN PARTRIDGE.

Correct the Errors following, that have escaped the Press.

PAge 5 line 31. read *Trims.* p 9 l. 22. r. *overflow* p. 13. l. 36. r. *he aims at.* p. 25. in the Scheam, r. ☉ 13.55. p 31 l.2.r. *Horary times* p 41. l 14. r. *occasus* p 80. l. 30. r. *dominium* p 81. l. 14. r. *'Tis* p. 84. l. 22. r. *Jupiter in Libra.* p 95. l. 6. r. *variata* p. 115 l. 20. r. *want,* p 135. l. 31. r. *are hindred.* p. 155. l. 15. r. *for that year.*

OPUS REFORMATUM

I Shall not enter into an Argumental Contest about the Art of Astrology in general, but leave that Work for the more florid Pens to discuss. Neither will I at this time undertake to demonstrate the Motion by which Directions are made, nor the Principles of this Art; nor yet those things that we call Causes Astrological; they being not only intended, but also more proper for another Treatise: I having designed here to shew some of those visible (I had almost said palpable) Absurdities, that some of the greatest Professors, not only of our own Nation, but others also, may justly be accused of. Now, if Directions, those things that we call Causes of Accidents in the Life of Man, do really produce an Effect at any time, then must they certainly at all times give something proportional to their Natures, and the Adjuncts that do attend them, or else some Rules of Exceptions laid down, by which we may judge and distinguish when they will or will not answer the Rules given us by our Authors on the Effects of Directions. I know very well, that the same Direction shall not have the same Effect at one time that it hath at another, and I think I know the reason why; but yet there shall be an Effect, and such a one too, as shall be agreeable to its own nature, and part of Heaven. And to this purpose, *Guido Bonatus* speaking of things of this kind, says, *Causa enim perfecta, perfectum inducit Effectum*: Which is indeed really true, not only in this of Astrology, but also in all other Philosophick matters in nature. For if we own a thing to be the real Cause of any other thing at one time, when perhaps it shall pass by twenty times afterward without the least show of an Effect; is to tell the World in plain terms, That we neither know nor understand what we mean ourselves; or else by reason of our Ignorance we are not able to distinguish between a Cause

and

and an Effect, according to our own Principles in that Art which we pretend to; which gives our Adversaries just Cause to say, *Aut enim Astrologi non Intelligunt, aut si-Intelligunt graviter Errant.*

For I am persuaded, if the Astrologers, or such as are so esteemed, were asked, How many of those Directions, that they call Mortal ones, have in divers Nativities passed over without giving Death, or any Disease to the Injury of the Body; they would be apt to confess, As many of them have missed as hit, and yet they are very well satisfied with their method, and go on as confidently, as if they had never found either error or disappointment, as you shall find That further examined and proved throughout this Treatise; for I have made choice of this Subject, as the properest I could pitch upon to bring me readily to the point in hand, that is, to expose these Fooleries and Absurdities, which I find not in one, but most of our Authors: Nay, our Enemies too are not without their Absurdities, as we may see by *Heminga* in the Nativity of Pope *Paul* the Third, page 92, wherein among the rest of his Objections, he tells us of some reputed dangerous Directions that the Pope had passed, and yet did no injury to his Life; and one of those he mentions, was the *Ascendent* to his own *Square*; *A very learned Objection!* And I think no ways likely to give any thing good or bad, and therefore muchless Death; but I do not so much blame *Heminga* (tho' a very Learned Man, and well read in the Art of Astrology) as I do *Ceresarius* of *Mantua*, who wrote the Predictions that *Heminga* carps at, in which he hath these words, *D. V. R. graviter se habebit cum magno Vitæ discrimine quæ dies erit 4 vel 5 Maii, 1549. ex directione Horoscopi ad suum trinum qui pro quadrato habetur, eo quia est in signis brevium Ascensionum.* I must needs say, it is a very odd sort of Astrology to my ears, to hear them talk of the Ascendant to its own Trine, and this by so eminent a Man as *Paris Ceresarius* was; and what is yet more strange, that he should from hence predict danger of Death. And besides, we find the same thing printed in *Cardan* about this Popes Nativity, where he takes some little notice about those Directions, but says not one word of that about the Ascendant to his own Trine, which makes me doubt whether he did not countenance that Opinion also. Now, pray let me ask any man what can be expected from such like Directions as these? and whether the *Sextiles*, *Squares* and *Trines* of the *Dragons Head* and

Opus Reformatum.

and *Tail*, are not as proper and effectual as these are? For tho' I do allow that there are such points, as *Sextiles*, *Squares*, and *Trines* to the *Ascendant*, *Midheaven*, &c. taken *in Mundo*, or at leastwise in their imaginary way in the *Zodiack*, yet what is there to irradiate those points or parts of the Heavens? for the Ascendant and Tenth can emit no Rays, and therefore can give no Power to the other parts of Heaven to become serviceable after this manner as they pretend to; therefore I say, if these Points were ever fit for the use here pretended, they must be ever so in some measure, more or less; but in all my Practice I could never find it; and I am sure there is no ground nor reason to believe it, let them say what they will; yet by these and such-like ways, young Students are seduced and led by the Nose with these Tongs of Authority. And therefore let this serve for an Instance in general, That there are Methods used, which are both Vain and Improbable; for every Cause must have its Effect, or else it is no Cause.

To these I might add those Directions that are so often made use of in all Nativities, and with as little success as these are, as will appear by what follows, so far as it concerns this Nativity I am about to handle. For if we allow those Reasons there alledged to be true, then we shall find abundance of Nativities to be above the Order of Nature, and reach of the Stars, or else the Stars have done their duty negligently and by halves, when we shall find so many people have escaped the Ascendant to the Squares and Oppositions of *Saturn* and *Mars*, and this poor Gentleman fall by it, which is indeed a perfect piece of Impossibility, if the Rules of the best Masters of it are true, and the Experience of those that have tried them, the same. Now to satisfie you yet further, that their Directions for Sickness, Death, and other Accidents, are generally vain and impertinent, and that there are very few, if any of them, that are really setled in their own judgment and opinion, how to determine those things according to Rule and regular Method; do but carry a Nativity of any person that is dead, to any of them, and desire the Reason of his Death Astrologically, they shall immediately give you some sham story or other either of the Moon to the Square or Opposition of *Jupiter* and *Venus*, Rulers of the Eighth House, the Ascendant to the *Dragons-Tail*, or to the *Antiscion* of some ill natur'd Star; nay, they shall assign you some Direction to the Ascendant to kill, when the Sun and Moon are both in Aphetical places; or else

else Directions to the Sun or Moon, placed in the Third, Fourth, or Fifth Houses under the Earth, which are indeed neither agreeable to Reason, Nature, nor their own Rules published from their own hands: For do they not tell you long stories of the *Sun, Moon*, and *Ascendant*, (and some the *Midheaven*) being *givers* of *Life?* And did you ever know them keep to the use of them, unless it was to serve a turn when nothing else would do? Which is plain to me, that they do not understand their own Rules, or else they do not believe them. To my knowledge there was (as in the case of the Protector) a Figure of *Charles* the Second's Birth generally agreed on, and believed by all those that professed Astrology, and by which a certain person did predict his Death in 1685, and by which Figure they all said he would live to 70 years of Age; but since his Death, you may go to twenty of them, and perhaps every one of them shew you a different Figure, and assign different Causes for his Death; they being as much confounded about that Prince's Nativity and Death, as ever they were about the Protector's: Of these and such-like stories as these are, I could give you a great number, which will serve for no other use but to shew you, that Ignorance becomes *Powerful*, when it grows *Popular* and *General*, at which time it is usually guarded by *Impudence* and *Error*, and by their assistance it commonly takes *Truth* by the beard. I shall therefore conclude these things with this Axiom,

> *That every Cause must have a Certain Effect; and by that Rule, any Direction that hath Power to kill at one time, hath at another, or else a good substantial Rule to shew reason to the contrary.*

It hath been the common custom of our Modern Pretenders to Astrology, to impose on the world, and abuse the Art they pretend to, by Printing the Nativities of dead persons for true ones; for when they are laid in their Graves, it is presumed that nothing can happen afterwards able to contradict the Authority of their Rules, in the pretended Correction of the deceased man's Geniture; for now all Accidents cease, and the common Professors rest satisfied, that what was done was true, they not being able or willing to make any farther Enquiry after it, nor perhaps can they? From hence they pretend to give reasons for all the past actions of Life, Famous or Infamous, Health, Sickness, and last of all, Death it self; making every thing appear as plain as the Sun upon the Meridian, especially to those that do not understand it. And left any of those advantagious notions should be lost, they are printed and published to instruct the young *Tyroes* and Students in this Science, where they may find the Nativity printed, and the Reasons thereof annexed; with choice Rules and Aphorisms fit to be considered by those that are Beginners, that they may be led out of their way; and by the Old ones, that they may be confirmed in their Errors: For those Nativities that are commonly printed, are made by the Astrologers; they often differing from the true time, one, two, or three hours, and sometimes more: So he did, that *promised his Client in print, he should live one or two and thirty years longer, and the poor Gentleman was dead before the Book was published.* So that it is safer to take a Nativity by guess only, than by their Correction, and perhaps nearer the truth: Not to mention the story of Sir *F. H.* or Mr. *P.* with many others, that may fairly challenge a place in this story, besides this Gentleman, whose Nativity is the subject of this Treatise; and hath been as unfairly used by them, as any man whatever. For as long as he lived, they let him have *Pisces* ascending, and *Mars* in his Ascendant, which they thought was a Position very suitable to his Grandeur and Courage, and for one that was so great a Warriour. And this passed very well among them for some years, without any distrust of the truth of it; and by that Figure they could prove all his Sickness, Honours, Victories, &c. But at last he died; and to the amazement of the whole Society, without any Direction to kill him; which without doubt put them out of their Terms for a while, till they had agreed upon making him a New Nativity; for it was in vain for them to believe that any man would think that to be his true one, when they had no Direction, (no, not a sham one) to make the world believe that he dyed by Order from the Stars; and that was strange, that they had no direction at that time; for they are seldom unprovided of the Ascendant to the Square or Opposition of *Jupiter* or *Venus*, the Ascendant to his own *Sextile*, *Square*, or *Trine* in Signs of Long or Short Ascention, as occasion serves; or the *Sun* or *Moon* to the *Square* of the *Dragons-Tail*, or such-like stuff as this is; and tho this may seem nauseous and fulsome, to hear such

fooleries

fooleries as these are, yet I do assure you they do make use of such things, and worse, if worse can be, in point of reason: But at this time it seems, they had not such Directions as they thought probable to pass among the rest of the Society; and therefore a new Nativity must be found out, and it must be such a one too that proves his Death, tho it prove nothing else.

And the next they pitched upon, was farther from the true time of his Birth, than the former was; for now they make him *Aries* Ascending, and the *Sun* in his Horoscope in *Taurus*, and *Saturn* and *Mars* in Opposition from the Cusps of the first and seventh Houses, and in Square to his Tenth, and *Jupiter* in Opposition to his Midheaven, and in Square to his Ascendant, which would make but an untoward Nativity, (according to their own Rules, and *Gadbury*'s in particular, printed by himself, but all borrowed), for a Person of his *Courage, Conduct, Bravery*, and *Presence of mind*, in his most dangerous Undertakings: For *Mars* on the Ascendant must be allowed to shew his Manners, Disposition, and Temper, by being in that Angle; as you may see, *Doctr. Nativ.* pag. 91. and then his being in Opposition to *Saturn*, and in Square to *Jupiter*, must make a very odd temper'd man, *Morose, Peevish, Rash*, and *Unsuccessful* in his general Endeavours, and withal *Sickly*; vide *Cardin. Cœli*, pag. 34. §. 78. in his own words: To which I will add, That the Opposition of *Saturn* should make him *timorous* and *fearful*, and by consequence a *little Cowardly*, and of a *Base spirit*; but I could never hear his Enemies charge any of these things in the least on him; but they say that he was *Brave, Bold*, and *Generous*; that he never had any *Fear* or *Terror* upon him, but always beat that into his Enemies; and when he took them, used them more like Gentlemen at liberty, than Prisoners; but besides, they all allow, that the Lord of the Tenth in Opposition to *Mars*, and both in Square to the Midheaven, is a fatal Position to any man's Honour when born to it; and then pray how should such a Position give such Grandeur and Power as he advanced to, if their Rules are true? vide *Doctr. Nat.* pag. 164. For it is certain, that *Saturn* and *Mars* in Opposition from the First and Seventh, would make him a very ill-natured man, and subject to many Misfortunes; and indeed I could spend some Pages after this manner from their own Authors and words, directly opposite to this Position, and very probable to prove, that this which was then printed, was not the Protector's true Nativi-

Opus Reformatum.

tv: but I shall leave all these Arguments and Reasonings, because I have better to insist upon, which will better serve, and more demonstrably prove the Falsity of that Figure, and the Unskilfulness of him that made it; and so I come to the matter more nearly.

The Figure of this Great Man's Nativity is owned by a very worthy Gentleman, one *J. Gadbury* by name, and by him printed in his crowd of Errors, called *Collectio Geniturarum*, or a Collection of choice Nativities, that is, of his own making; now this I could have passed by, and look'd on it as the effect and oversight of his Juvenile years; but he prints the same again in his *Card. Cœli*, after five and twenty years, to shew that he was still the same man, and that he had no more skill in his own Profession in 1685, than he had in 1659; and by doing that, he seems to me to justifie all the Errors of his Collection, because he hath hitherto given us no Caution concerning any of those Errors in that book, of which these of the Protector's are some of the greatest; and to say the truth, this of his *Cardines Cœli* is as full of Fooleries and absurdities, as the other, which I shall endeavour more fully to evince, before I conclude this Treatise.

The time he sets this Figure for, is the twentyfifth of *April* at almost forty seven minutes after three of the Clock in the Morning 1599. and upon that Position he spends a whole Page to tell his Reader, that there are several things concur to prove it true, besides the Directions he after mentions; as the Opposition of *Saturn* and *Mars* from *Aries and Libra*, the three Superiours in their own Dignities, and above all *Cardinal Signs*, possessing the four Angles of the Figure; which in the Nativity of *Charles Gustavus*, as well as in this of the Protector's, was (as *Gadb* says,) fully verified. And from these two Fictitious Nativities (for such they both are) he confidently forms this notion into an Astrological Aphorism, and prints it in his *Choice Collection*, Aphor. 18. of which more hereafter; and after abundance of sorry stuff besides, he concludes with these words: ' Presuming that divers Artists will be ' curious in scanning this Geniture, I shall for their assistance, ' and prevention of trouble, present them with a Catalogue of ' several Accidents of his Life, and the Directions, &c. that were ' (in an Astrological sense) the proper Occasions of them, and ' (*with no small pains to me*) they are these following.

And

Opus Reformatum.

And here I desire the Reader, and all that pretend to be Artists, to consider his reasons for the Correcting this Nativity.

1. In the Year 1640, this Native's Grandeur began, for then he was first called into publick business, by being chosen a Member of Parliament; to signifie which he had [as *J. G.* says] his Mid-heaven to the *Dragon's Head*; now, is not this a probable thing, that this Node should give greater advantage than the M. C. to the Trine of *Saturn* and Sextile of *Mars*, nay the greatest of all, for this was the beginning and ground of all the rest of his Honors and Preferments both in the State and Army. Now if you will but consider, this *Dragons Head* and *Tail* are nothing but the Intersections of the Ecliptick and Orbite of the Moon at opposite Points, and those two Circles are but imaginary, and therefore the two Nodes cannot be otherways: Again, Why one of these Points should be a Fortune, and the other an Infortune, is a Mystery that the greater Masters of this Science still reserve in their own bosoms. But to the Question in hand. Pray what is the reason that the *M. C. ad Caput* should give such present honour, and lay the ground-work for the future, when the M. C. to the Trine of *Saturn*, and Sextile of *Mars*, went a little before it, and gave nothing at all, as we know of: and yet this Native designed by God and Nature to be so great a Man as he after proved, and that too, from the nature and principles of those two Stars, *Policy, Power* and *Courage*: And indeed I would intreat honest *John* to present the World with some Treatise that might resolve and unfold these secret *Nostrums* not yet known to the unbelieving World, as I suppose he calls the great, if not the greatest part of the Nation. But did this *Dragons Head* give this? if it should happen to prove true, I profess it is a most admirable Discovery; but I doubt this is the first Experiment, and judg it will be the last too of its kind; for whosoever shall have occasion to try it in another Case of the like nature, will find themselves wretchedly deceived and cheated. For throughout his Choice Collections he never tells you a word of any one being preferred by the M C. ad ☋, but of that *Minister's* being elected Fellow, *pag.* 114. but to tell you the truth, it was not on that, but the A(scendant to the body of *Venus*, as he tells you himself, but he doth not tell you one word of the effect of the M. C. ad ☋ in Dr. *George Starkey's* Nativity. However, he tickled off his Friend Mr. *Blyn-*

man with *Imprisonments* and *Scandals* upon the *M. C. ad Caudam draconis*; but to tell you plainly, those Accidents (if the Figure is true) were from the *Sun ad oppositum Saturni*, who is the real Author of such things as those, as the Case then stood; and he hath let Mr. *Eastwood*, pag. 170. pass by his *M. C. ad* ☌ without any remarkable effect, which shews a kind of plaguy Ill-nature in him, to let the young man at 20 years of Age pass without some good effect of it: sure he might have deserved something at that Age, as well as *Oliver*, to have all at forty. In a word, I think he hath knocked two or three little Babes on the head besides with the *Dragons Tail*; which is as useful as the other in its place, and serves sometimes at a dead lift. But let him prove to me if he can, why the Head and tail should not be both of one and the same nature, if they have any influence at all, or power to give good or evil in direction; I confess I could never find it.

2. *Secondly*, In the Year 1642. he was preferred to the Command of a Collonel of Horse; having before, like an honest Gentleman, and true *Englishman*, raised a Troop of Horse at his own Charge, and served in his own Person to defend his Country against the then growing Popish Interest, which like a Deluge was like to overthrow all. He had then, says *J. G.* the *Moon* directed to the *Scorpion's Heart*, but whether with, or without Latitude, he hath not told us: but let it be which it will, it is wholly false; for the *Moon's* pole of Position in that place in his Figure is about 50, and her Oblique Ascention under that Pole in the opposite point is about 350 d. 18′. so that the Ark of Direction with Latitude, is 37 d. 28′. and without Latitude it is 45 d. 14′. which according to *Natbod*'s measure, will give more than 45 years: and therefore neither of them can come up in the Year 1642. as he pretends. But suppose it did come up then, why must it give such considerable Preferment as a Collonel of Horse, which to him at that time was very great, both as to his Command and Trust reposed in him? why should it not give trouble or sickness to him; the death of his Wife, or Mother (if he had one living) as well, or rather than give honour and preferment? for in the Nativity of the *French* King, pag. 40. of his Collection, he gives him a violent Fever on the direction of the *Ascendant* to the *Scorpion's Heart*, without any thing else to assist it, except a Transit of *Mars* on the *Moon's* Radical place. And in *pag*. 43. in the Revolution of *Gustavus* the Second, it is there brought in as

an Argument of death; the *Sun* and *Saturn* in Conjunction near the *Cor* ♏, is there called violent because of the *Antares*. And in the Nativity of the Prince of *Orange*, pag. 54. it is there made use of to kill his Mother, and to give him a great deal of trouble; but to assist it he tells us, that the *M. C.* came up then to the Square of *Saturn*, which is notoriously false, for there was no such direction at that time, or near it. Yet after all this *Stuff* and *Foppery*, when he comes to Dr. *Gouge*'s Nativity, pag 107. he sends him to *Cambridge* upon no other Direction, but the *Sun* to the *Scorpion's Heart*, and nothing else to assist it. Thus you see what an Excellent Astrologer Mr *J G* is, and how obedient the Stars are to those who can skilfully command them; make them kill one, give another trouble, send a third to *Cambridge*, and make a fourth a Collonel of Horse: But if all he says were allowed in the *Protector*'s Case, it serves nothing at all to the Correction, nor to prove the time of his Figure true; for all men that know any thing of Directions, know very well that this Direction would have been nearly the same, had the time been taken later or earlier: but I wonder why *J. G.* should exclaim against *Cromwell* for sinking the Oath of Allegiance to his Sovereign, as he calls him, when that *King* had broke and sunk his Coronation Oath long before, and we all remember very well who it was that did it since also in the Year 1586. and 1687. to almost the Nation's ruin, and destruction of the Protestant Religion.

3 *Thirdly*, In the Year 1643. he was made *Lieutenant-General* to the *Earl* of *Manchester*; at which time he says he had the *Moon* directed to the Trine of *Mars*; but this is also extreamly false, because there is no such direction as he pretends to at this time; which any one may see by working those Operations, in which the Ark without Latitude, which is the only Direction that he knows in that way, is 48 d. 26′. and the Ark with Latitude is almost 41. both which are far distant from 1643. and cannot come up at that time he mentions, nor near it. but it it did, it cannot correct without some other to agree with it to the Angles.

4. *Fourthly*, He tells us, that he quarrelled with the Earl of *Manchester* his General, and preferred divers Informations against him in Parliament, and managed it so well, that he carried his Point, and came off with honour; the Cause of this was (he says) *Saturn* being on his Ascendant, and the Radical place of *Mars* in Opposition

position to his own, and the Ascendant directed to the Terms of *Mars*. Certainly this Man was infatuated when he wrote this Nonsense; for I have more Charity for him, than to think he had so little Skill or Sense to believe this, and not know better; but tell us of a Transit of *Saturn* by *Mars* his Radical place in opposition to his own. Why, what was this to *Cromwell*? why did not (if this is true) *Saturn* do him a mischief the last year, when he got his Lieutenant-General's Commission, for he was then Stationary on the Radical place of *Mars*, and no harm observed. Well: but the Ascendant was also afflicted by direction; how so? why it came to the Terms of *Mars*; Ay, this is something like to do the feat. did ever any Soul hear an Infallible Son of an Infallible Church give such Reasons as these are? In the last year he says the *Moon* to the Trine of *Mars* gave him Preferment, and is that Direction so soon over? will it not continue in force one year? and if it doth, pray why should the Terms of *Mars* be alledged as an Injury to him, and he under a very good Martial Direction? Why should not the Trine of *Mars* give the Contest (if there was such a Direction at that time, as he says there was) more likely than the Terms of *Mars*, it ending in his Advantage and Honour? which cannot be allowed such an Affliction as he seems to insinuate by the Transit of *Saturn*. But why must the Ascendant to the Terms of *Mars* be brought in now as a cause of difference? Doth it always give Quarrels and Contests? Did it also give Quarrels, Contests, and Difference, when the Ascendant came to the beginning of *Cancer*, which was the Terms of *Mars* also, which was two or three years afterward? I doubt it; and I think it would be worth while to ask the Gentleman, if it did not fall in pitted and smoaky degrees, if so, then it is beyond all question and doubt; but the truth of all is, there was nothing else to sham in at this time, and therefore this must do; yet I do think there is no man will look upon this as a good reason and argument to prove the Nativity true.

5. *Fifthly*, In 1645 he says *Oliver Cromwell* was made Lieutenant-General to Sir *Thomas Fairfax*, and this under the Direction of the Moon to the Sextile of *Saturn*, Lord of the Tenth House; and indeed it was well he was Lord of the Tenth, or else he had certainly lost his Honour and Preferment at that time; however, that is also false, there was no such Direction at that time, and that for the Reasons before-mentioned.

6. *Sixthly*,

6. *Sixthly*, In 1648, for his contending with the Parliament, and some other things, he says he had his Sun to the Square of *Saturn*, and the part of Fortune to the Opposition of *Venus*: As for that of *Venus*, I am sure 'tis false, for he is not able either to take or direct the part of Fortune; and what is more, if the part of Fortune were truly placed in that Figure, it should be in about 11 or 12 degrees of *Leo*, and he hath made it in one and twenty; and for that Direction of *Saturn*, if it should be true, it doth not at all help to the Correction.

7. *Seventhly*, In 1649 he went over to *Ireland* to oppose the Popish Rebels in that Nation, and defend the Protestant Religion; and as *Gadbury* says, he had a Flux and Feaver there, for these things he gives him the Moon to her own Square, and the Contrantiscion of *Jupiter*; alas, poor man! he never knew yet how to take an Antiscion or a Zodiacal Parallel, which you please; and I will venture an even Wager of what he will, that he doth not know how to direct the Moon either to an Antiscion or Contrantiscion of any Planet; so great is his Confidence and Ignorance in pretending to a thing he understands not. And furthermore, had the Moon been so directed at that time, as he says she was to those two directions, I am certain he would have had neither Flux nor Feaver at that time, if *Ptolomy* says true; but you must bear with his Ignorance, for if he knew better, he would do better.

8. *Eighthly*, In 1650 and 1651, he beat the *Scots* at *Dunbar*, and the *Cavaliers* at *Worcester* to their hearts content; for this he gives him the Sun to his own Sextile; but how he doth make it do, I cannot tell, for the Ark of direction is 53, 46, and gives about 54 years, and he was now but 51 and 52 years of age; which is a great difference in point of time; but he doth not tell you one word of the Sun to the Square of *Mars* and *Saturn*, nor their effects, one of which happened at 48 years of Age, and the other at 51; and tho he could not tell what they gave, yet he might have told us what the reason was that they did not kill, or at leastwise give Sickness, as well as the Moon to the Contrantiscion of *Jupiter* and her own Square; or why the Sun to the Square of *Saturn* and *Mars*, should not give loss of Honour, and damage to Reputation, as well as the *M.C.* to the *Dragons-head*, gave the greatest of Honour; but these, I suppose are *Nostrums* lodged in his own Carkass, and are not to be made known till the publicati-

on of his body of Tautology, or a more convenient time: Now if this Nativity that he hath printed, were true, then the Sun is positively Giver of Life, which if so, he hath (according to *Ptolomy*) not only the principal Government of Honour and Grandeur, but of Health, Sickness, Life and Death; and therefore it is the greatest wonder to me, that under two such directions there should be no effect attend him either of Sickness or Scandal; but these are small things with honest *John*.

9. *Ninthly*, In 1653, in *December*, he was Proclaimed *Protector* of *England*; he had now the Sun directed to the body of *Jupiter*, Sextile of the Moon, and the part of Fortune to the Sextile of *Venus*, those directions, I confess, are probable for such an effect, and the former comes too at the time he says it doth; but the last of the three he knows nothing of it.

10. *Tenthly*, In 1654 he concluded a Peace with *France*, and makes a League with *Sweden*; and for that *Gadb.* says he had the part of Fortune to the Trine of *Mars*; but that cannot be allowed; for if he had lived twenty years longer than he did, that direction would not have come up; so improbable a Direction that is to be alledged for this time; but alas, poor man! 'tis his want of skill.

11. *Eleventhly*, In 1656. he called a Parliament, and they desired him to take upon him the Title of *King*, which he refused; for this he had (as *Gadb.* says) the part of Fortune to the Sextile of *Saturn*, Lord of the Tenth. I have little occasion to say any thing more to this, because I told you before, that he can neither take nor direct that Point.

12. *Twelfthly*, In 1657. he sent Six thousand men over into *Flanders*, under the Command of Sir *John Reynolds*, by whose means he became Master of *Dunkirk*, he had then the Sun directed to the Sextile of *Mercury*; and why should not this Sextile of *Mercury*, being in Signs of long Ascention, be equal to a Square? if so, why should it give any good at all? But let it be the one or the other, this as well as the rest can by no means serve to prove the Figure true, which is the thing he aims it.

13. *Thirteenthly*, In the year 1658, on *September* the Third, this great General and Statesman died of an Intermitting Feaver at first, but afterward Continual; which *Gadbury* tells us was caused by the Ascendant (who is, says he in this Nativity, Giver of Life) directed to the Square of *Mars* in *Cancer*, his fall; the

Sun

Opus Reformatum.

Sun to the Head of *Hercules*, and the part of Fortune to the Square of the Moon. As for this last of the ⊕ to the Square of the Moon, that cannot be directed to the Aspects in the Zodiack, becaufe oftentimes that doth not move in it, nor he knows no other way of directing. And for the Sun to the Head of *Hercules*, 'tis a fmall Star of the Second Magnitude in 18 degrees of *Cancer*, and almoft 7 degrees of North Latitude; but he directs it here without Latitude. If this hath any force to kill without Latitude, why did not the Sun to that Star with Latitude kill, it coming up with the Square of *Saturn*, and the ⊕ to the Oppofition of *Venus*, in the year 1648? For it would be more able to kill when the Sun was afflicted by two violent Promittors, than by one; and the rather, if the Sun fhould prove *Hileg*; as I believe you will find it is in this Figure of his making? And here by the way, I muft take the liberty to queftion this trifling Gentleman how he proves the Afcendant to be *Giver of Life*? For in his borrowed Rules in the *Doctr of Nativ.* he tells us that the Sun in the Afcendant is *Hileg*, and I hope he will not make two *Aphæta*'s in one Nativity. And alfo *Origanus* in *Introduct. par. 3. cap. 2* preacheth the very fame Doctrine, fo doth *Argol, Pezelius, Ranzou*, and all the reft of our Authors; but above all, the Great *Ptolomy*, in his *Quadripartitum, lib. 3. cap. 11* and *cap. 13.* where he is particular and very pofitive, when he fays, *Cùm autem quærimus in his locis potentiffimum, primus erit Medium Cæli, deinde Horofcopus, &c.* So that you fee the Horofcope is one of the chiefeft prerogatory places; and yet this worthy Gentleman, contrary to the Rules printed by himfelf, and all our ancient Authors, rejects the Sun in the middle of the Afcendant, and confidently or ignorantly tells us, That the Afcendant is Giver of Life, or *Hileg*; and this for no other reafon, (as I can fee) but to give countenance and credit to his own erroneous practices, and to lead (like *Jack with a Lanthorn*) other men out of the way, into thefe bogs of Error. In fhort, I do affirm, That the Sun within five degrees above the Cufp of the Afcendant, till within five degrees of the Cufp of the Second; or rather, to fpeak in *Ptolomy*'s terms and meaning, within the compafs of his double Horary times there, he is to be accepted for Giver of Life; provided the Moon is not in an Aphetical place above the Earth, or the part of Fortune. &c. qualified for that power? But in this Figure of his, the Sun is beyond all doubt Giver of Life, he being in the very middle of the Houfe, and having there no Competitor.

Hence

Opus-Reformatum.

Hence that which *Gadb.* asserts in this case, is a palpable falshood, which might have been excused in a Novice; but in an old *Bell-weather* it ought to be reproved, and that sharply too: But let it go how it will, it was a credit for *Crommell*, that his Foes could find nothing to kill him but the Head of *Hercules*, joined with a fictitious Direction, and that is the Ascendant to the Square of *Mars*, which in reality could not come up before Ninety years of age, or thereabouts.

But the main Direction that Mr *John* lays all the stress of the matter upon, is the Ascendant to the Square of *Mars* in the Zodiack, which is, (to say the truth), no direction at all, for you may as well direct the Ascendant to the Antiscion of any Planet, as to an Aspect in the Zodiack; they being both impossible to be done by any one, *John* excepted. But suppose it were allowable, and that there was such a Direction in Nature, as he there tells us there is, yet that Direction could not kill; for if he pleaseth but to read *Ptolomy*, Lib. 3. Cap. 13. *Quadripart.* he there tells us, That if the Rays of *Jupiter* or *Venus*, fall within eight or twelve degrees after a Malefick Direction, that Direction cannot kill: Now in this case, here is but one Malefick Direction to the Ascendant, and that is the Square of *Mars*, which is succeeded by the Ascendant to the Sextile of the Sun, the *Body of Jupiter*, Sextile of the Moon, and Sextile of *Mercury*, and they all nearly in Aspect to *Jupiter*, and for that reason partakers of his nature in a great measure; therefore how this body of Directions should (contrary to all good and Authentick Rules) Kill, seems to me a Mystery; and what is more, that he should dye of such a Disease as an intermitting Feaver or Poyson: for it is not *Mars*, but the *Sun* and *Jupiter*, that do specificate the Disease; and how they two should kill, but especially after that manner, I hope my Friend *John* will explain in his twenty years promised *Body of Tautology*, when he thinks convenient to print it; and also in that Book to give us full direction for the understanding his pitted *Azimeen*, and smoaky Degrees; which, perhaps, may have a great hand in killing this Gentleman, tho he hath not mentioned it, nor do we understand it, which is worse.

But seeing Astrology is allowed and owned by some of the most Learned, to be a bundle of Experience improved into Rules by continued observations of those Accidents and Effects that did always attend different Directions and Positions: Hence it then follows,

follows, *That like Causes must always have like Effects*, or else Rules of Exception laid down to know when they shall, and when they shall not give those common Effects that they all tell us of: For if the Ascendant, Sun or Moon to the body, Square or Opposition of *Saturn* and *Mars*, shall kill in two or three Cases, and miss in ten or twelve, it leaves Astrology an idle, foolish, and reproachful Study, being uncertain and vain, and therefore not to be studied nor defended by any but men of a Reputation equal to it self. For if the Ascendant to the Square of *Mars*, in this pretended Nativity of the *Lord Protector's*, should kill when the Body of *Jupiter*, Sextile of the *Sun* and *Moon*, &c. are so near, *then I do affirm, That nothing can hinder it at any time, but it must always certainly kill*; which if true, then pray observe what follows, taken out of that Learned Treatise, called *Collecti Genitura*, a Book full of Contradictions and Error, as to the Principles and Truths of Astrology; which I shall more fully detect hereafter, but give you a glimpse of it now, to shew you what a sort of man he is, that pretends to be the Leader and Top-man of the Society of Astrologers in *England*, and how he and his Notions ought to be believed.

1. *First* then; In the *Nativity of Queen Mary*, pag. 11. the Ascendant to the Square of *Mars* did not kill, tho' it was assisted by the Bodies of *Mercury* and the *Sun*, and they both Malefick and Peregrin: nor did the Square of *Saturn* afterward kill her.

2. In the Nativities of *Ann* Queen of *Hungary*, pag. 28. *Lewis* the XIII*th*. King of *France*, pag. 34. and *Charles Gustavus*, King of *Sweden*, pag. 35. he lets those three out-live the Ascendant to the Body of *Mars*, which must be undoubtedly more violent than the Square; and in two of the three it came up young.

In the Case of *Frederick* King of *Denmark*, pag. 37. it did not kill, tho' it fell near the Lyons heart.

3. In the Nativity of the *Earl of Essex*, pag. 45. we have a most admirable Instance; for there the Ascendant to the Squares of the *Sun*, the *Moon*, and *Mars*, all together, had not Power and Strength enough to kill, and yet no assistance from *Jupiter* and *Venus* to help or save; when you see in the Case of *Cromwell*, that the single Square of *Mars* did the business, tho' the Body of *Jupiter*, &c. were very near to the place. This is *Brick-Court Astrology* with a witness! *Risum teneatis*.

4. In

Opus Reformatum.

4. In the Case of *Casimir King of Poland*, pag. 46. it did likewise fail, tho *Mars* was there among the *Pleiades*, and for that reason the more violent.

5. In the Nativity of *Charles Tortenson*, the great *Swedish* General, pag. 48. where *Mars* is in Conjunction with the Sun, Lord of the Eighth, and in Square to *Saturn* in the Eighth; yet this worthy Gentleman lets him out-live the Ascendant to the Square of *Saturn*, Bodies of *Mars* and the *Sun*, and sends him to the other world on the Ascendant to the Opposition of *Saturn*. In this Nativity Honest *John* hath shewn as much of his Ignorance (as to the Rules of Astrology) as in any one Case throughout the whole Book besides; for here he gives the Ascendant the Power of *Hileg*, and yet both *Sun* and *Moon* in Aphætical places, the one in the first, and the other in the seventh.

6. In the Nativity of the *Dutchess of Sfortia*, page 64. the Square of *Mars* did not kill, but the Ascendant to the Opposition of the *Moon* and the Sun to the Square of *Venus* did, and yet neither of them Givers of Life; neither did the Ascendant to the Square of *Mars* kill in the Nativity of *Don John of Austria*, pag. 65.

7. In the Nativity of *George Duke of Albemarle*, pag. 70. neither the Square of *Saturn* or *Mars* to the Ascendant could kill him, and yet *Mars* Lord of the Eighth House.

8. In the Case of *Pope Paul* the 5*th*. the Ascendant to the Square of *Mars* did not kill; and yet the Opposition of *Mercury* out of the Eighth House fell near the same place.

9. In the Case of *Pope Gregory* 15. pag. 81. the Horoscope to the Square of *Mars* did not kill, and yet that Angle Giver of Life; but the Square of *Mercury* did it to the purpose a while after. I suppose *Mars* was Popishly inclined at that time, and therefore would not hurt his Ghostly Father; but *Mercury* appeared to be a downright Heretick, and had no respect either to his Age or Infallibility.

10. In the Nativity of *Cardinal Peter Bembus*, pag. 85. the same Aspect did not kill, and yet *Mars* Lord of the Eighth. I really judge that he was a Papist in those times; what think you *John*, was he or no? You are the better Judg of the two, because you are of that Persuasion.

11. In the Case of Mr. *Thomas Gataker*, pag. 102. the Square of *Mars*, and Opposition of the Sun out of the Eighth, would not do; but the Opposition of *Saturn* did it afterwards.

D   12. In

Opus Reformatum.

12. In the Nativity of *Judg Reeves*, pag. 121. the Square of *Mars*, Opposition of the Moon, and Body of *Saturn*, could not kill: but after that, something else did it.

13. In the Case of Dr. *Richard Laford*, pag. 133. he out-lived the Ascendant to the Square of *Mars* and the *Sun*, both which Aspects fell near the *Lyons-heart*.

14. In the Geniture of Mr. *Stephen Rogers*, pag. 138. the Ascendant was directed to the Square of *Mars*; and yet that could not kill him, although the Square of the Moon gave her assistance.

15. In that of Major-General *Lambert*, pag. 167. he passed the Ascendant to the Square of *Mars*, and divers years after, to the Square of *Saturn* and the Moon, and lived many years afterward.

16. In the Case of Dr. *Geoffrey le Neve*, pag. 178. he likewise out-lived the Ascendant to the Square of *Mars*, and to the Square of *Saturn* after that also.

17. In the Nativity of Mr. *John Booker*, pag. 187. you will there find that he out-lived the Ascendant to the Square of *Mars*, Square of the Sun, Square of the Moon, and Square of *Mercury*, and lived many years afterward.

18. In the Geniture of Mr. *Will. Leybourn*, pag. 187. you will find that he also hath out-lived the Ascendant to the Square of *Mars* and *Mercury*, and yet these fell near the Cusp of the fourth House, and in *Cancer* likewise; as it did in that Figure Honest *John* gave us for the true one of *Oliver Cromwell*.

19. In his own Nativity, pag. 190. he out-lived the Ascendant to the Opposition of *Mars*, and lives yet, as I suppose.

20. In the Nativity of Mr. *John Mallet*, pag. 180. he outlived the Ascendant to the Square of *Mars*, but unhappily dyed afterward on the Ascendant to the Square of *Saturn*, as Honest *John* says.

Thus I have given you above Twenty Examples of that Aspect and Direction out of his own Book, where it did not kill: and I could have given you more out of the same also, if I had not thought these over and above sufficient to prove the Improbability of what this trifling man puts upon us for truth. Now let any impartial man seriously consider the Reasons that he gives to prove his Figure true, (which he says cost him so much pains) and especially that for his Death, and compare the Collection of

Examples

Examples I have here made, with those Reasons he hath given, and then tell me, Whether the *Ascendant to the Square of Mars* is a Direction fit to be believed and depended on, for the Death of *Oliver Cromwell*: For you see here is twenty to one against it; and if like Causes have not like Effects, (without Rules of Exception), then I will certainly renounce Astrology, and believe it no more. And I dare further assure you, That the Astrology which is generally made *Use of*, *Studied*, and *Practised*, is rather fit to be laugh'd at, than believed; as you may easily see by the silly shams of *Gadbury*, if you compare one thing with another throughout his whole Book, called the Collection, which in a short time I shall also expose.

And for me to believe that this Gentleman died on the Ascendant to the Square of *Mars*, after so plain a Conviction of the Error, when there are Twenty Examples under his own Hand to prove where and when it hath missed of that Effect, is to tell all mankind, That I am an Ignorant, Credulous Fellow, void both of Reason and Skill, and fit to be imposed upon by any one that is willing to attempt it. And for my part, when I consider that there are a great number of Ingenious persons of all Qualities and Degrees in this Kingdom, who understands Astrology very well, and have observed the Shams and Cheats of this Impostor, I wonder they were never called in question, and exploded before now; for they will serve for no other use, but to lead the young Students out of their way, and bring an Odium upon the Science it self, when it is read by such Men, who when they observe its incoherence, are readily apt to make use of it, or any thing else they can pick up to brand it with Infamy; for which end they need not trouble themselves to read Books written against it; for let them peruse but our own Authors, and they will not fail to find stuff enough to make themselves merry at; and yet for all this, *There is a True Astrology in being*: Little Thanks to our Modern Authors.

Object. But perhaps here may rise an Objection, and I would not have any thing left in the dark, that now occurs to my memory: For perhaps some may say, Do you believe that it is possible for the Ascendant to the Square of *Mars*, to kill at any time? or do you think it can never kill?

Answ. Yes; That I can attest upon experience, that it doth kill; and I can tell you several Nativities in honest *John's* Collection, that have dyed on the Ascendant to the Square of *Mars*, and Square of *Saturn*, tho unknown to him; but it must be in such Nativities where the Horoscope is Giver of Life; for no Point can be directed for Death, but the *Hileg*; and therefore whosoever practiseth contrary to that Rule, erreth, and will never do any thing well; and you shall see more on that subject. That no man ever yet made any famous Prediction of Death, but when he directed and made use of the Giver of Life in his Operation and Judgment.

Thus have I made it as plain as possible it can be, to any Artist, or other Pretender to Astrology, That the Rules and Reasons made use of to prove the truth of the Protector's Nativity, are false and erroneous, and built upon such Principles as are not true in themselves, neither will they hold true in other Positions, to effect what they are brought here to prove: And also the major part of the Directions that he there talks of, will serve to any other Position within half an hour or an hour, with a little variation; but for the first, the fourth, the tenth, and the thirteenth, being those that do depend particularly on the truth of the Figure, they are so ridiculously false, that they need no other Arguments to expose them, but their Non-effect in other Genitures; and therefore I do advise all Ingenious, Laborious Artists, to compare one thing with another after this manner, in those books sent forth into the world by our Modern Authors; and at last try in their own Practice, whether those Rules will hold or not; and also let them consider, whether they are not imposed upon in divers other cases, as well as in this Nativity.

Lastly, I would advise Mr. *John*, seeing *Mars* hath played these Tricks, and cheated him so, to proceed against him by a Form of Law, as he knows how, without doubt; and the Booksellers of *London* say he hath very good skill in *Scandalum Magnatums*, for which they desire him to remember the Earl of P.

First then. Let him bring a *Quo Warranto* against him, and take away his Charter, (he knows where to have Judges for that purpose,) unless he can shew good reason why he hath done his duty so negligently, partially, and basely, killing one part of mankind, and letting Twenty escape, that lay at his mercy; by which means he hath brought Catholick *John's* Reputation into

doubt

doubt and question, for which he can never make him satisfaction, unless he can help him to a greater share of ——— And in the next place have him before Father *Peters*, and Inquisition him; for I doubt the Knave is not found in the Faith, but hath a plaguy share of Heresy and Disobedience. How! serve honest *John* so! But it will be so sometimes when Papists deal with Heretical Stars.

And then let him draw up an humble Address to Monsieur *Tiran*, in the Name of him, and his Society, in *quo humiliter Monstretur*; that he hath for a long time drove on a Trade of Lying, (but not a word of his Ignorance) being cheated and abused by a sort of obstinate and disobedient Stars. And that if now at last he pleaseth but to give his *Mandamus*, that *Saturn* and *Mars*, &c. may henceforward obediently comply with all the Astrological Rules in fashion, that he shall be in duty bound to shew himself full as skilful as ever.

And so I come to present you with the true Nativity of this Great General, without Sham or Trick; and the Directions shall also have an equal Effect in other Nativities, according to the *Hyphothesis* before laid down.

THE

THE
NATIVITY
OF
𝔒𝔩𝔦𝔳𝔢𝔯 𝔆𝔯𝔬𝔪𝔴𝔢𝔩𝔩,
Lord Protector of *ENGLAND*.

Fairly and faithfully handled according to the true Principles of Astrology.

THE time of this Great Man's birth, according as he gave it himself, was on St. *Mark's* day in the year 1599. *Summo Mane*, at *Huntington*, whose Latitude is 52 deg. and a few minutes; and this is the estimate time given.

Now the main point is, how we must understand this short Sentence, *Summo Mane*; and it can in my Judgement have no other meaning than very early in the Morning, that is, in the very top of the Morning, or suddenly after Twelve, for so the word seems to import; and inded I can give it no other Interpretation but this; for the word *Summo* must be there taken *Adverbially*, and derived from the *Adjective Summus*, which in that sence it is here spoken, signifies the very highest, extream, utmost, top, &c. of the Morning; tho I confess the word Morning takes in all the whole

time

time from Twelve, or Midnight, till Twelve at Noon; but if he had been born after *Sun* rising, I am very apt to believe he would have used another way of expressing it, as by *Ante Meredium*, &c. but if before *Sun* rising, as indeed they all agree he was, then I can take it in no other sence but this that I have already given, The top of the Morning, and the time pitched upon, is at about 5 minutes after one of the Clock, and to that time the Planets places, both in Longitude and Latitude, are calculated by the Caroline Tables, as followeth,

	Longit.	*Planetar.*			*Lat.*	*Plan.*		*Par.*	*Plan.*
	deg.	m.	sec.						
♄	11	47	2	♎	2	54	No	2	1
♃	15	4	19	♋	0	24	No	23	5
♂	10	25	29	♈	1	04	So	3	9
♀	29	51	49	♉	0	29	No	20	40
☿	16	19	25	♉	0	18	No	18	3
☉	13	55	10	♉	0	00	00	16	5
☽	14	35	40	♍	2	31	So	3	46
☊	15	51	28	♒	0	00	00	0	00
☋	15	51	28	♌	0	00	00	16	00

From their Longitudes and Latitudes thus found, are their Parallels, or Antiscions obtained, as here you may see.

♄	5	2	♎	5	2	♈	24	58	♓	24	58	♍
♃	10	48	♋	10	48	♑	19	12	♊	19	12	♐
♂	17	55	♈	7	55	♎	22	5	♍	22	5	♓
♀	2	10	♊	2	10	♐	27	50	♋	27	50	♑
☿	20	56	♉	20	56	♏	9	4	♌	9	4	♒
☽	20	31	♍	20	31	♓	9	29	♈	9	29	♎
☉	13	57	♉	13	57	♏	16	3	♌	16	3	♒

Now to gain the Cusps of the Twelve Houses, I proceed in the method following, by taking the right Ascention of the *Sun*, and the right Ascention of Time, and adding them together, gives

gives the right Ascention of the Mid-Heaven; to which adding thirty Degrees, gives the Oblique Ascention of the Eleventh House; and so by the addition of thirty Degrees, we gain the other six of the Oriental Houses, as in the following Example.

Ascent. Recta Solis	41 26		
Ascenti Rect. Temporis	196 14		
Ascent. Rect med. Cœli	237 40	♏ 29ᵈ 52′	
Adde	30		
Ascen. Obliq. Dom. 11	267 40	♐ 18	
Adde	30		
Ascen. Obliq. Dom. 12	297 40	♑ 5	
Adde	30		
Ascen. Obliq Ascenden.	327 40	♑ 26 19	
Adde	30		
Ascen. Obliq. Dom. 2	357 40	♓ 26	
Adde	30		
Ascen. Obliq. Dom. 3	27 40	♉ 6	

Many of our Modern Professors have made a great noise about taking the Minutes and Seconds for the Cusps of every House, which I think are both useless and impertinent; for what use do they make of them, when they have taken them? none, as I know; however, I will give you a short Example, and leave the rest for those that think them useful.

For the M.C. I take the difference between the two *Arks*, greater and lesser, then the Right Ascention of the M.C. and that is 62. Then I take the difference between the next Less, and the Right Ascention, and that is 54; then I say by the Rule of proportion, If 62 gives 60, 54 shall give 52, which leaves the Cusp of the Tenth in 29 deg. 52 minutes of *Scorpio*.

And for the Cusp of the Ascendant, I also take the difference as before between the two *Arks*; greater and lesser than the Oblique Ascention of the Ascendant, and that is 44 Minutes; and also between the lesser *Ark* and the Oblique Ascention, which is 14 Minutes: then I say as before, By the Rule of Proportion, if

44 mi-

Opus Reformatum

44 minutes gives 60 minutes, 14 minutes shall give 19 minutes, which tells us, that the Cusp of the Ascendant resteth in 26 degrees and 19 minutes of *Capricorn*, under the Pole 52. I omit to take notice of the Equation for those few minutes above 52. the Pole of Birth, and therefore the figure without any further operation, is as followeth;

A 237. 40. R

Natus
Die 25. Aprilis, Hora 1.
Minut 4. Second. 56.
Mane, 1599
☽ a △ ⊙ ad ✶ ♃ △ ☿
Latitude, *Huntington*.

Opus Reformatum.

A Table of the Directions in this Nativity, with the several Arks thereof, the measure of Time agreeing to each of them, and the year of our Lord when they began to take effect.

Nomina Directionum.	Arcus Directi. Gr. Mi	Mensur. Directi. An. M.	Anni Dom
Sol ad Terminos ♃	0 57	0 11	1600
Sol ad ✶ ♃ in Zodiaco	1 00	1 00	1600
Luna ad ✶ ♃ in Zodiaco cum Latitudine	1 13	1 3	1600
Luna ad ✶ ♀ in Zodiaco cum Latitudine	1 52	1 11	1601
Sol ad Corpus ♀	2 8	2 2	1601
Luna ad Terminos ♃	2 44	2 8	1601
Luna ad Terminos ♂	4 17	4 5	1603
Luna ad ✶ ♃ Zodiaco sine Latitudine	4 34	4 8	1603
Luna ad parallelum ♃ mundo dd	4 40	4 9	1603
Sol ad □ ♃ in mundo dd	4 54	5 1	1604
Luna ad △ ♀ Zodiaco sine Latitudine	5 17	5 5	1604
Sol ad Sesquiquadratum ♄ in mundo dd	6 5	6 3	1605
Sol ad parallelum ♀ in Zodiaco	6 23	6 7	1605
Luna ad parallelum ♄ in Zodiaco	6 25	6 7	1605
⊕ ad parallelum ♄ in Zodiaco	6 25	6 7	1605
Ascendens ad ✶ ☉	6 27	6 8	1605
Luna ad Semiquadratum ♃ mundo dd	6 38	6 10	1606
Luna ad parallelum ♂ in Zodiaco	7 16	7 5	1606
⊕ ad parallelum ♂ in Zodiaco	7 16	7 5	1606
Sol ad pleiades cum Latitudine	7 43	7 11	1607
Luna ad △ ♀ in Zodiaco cum Latitudine	7 43	7 11	1607
⊕ ad parallelum ♂ mundo dd	7 48	8 00	1607
Luna ad Terminos ♄	7 49	8 00	1607
Luna ad Terminos ♄	7 56	8 1	1607
⊕ ad □ ☉ mundo dd	7 57	8 1	1607
Luna ad parallelum proprium	8 5	8 3	1607
⊕ ad parallelum ☽ in Zodiaco	8 5	8 3	1607
Sol ad Terminos ♄	8 17	8 5	1607
Luna ad □ ♀ in mundo dd	9 14	9 5	1608
Medium Cæli ad △ ♂	9 30	9 8	1608
Sol ad Pleiades sine Latitudine	10 9	10 4	1609
Medium Cæli ad △ ♃	10 26	10 7	1609
⊕ ad parallelum ♄ mundo dd	10 29	10 8	1609
Luna ad Terminos ♀	10 43	10 11	1610
⊕ ad △ ♂ in mundo dd	11 12	11 5	1610
⊕ ad Corpus Jovis dd	11 37	11 10	1611
Luna ad ☍ ♂ in Zodiaco cum Latitudine	12 13	12 5	1611

Nomina

Opus Reformatum

Nomina Directionum.	Arcus Directi Gr. Mi.	Numer. Annor. An. M.	Anni Dom
Medium Cœli ad ✶ ♄	12 13	12 5	1611
Luna ad △ ♀ in Zodiaco sine Latitudine	12 19	12 7	1611
Luna ad Corpus ♄ in Zodiaco cum Latitudine	14 52	13 1	1612
Sol ad Terminos ☌	13 00	13 3	1612
Luna ad □ ♃ in Zodiaco cum Latitudine	14 27	14 9	1614
Luna ad Terminos ♃	14 51	14 10	1614
Sol ad Corpus ♀ in Zodiaco	14 48	15 1	1614
Sol ad Terminos ♀	14 55	15 3	1614
Luna ad ✶ ♃ in mundo dd.	16 13	15 7	1615
Luna ad Spicam ♍ cum Latitudine	16 24	16 9	1616
Sol ad quintilem ♃ mundo dd.	16 25	16 9	1616
Sol ad Parallelum ♀ in Zodiaco	16 57	17 2	1616
Ascendens ad Semiquadratum ☉	17 52	18 1	1617
Luna ad ☍ ☌ in Zodiaco cum Latitudine	17 48	18 00	1617
Luna ad Terminos ♀	17 54	18 1	1617
Luna ad Corpus ♄ Zodiaco sine Latitudine	18 29	18 9	1618
Sol ad Parallelum ♃ motu rapto	19 27	18 9	1619
Ascendens ad Semiquadratum ♀	19 42	20 00	1619
Sol ad Aldebaran sine Latitudine	19 43	20 00	1619
Ascendens ad Semiquadratum ♃	20 11	20 3	1619
Luna ad □ ♃ in Zodiaco sine Latitudine	20 16	20 6	1619
Ascendens ad Sextilem ♀	20 18	20 10	1620
Sol ad △ ♄ in mundo dd.	20 36	20 10	1620
Luna ad Terminos ☌	21 15	21 7	1621
Luna ad Terminos ☌	21 23	21 9	1621
⊕ ad quadratum ♀ in mundo dd.	21 35	21 00	1621
Sol ad Terminos ♃	21 50	22 3	1621
Ascendens ad ☍ ☽	22 26	22 6	1621
Medium Cœli ad □ ☽	22 24	22 8	1621
Sol ad ☌ ☌ mundo motu Conver.	22 15	22 9	1622
Luna ad Spicam ♍ sine Latitudine	22 52	22 10	1622
Sol ad Aldebaran cum Latitudine	23 42	23 1	1622
Luna ad quintilem ♃ mundo dd.	23 55	24 5	1623
Sol ad ✶ ♃ in mundo dd.	24 21	24 8	1624
Luna ad Parallelum ♀ in Zodiaco	24 47	25 4	1624
⊕ ad Parallelum ♀ in Zodiaco	24 47	25 4	1624
Sol ad ✶ ☌ in Zodiaco	25 5	25 9	1625
⊕ ad Sesquiquadratum ☌ in mundo dd.	25 6	26 00	1625
Luna ad Terminos ♀	26 13	26 5	1625
Sol ad △ ♄ in Zodiaco	26 38	26 11	1626
Luna ad Sesquiquadratum ☌ mundo motu Convers.	26 42	27 00	1626
⊕ ad Parallelum ☉ dd.	27 50	28 4	1627
Luna ad Terminos ♀	28 41	28 11	1628
Luna ad Semiquadratum ♄ mundo motu Convers.	28 45	28 11	1628
Medium Cœli ad △ ☉	29 17	29 1	1628

E 2   Nomina

Nomina Directionum.	Arcus Directi. Gr.	Mi	Numer. Annor An.	M.	Anni Dom
Sol ad ⚹ ♀ mundo motu Convers	29	27	29	9	1629
Sol ad □ ☽ in Zodiaco	29	33	29	10	1629
Ascendens ad △ ♃	29	36	29	11	1629
Luna ad Parallelum ♀ in Zodiaco	29	45	30	1	1629
⊕ ad Parallelum ♀ in Zodiaco	29	45	30	1	1629
Sol ad Terminos ♀	29	51	30	3	1629
Luna ad ☍ ☉ cum Latitudine	29	54	30	3	1629
Sol ad ⚹ ♂ mundo dd.	29	59	30	4	1629
Luna ad Sextilem. proprium cum Latitudine	30	20	30	8	1630
Ascendens ad Semiquadratum ♀	30	37	30	11	1630
Medium Cœli ad △ ☿	30	38	30	11	1630
Luna ad △ ♃ in Zodiaco cum Latitudine	30	38	30	11	1630
⊕ ad △ ☉ mundo dd.	30	47	31	1	1630
⊕ ad △ ☿ mundo dd.	31	6	31	5	1630
Luna ad ☍ ☿ in Zodaico cum Latitudine	31	24	31	9	1631
Luna ad parallelum ♄ motu rapto	31	39	32	10	1631
Luna ad Terminos ♃	33	6	33	2	1632
Sol ad Semiquadratum ♃ mundo dd.	33	44	33	10	1633
Luna ad Terminos ♃	33	52	34	00	1633
Sol ad parallelum ♃ in Zodaico	34	13	34	6	1633
Sol ad Parallelum ♃ mundo dd.	35	6	35	2	1634
Luna ad □ ♃ in mundo dd	35	23	35	6	1634
Luna ad Parallelum ♃ in Zodiaco	35	24	35	6	1634
⊕ ad Parallelum ♃ in Zodiaco	35	24	35	6	1634
Sol ad Parallelum ☽ motu rapto	36	33	36	7	1635
Luna ad ☍ ☉ in Zodiaco sine Latitudine	37	7	37	1	1636
Luna ad Terminos ♄	37	22	37	4	1636
Luna ad ⚹ ☽ in Zodiaco sine Latitudine	37	34	37	6	1636
Luna ad △ ♃ in Zodiaco sine Latitudine	37	54	37	10	1637
Ascendens ad Corpus ♂	38	16	38	2	1637
Medium Cœli ad □ ♂	38	16	38	2	1637
Luna ad Parallelum ☿ motu rapto	38	30	38	5	1637
Sol ad quintilem ♀ motu Convers.	38	35	38	6	1637
Luna ad ☍ ☿ in Zodiaco sine Latitudine	38	42	38	8	1637
⊕ ad Parallelum ♀ mundo dd.	39	39	39	8	1638
⊕ ad Semiquadratum ♃ dd	40	22	40	3	1639
Sol ad Terminos ♄	40	33	40	5	1639
Luna ad ☍ ♀ in Zodiaco cum Latitudine	40	46	40	8	1640
Medium Cœli ad △ ♀	40	52	40	9	1640
Luna ad Terminos ♃	40	53	40	9	1640
Luna ad △ ♂ mundo motu Convers.	40	55	40	10	1640
Ascendens ad ☍ ♄	41	21	41	2	1640
Medium Cœli ad □ ♄	41	21	41	2	1640
Luna ad parallelum proprium motu Convers	41	47	41	8	1640
Sol ad parallelum ♃ mundo motu Convers	41	48	41	8	1640

Opus Reformatum.

Nomina Directionum.	Arcus Directi. Gr. Mi.	Numei Annor. An. M	Anni Dom
⊕ ad Sesquiquadratum ♀ mundo dd	42 32	41 10	1641
⊕ ad △ ♀ mundo dd	42 15	41 10	1641
Sol ad □ ☽ mundo dd	42 12	42 00	1641
⊕ ad Sesquiquadratum ☉ in mundo ad	43 02	42 00	1641
⊕ ad Cor Leonis dd	43 41	43 5	1642
Luna ad △ ♃ mundo dd	44 26	44 2	1643
Luna ad ✶ ♄ mundo motu Convers.	44 34	44 4	1643
Luna ad Parallelum ♀ motu rapto	44 40	44 5	1644
Sol ad Semiquadratum ♀ mundo dd	45	44 11	1644
Sol ad ✶ ☉ mundo motu Convers.	45 11	45 10 3	1644
Luna ad Cor ♏ in Zodiaco cum Latitudine	45 36	45 1 4	1644
Sol ad Terminos ♂	45 57	45 7	1644
Sol ad Parallelum ♂ motu rapto	46 3	45 8	1645
⊕ ad Parallelum ♃ motu rapto	46 7	45 9	1645
Sol ad ✶ ♀ in mundo dd	46	45 9	1645
Luna ad □ ♀ Zodiaco sine Latitudine	48 30	48 1	1647
Medium Cæli ad □ ♃	48 44	48 00	1647
Ascendens ad □ ♃	48 44	48 4	1647
⊕ ad ✶ ♃ mundo dd	49 55	49 6	1648
Medium Cæli ad △ ☽	50 27	50 00	1649
Luna ad △ ♂ in Zodiaco cum Latitudine	50 39	50 2	1649
Luna ad ✶ ♄ in Zodiaco cum Latitudine	51 43	51 4	1650
⊕ ad Corpus Lunæ dd	52 00	51 5	1650
Ascendens ad Corpus ☉	52 9	51 6	1650
Medium Cæli ad □ ☉	52	51 6	1650
Sol ad □ ♀ mundo motu Convers.	52 8		1650
⊕ ad Sesquiquadratum ♀ mundo dd	52 16	51 10	1651
Ascendens ad Corpus ♀	52 13	51 8	1651
Medium Cæli ad □ ♀	52 30	52 1	1651
Luna ad Cor Scorpii sine Latitudine	53 3	52	1651
Luna ad Terminos ♀	53 3	52	1652
Luna ad △ ♃ in mundo dd	54 33	53 11	1653
Sol ad Terminos ♀	54 45	54 1	1653
Luna ad □ proprium Zodiaci cum Latitudine	54 46	54 1	1653
Sol ad ✶ ♀ in mundo dd	55 36	54 9	1654
Luna ad △ ♂ in Zodiaco sine Latitudine	56 16	56 5	1655
Sol ad □ ♂ in Zodiaco	57 12	56 8	1656
Sol ad Parallelum ♃ in Zodiaco	57 53	57 1	1656
Luna ad ✶ ♄ in Zodiaco sine Latitudine	58 29	57 8	1657
Sol ad □ ♄ in Zodiaco	58 59	58 2	1657
Sol ad quintilem ☽ mundo dd	59 13	58	1657
Luna ad Parallelum ♂ mundo dd	59 56	59 2	1658
Luna ad Parallelum ♂ mundo dd	60 7	59 4	1658
Sol ad □ ♂ in mundo dd	60 54	59 9	1659
Luna ad □ ☽ in Zodiaco sine Latitudine	61 3	60 3	1659

Nomina

Nomina Directionum.	Arcus Directi. Gr. Mi.	Numer. Annor. An. M	Anni Dom
Sol ad ✶ proprium, in Zodiaco	60 18	60 6	1659
Luna ad Parallelum ♄ mundo dd.	62 18	61 6	1660
Luna ad Parallelum ♄ mundo dd.	62 51	62 00	1661
Sol ad ☐ ♄ in mundo dd.	63 18	62 6	1661
Luna ad ☐ ♄ mundo motu Conver.	66 56	66 00	1665
Luna ad ☐ ♂ mundo motu Conver.	69 17	68 3	1667

Having finished the Table of Directions, give me leave to say a word or two about the Directions of the *Sun*, as it is delivered and approved by the best Authors in that way and method. The Directions of the *Sun* under the Earth are different from those above the Earth, and that two ways: First, By being in the *Crepusculine Circles*: And secondly, By being in the *Obscure Ark*; and the cause of this difference is from the *Sun's* being nearer too, or further from our Horizon or Hemisphere, or rather (which is more proper) according to the Intension of his Light toward our Hemisphere; for when he is in the *Crepusculine Circles*, he doth much more affect us, and his Directions are more forcible than when he is in the *Obscure Ark*. Now, in the Operation for the Directions in the *Obscure Ark*, the main thing is, the *Part proportional* for the occurrent place. But in that for the *Crepusculine Circles* ascending or descending, the chiefest thing to be obtained, is the *Ortive difference*; and both these are to be applied, as directed to compleat and perfect those Directions in the *Zodiack*. And these things will appear the more plain, if we consider a few things about Directions, with the real and natural Motions thereof. The Prorogatory Virtue of the *Sun* or *Moon* remains immovable in *Mundo*, movable in the *Zodiack*, which is plain; because the Nocturnal Ark is either extended or contracted, according as they by their directional Motion shall change and alter their Declination, and by the same reason make their distances greater or less from the two next Angles; from whence ariseth that diversity and variety of Operation in working the *Sun's* directions true, which is a Mystery not known to many.

But yet further to illustrate this truth; Suppose the 15th Degree of *Aries* should ascend under the Elevation of 52, at which time, about six degrees of *Cancer* will be on the *Imum Cœli*; the

Seminocturnal

Opus Reformatum.

Seminocturnal Ark of the end of *Aries* in Horary Trines is 75 d. 30′ of *Taurus*, 63 d. 41′: and of the end of *Gemini* 57 d. 30′. By which you see the difference between the Seminocturnal Ark of the 30th degree of *Aries*, and the 30th degree of *Gemini*, is 18 degrees, which is the 20th part of the whole Circle, which in one Quadrant must of necessity form another Oblique Ark of difference in the distance between the 30th degree of *Aries* (where we will suppose the *Sun* to be) and the end of *Gemini*, the place of a Promittor, either Body or Aspect; and that the Nocturnal Circle of the 30th degree of *Aries*, from which the *Sun* moves by direction, is greater by 18 degrees, than the 30th degree of *Gemini*, to which Point the *Sun* must come to meet the Promittor: And this is such a difference, that neither the Circles of Position, nor the Horary Times will, or can regulate, because they are both formed from the same Principle; and the reason of it really is that which I spoke of before; That the prorogatory virtue remains fixed in *Mundo*, but moveable in *Zodiaco*. And by reason of that mobility, it makes a variation in its Circle by reason of its Declination; for at that time before mentioned, of 15 degrees of *Aries* ascending, the *Sun* being in 30 of the same Sign, under the Pole 52. the distance of the *Sun* from the Ascendant will be 6 degrees, 38 minutes: but when the Direction is finished to the 30th degree of *Gemini*, the *Sun* will be distant from the Ascendant but 5 degrees, 3 minutes; so that your own Reason will tell you, if his distance grows less, his Pole must grow greater; and then where is the truth of your direction? And let this suffice to have spoken of the ground of direction which hath fallen in by accident, it not being intended at first; perhaps I may take a time to discourse it larger and plainer.

The *Sun* (as it is agreed on by all) when he is above the Earth, exerts his Power more, and his Influence is greater, and more effectual to us in all Cases, whether he be Significator or Promittor, than when he is under the Earth; if so, then when he is under the Earth, by how much nearer he is to the Horizon, by so much the more (especially in the Crepusculine Ark) the Power and Influx of his Light and Vertue affects our Meridian; and according to the intension of his Light, so is his vital and Prorogatory Power.

But now in this Nativity, though the *Sun* is under the Earth, yet his Accidents are such, that will not admit him to any general

Rule

Opus Reformatum.

Rule that I have seen in order to direction; for at the time of his birth we find the *Sun* in the third House distant from the Ascendant 52 degrees, 29 minutes, and in that point of the Zodiack his Obscure Ark is one hour 44 minutes, and his Crepusculine Ark is two hours and 49 minutes, which together make up his Nocturnal Ark four hours 33 minutes. Hence you see at the time of birth we find the *Sun* within the Limits of his Obscure Ark, and by that he ought to be directed so long as he hath any, which terminates in the beginning of *Gemini*, when he is increased in his North Declination about 4 degrees and 8 minutes, so that then his Nocturnal Ark is abdicated; and he within the Crepusculine Ark, where he ought to be directed also, different from the former method: but at that time also the method mentioned is obstructed, for the Nocturnal Ark is but one continued Crepuspulum, and admits of no operation; because the Ortive difference is not to be gained as in other Nativities. That is, in other Nativities of different Positions, or different Elevations, or at other Seasons of the year; (for all Nativities of the same Position and Elevation are liable to the very same Circumstance, when the *Sun* is near the Solstitial Tropick, and under the Earth, as here in this now under consideration.)

Now the whole curiosity and difficulty (as I said before) in working Directions of this sort and nature, is to gain the true *Ortive difference* that is proportionably allowable for each Ark of distance, and to apply it according as it ought to the Ark of Direction, by which means the true Direction is produced and obtained. But this cannot be performed in this Nativity, and therefore I will propound another way, which to me seems rational. In this Case, and that is to direct the *Sun*, as if he were in the Crepusculine Circles without the *Ortive difference*. For though we cannot direct the *Sun* as he ought to be; yet we ought to pursue the tract and method of Truth as far, and as near as it is possible; in order to obtain what we expect from the distance and Ark of Direction: which if it be done (for all the preceding Directions of the *Sun* in the Zodiack are performed, according to *Ptolomy*, by the Oblique Ascention, taken under the true Pole of position; And those Directions in *Mundo* are performed by the usual way of Proportion, &c. without the Obscure Ark) we shall find a considerable difference when we compare the Directions following, which are wrought after that method, with those performed after the usual

usual manner, and inserted in the Table of Directions preceding. For indeed the Directions of the *Sun* there wrought have no great matter to do in the publick Transactions, and Mutations of this Native's Life; unless we do allow (as a certain Bounce among us hath done) *That bad Directions in Violent and Eminent Nativities, give glorious and eminent Effects; and that they do not shew their Effects by injuring the Native, but those who are his Enemies, and with whom he doth contend.* which is a pretty sort of Cant, that the Effects of the Stars shall in one Nativity from the same Ray and Direction, give *Sickness, Loss of Honour, Imprisonment,* and, perhaps, *Death* in the conclusion, to the Native; and in another Nativity to his Enemies only: a very likely Story, and just such stuff as the rest of his is, who hath imposed this upon the World.

But as to the *Sun*, he is the principal Significator of all Honour, Grandeur and Reputation, as well by Direction as by Position; for as the *Moon* is significator of all common and general Actions of human Life, so the *Sun* is significator principally of those of Honour, &c. Hence we may very well expect the *Sun* to give something considerable in this Great Man's Nativity: for I think every one allows the Accidents and Contingencies of human Life are brought to pass, and produced by directions, as the only effect of Motion; and therefore as this Native hath had great and prodigious Effects, so the Directions ought to be something in proportion to what was produced; for from poor weak Directions there can be but small and inconsiderable Effects produced. However, I do not lay this down as absolutely necessary to be followed; I only propound it, as being an unusual Case, that you, whoever you are that understand it, may judge which is the most probable; though I am satisfied that the Directions of the *Sun* in the Crepusculine Circles are true, but in this Case we have no Rule, and therefore this method is offered as a supply to that defect: that is, whither the *Sun* directed after the method and manner when he is in the Crepusculine Circles without the *Ortive difference* (when it cannot be had, as here) will not nearly correspond to Truth, as in other parts of the Zodiack where it can be taken. In which thing I submit my self to those skilful in that way and method, and only enter it down as an Essay to a better discovery; for I am well assured, that the best method of directions yet discovered, may admit of correction and emendation, if the Professors of this Study would be pleased to take pains and labour in it;

F but

Opus Reformatum.

but one part of them are ignorant, and the other idle, and so the work lies by: but for the common way, as it is a very easie one, so it is a very false one; and he that pretends to Astrology, and hath not found himself cheated by his own Rules in Directions, &c. some hundreds of times, I think he hath taken but very little pains in those Operations, or else by the help of a bad memory he hath forgot them: but it serves the turn; and so long as none knows better, every one is contented, and, I suppose, most of them are so far from mending of it, that were there a better produced, they are so fond of their Errors, that they will not part with their old one, and therefore let them go on and see what they can make of it; and whether this I have here done pleaseth or not, I care not; under which consideration, I come now (as I promised you) to give half a score Directions to spend your Judgment on, and to consider what prospect they have to Truth: yet I do not expect every one to be capable of judging whether it be true or false, and therefore would not have every little *Capricio* think that I call for his Opinion, or would have him busily concerned in giving his Judgment about the matter, before he apprehends it: And yet without setting a Figure, I can tell you I must expect such usage, and that from such People too, who I can assure you (some of them) are no small Fools.

Nomina Directionum	Arcus Directl. Gr. Mi	Numer. Annor.	Anni Dom.
Sol ad ✶ ☌ in Zodiaco	17 43	18 60	1617
Sol ad Trine ♄ in Zodiaco	18 51	19 9	1618
Sol ad □ Lunæ in Zodiaco	21 16	21 7	1620
Sol ad □ Martem in Zodiaco	48 27	47 10	1647
Sol ad parallelum ♃ in Zodiaco	48 55	48 4	1647
Sol ad □ Saturni in Zodiaco	50 8	49 8	1648
Sol ad ✶ proprium in Zodiaco	53 49	52 3	1651
Sol ad ✶ Lunæ in Zodiaco	52 41	53 11	1652
Sol ad Corpus ♃ in Zodiaco	54 18	53 8	1653
Sol ad ✶ Mercurii in Zodiaco	55 52	55 2	1654

These things being thus performed, and done, Let us now examine the whole Work, and see how the Directions do agree with his Accidents, from the Year 1646 to his death; for we have none particular and significant before he was 40, or 41 years

of

of Age, the former part of his Life being to me unknown; neither is there any solid Account of any of note by those that have written his Life, and therefore I shall make use only of those Accidents that are certainly true, and generally known to all Mankind, and they are those that do generally relate to the Publick.

Anno 1640. He was by his Country chosen a Member in that Parliament that King *C.* I. called to sit in *November*, and this was the first step he made into the Publick; but I cannot own this to be so great a preferment as some do, because it is attended with labour, trouble and charge, yet I must acknowledge that this laid the ground-work of his future Rise and Grandeur: He had then the *Moon* directed to the Opposition of *Venus* in *Zodiaco*; *Moon ad Trinum ☌ in mundo dd.* and the Mid-heaven *ad △ ♀* and *□ ♄*, and in his Revolution for that year *Jupiter* was in exact Sextile to his Radical Mid-heaven: thus you see he had both good and bad Directions in this year, and therefore I do not doubt but he had some strugling and contest in his Election, as well as in his other Affairs.

Anno 1641. Like a True *Englishman* he raised a Troop of Horse at his own Charge to assist the Parliament, and defend his Country against Popery, which was then coming in like a flood: he had then the ⊕ *ad Sesquiquadrat* of ♀ *dd.* and to the △ ♀ *dd.* the *Sun* to the square of the *Moon*, and the ⊕ *ad Sesquiquadrat* of the *Sun*, and with these he had also an unlucky Revolution.

Anno 1642. He had a Commission for a Regiment of Horse, which Regiment he raised in his own Country of Freeholders, and Freeholders Sons, who did really go out in point of Conscience to serve their Country in that time of danger: he had now the ⊕ *ad Cor* ♌, and a very good Revolution to assist him.

Anno 1643. He was very active in the North, where he opposed the Earl of *Newcastle*, and to that purpose joined with the Lord *Willoughby*, and did the Parliament and whole Nation gallant Service. In this Summer he also took *Stamford* from the King's Forces; and this was the first year that he was taken notice of in publick, and esteemed by the Parliament, because they found him faithful; he had now the *Moon ad △ ♃ in mundo dd. Moon ad ✱ ♄ in mundo dd.* and *Moon* also *ad parallelum ♀ in mundo Motu Rapto*; with these he he had also a most admirable Revolution, for the *Moon* was on his Radical Mid-heaven in Trine to *Venus*; and both *Mars* and *Venus* in Trine to his Mid-heaven, with other advantageous Positions. I remember *Honest John* exclaims against him in this year for his whining and dissimulation in Religion, which I confess, if true, was a very ill thing; but *prithee John* tell me one thing, Was this Hypocrisie at *White-hall*, in the Year 1643. greater than that at *Breda* in 1658. when none but the good men must beg a blessing on the good Creatures? &c. And when one of those good Parsons asked a *certain Gentleman* how they spent the *Sabbath-day*; why, says he, we spend the Morning in reading, and Private Devotion; but in the Afternoon they always met together, and every man took a portion or part of Scripture, and spoke from that; and when they had all done, then His Majesty took up every man's Notions delivered, spoke to them distinctly, giving his own Opinion of the whole matter, and after some Exhortations to a good Life, he himself concluded the day in Prayer, which made those good men say, that they had a King in Covenant with God. I think this enough without mentioning any thing of the *Scotch Covenant*, to inform honest *J. G.* that he might have forbore that Reflection on *Cromwell*, for you see it is an easie matter to give him a *Rowland* for his *Oliver*.

Anno 1644. He differed with the Earl of *Manchester*, one of the Parliament Generals, about the Conduct of a Battel. I think that of *Marston-Moor*, about which they accused each other; but *Cromwell* came off Victor, and still stood fair with the Parliament, making his own Case good. He had now the *Sun ad Semiquadrat* of ♀ *in mundo dd.* the *Sun* to his own *Sextile in mundo dd.* and the *Moon* to the *Cor* ♏ with latitude. In his Revolution he had the *Sun* in Conjunction with *Jupiter*, the *Moon* in Conjunction with *Saturn*, and *Mars* in Trine to his Radical Mid-heaven.

Anno 1645. *Cromwell* was made Lieutenant-General to Sir *Thomas Fairfax*, and did the Parliament and Nation admirable Service in the West of *England*, in *Oxfordshire*, and at *Naseby*. He had now the *Sun ad parallelum* ☌ *in mundo motu rapto*, the ⊕ *ad par* ♃ *motu rapto*, and the *Sun ad* ✶ ♀ *in mundo dd.*

Anno

Opus Reformatum.

Anno 1647. was a year of trouble and much labour to him about the Differences of the Army; his Enemies appear'd openly against him, and endeavour to out him by divers Aspersions; but at last he got an Impeachment against them in Parliament, and with much strugling he at last got clear with Honour and Reputation. He had now the *Moon ad* □ ♀ *in Zodiaco S. L.* the *M. C. ad* □ ♃ and the Ascendant to the Square of *Jupiter*; and in the Second Table he had the *Sun ad* Square of *Mars*, and parallel of *Jupiter*, which are indeed all of them very apt and proper Directions for such Troubles and Vexations as he then underwent. The Revolution for that Year was but indifferent, more of bad than good in it; for the *Sun, Moon* and *Saturn* was in Conjunction.

Anno 1648. was a Year of much Labour and Toil to him: for then was he imployed to reduce the *Welsh* Rebels, which he did effectually; after that he went against *Duke Hamilton* and the *Scots*, then in *Lancashire*, where he beat and took the *Duke Prisoner*; and toward the end of the Year he was chosen by the Parliament to go *General* for *Ireland*; he had now the part of Fortune to the ✶ of ♃; in his Revolution for that Year he had his *Moon* in Sextile to his Radical Mid-heaven, and *Saturn* in Opposition to it, ♀ on the radical place of *Mars*, and in Trine to his Mid-heaven, which I judge gave his Arms success.

Anno 1649. he went General for *Ireland* to rescue that poor Kingdom out of the hands of the Papists; who had so barbarously murthered 200000 of the Protestant *English* before in the Year 1640 and on *July* the 10th he set forward on his Journy, which God was pleased to prosper with success; and that gloriously too, as you may see by the History of that War; and especially his first Undertaking, which was at *Drogedah*, where he storm'd that strong Garison, and put them to the Sword, and by that means frighted the whole Country, and made other Towns easier to be taken. But during his continuance in this Kingdom, they say he had the Flux, yet by the blessing of God he did very well: He had now his Mid heaven *ad* △ ☽; the *Moon ad* △ ♂ *in Zodiaco C. L.* two very great Directions, and fit for such an Undertaking: his Revolution was but indifferent, but what was in it, was good: His *Moon* was in his Radical Horoscope in Trine to the *Sun*, and in ✶ to ♀ on the Radical place of his ♂.

Anno

Anno 1650. he was made *Lord General* of all the Forces in the Commonwealth of *England*, and was then sent into *Scotland* to reduce them to obedience. And on *July* the 22d he entred that Kingdom with a powerful Army; and on *September* the 3d following, he Chastised the *Scots* in that memorable and famous Batrel of *Dunbar*, where he flew 3000 and took 10000 Prisoners, and with them Lieutenant-General *Lumsden*, Adjutant-General *Bickerton*, Three Collonels, Eleven Lieutenant-Collonels, Nine Majors, Forty seven Captains, Seven Captain-Lieutenants, Twelve Cornets, Seventy eight Ensigns, Thirty Guns, Fifteen thousand Arms, and Two hundred Colours: He had now the *Moon* ad ✶ ♄ in Zodiace C. L. the ⊕ ad *Corpus Lunæ*, and the Ascendant to the body of the *Sun*, with the Directions of the last Year, which are not yet over. In his Revolution for that year, there is not any thing remarkable; all that is, we find the *Sun* in Conjunction with ♀ and *Mars*.

Anno 1651. the Valiant *Cromwell* beat the *Scots* at *Worcester*, where he took Duke *Hamilton* and Twelve Earls, Lords, and Knights, besides; Three Major Generals, and Four other Generals, Twelve Collonels, Sixteen Lieutenant-Collonels, Twenty one Majors, a Hundred and ten Captains, a Hundred and thirty six Lieutenants, Seventy six Cornets, Twenty one Ensigns, Ninety Quartermasters; NINE PARSONS, Nine Chyrurgeons, Thirty of the King's Domestick Servants, Eight thousand Prisoners, Two thousand slain, and a Hundred and fifty Colours taken, with all their Baggage, Ammunition and Artillery, together with the Plunder of the Town. He had now the *Sun* to the Square of ♀ *motu Converso*; ⊕ ad *Sesquiquadratum* ♀, *in mundo*, dd. the Ascendant to the *Sextile* of *Mercury*; and the *Moon* to the *Cor*. ♃ S. L. In the Revolution there is little or nothing considerable.

Anno 1652. we have but little account of his Publick Actions and Affairs in this Year; neither have we any Direction, except in the Second Table, the *Sun* ad ✶ ☽, but a very good Revolution, the *Sun* in Trine to *Jupiter*, the *Moon* in Trine to the Midheaven, and also in Square to ☿, in ✶ ♀ ✶ ♂ and △ to ♃.

Anno 1653. In the beginning of the year he dissolved the Parliament, and all the year afterward he was busie about the Affairs of the Nation, and in *December* he was made Protector. He had

now

now the Moon ad △ ♃ in mundo dd. Sun ad Term ♀ the Moon to her own Square in the Zod. C. L. and in the Second Table the Sun to the body of Jupiter; his Revolution for that Year was but indifferent.

Anno 1654. he made Peace with the *Dutch*, sent a Fleet to the *West Indies* under the Command of *Pen*, made a League with *Sweden*, &c. he had now the Sun to the Sextile of *Venus* in mundo dd. but in the Second Table the ☉ ad ✶ ♀; and indeed either of them may be allowed such an effect.

Anno 1655. His Army in the *West-Indies* was destroyed by the oversight of the Commander, the Fleet took *Jamaica*; he received Addresses from divers parts of the Nation, and he appoints a Committee to provide relief for the poor Protestants in *Piedmont*. He had now his Moon directed to the Trine of *Mars* in Zodiaco S. L. But a very ill Revolution, *Mars* on his Ascendant in Square to the Moon.

Anno 1656. there was a Plot against his Life by some of his Guards, and also to set *White-hall* on fire; but it was discovered, and *Sindercom* apprehended, and also condemned for it, but died in the Tower; and as it was supposed, he poisoned himself. The Protector also called a Parliament, or something like it, who confirmed him in his Title and Power that He had before. He had now his Sun ad □ ♂ in Zodiaco, and to the parallel of *Jupiter* in Zodiaco also; which are very like the Effects of this Year. In his Revolution he had his Sun in Conjunction with *Jupiter* and Trine of *Saturn*, and the Moon in Trine to the Sun and *Jupiter*; and in Conjunction with *Saturn*.

Anno 1657. He sent Forces into *Flanders* to fight the *Spaniards*, he took *Dunkirk*, &c. He had now the Moon ad ✶ ♄ in Zodiaco S. L. and the Sun ad □ ♂ in Zodiaco likewise. In the Revolution he had his Moon on the Radical Ascendant in Trine to Saturn.

But in *Anno* 1658. after the great Success of his Army in *Flanders*, the Confirmation of his Title, and many other Publick Affairs of State being dispatched by him; as the Relief of the persecuted

cuted Protestants in *Poland* and *Bohemia*, his preserving those in *Piedmont* from the *French* Persecution, &c. on *September* the 3d. he died of an Intermitting Fever, having been sick about a Month, and was taken at *Hampton-Court*, to which place he resorted once a week. I know some pretend he was poisoned, and also say they knew the man, which was one of his Physicians: and so let him be for me, for that doth not concern my business here in hand: If his Doctor did poison him, and then brag of it, I think he was a very Ill man; for whatever *Oliver* was, either as to his Power, Principles or Religion, if very bad in all, was no authority for him to commit a private murther, nor any way extenuate his Crimes of Murther and Blood ; but aggravated and made more hainous, as being done by his Physician; which would be of ill consequence, should such things grow into custom and approbation ; and whoever should encourage such a thing, would be very unwilling to suffer by the same way themselves ; therefore in a word, if the Physician did do it, I think he was the worst of men. About *June* this Year, the *Moon*, who is giver of Life came to the parallel of *Mars in Mundo Motu Converso*; and about the latter end of *August* following, he had the *Moon* to the parallel of *Mars in mundo motu directo*: and this followed by the *Moon* to her own Square in *Zodiaco Sine Lat.* the *Moon* to the parallel of *Saturn in mundo motu directo & motu Converso*; the *Moon* to the Square of *Saturn in mundo motu Converso*, also to the Square of *Mars in mundo motu Converso*. Thus you see he had seven Directions violent and malefick, (and not one good Direction between) to kill him : which not only in this, but in any other Case to the Giver of Life, shall do the same without shamming in the Ascendant to the Square of *Mars*, as our *Popish Conjurer* you see hath done ; and yet at the same time take the confidence to tell the World the *Horoscope* was Giver of Life, when the *Sun* is but eleven degrees 33 minutes distant from the Ascendant, which according to all the Astrological Authors that I have read, is, and ought to be Giver of Life. As you may see in *Ptolomy's Quadripartit*, Lib. 3. cap. 13. *Campanella*, Lib. 4. cap. 4. Artic. 2. with many others that I would desire the worthy Gentleman to look over, and examine them well, and after he hath done that, to resolve us what he means by that Expression in his *Doctrine of Nativities*, pag. 258. where he says, *The Sun cannot be Giver of Life, if he were in an Apherical place, because the Birth is Nocturnal.* Methinks it sounds a little odd.

But

But yet further to clear this point about the *Hileg*; because I have mentioned my Authority for it, I will also prove it plainly from my Author's words, with the Book and Chapter, lest he may reassume his accustomed gift of Impudence, and deny my Quotations, as he did in his *Reply* to my *Almanack* of 1687, when those Quotations were really true, as these are. The Translation that I use, is that of *Melancthon*, which is the best Translation of *Ptolomy* in being, and hath I think given the truest meaning of *Ptolomy*'s words; and if you please but to look into the 11th Chapter of that *Quadripartite*, and the Third Book, you will there find these words. *Cum autem quærimus in his locis potentissimum, primus erit Medium Cæli, deinde Horoscopus; postea undecima domus succedens Media Cæli, deinde occasius, postea Nonus domus Antecedens Medium Cæli.* In this Chapter he is labouring to prove, and also lay down by Rule the place of the Prorogator; and after he hath spent some time to shew the Prorogatory place in general, he comes in the words beforementioned to the particulars, and which of them do precede in Power and Order; and therefore says he, *When we inquire who is most powerful in these places, the first in order is the Midheaven; next after that the Ascendant, then the Eleventh House, then the Seventh, and last of all the Ninth.* And the reason why he is so particular in this Case, is because the *Sun* and *Moon* may be sometimes both in Prorogatory Places, and both contend for priority; therefore in such a Case these Rules are to be considered and compared with those of the 13th Chapter of the same Book; by which it may be decided which of the two have the real Power of *Hileg*, or giver of Life. Hence certainly our Author by taking such pains and care to lay down particular Rules how to elect the giver of Life, did intend a greater use to be made of it, than any of our late Pretenders, I perceive, are aware of, which seems more plain from the first Paragraph of the 14th Chapter, where he discourseth wholly of the Anaretical Point, and who or what he judgeth to be *Anareta*, yet he allows none to be directed to that point; but the *Hileg*, or giver of Life; and therefore he begins that Chapter with these words, *Invento Prorogatore, duo modi sumendi sunt*, &c.

Now, if this Doctrine be true, and that the Professors of this Science will be pleased to allow the Great *Ptolomy* a share in their good Opinions; then this *Lying Oracle* of ours is quite out of doors, and besides the Mark in his own Trade, when he tells the World, That *the* Sun *cannot be giver of Life, if he were in an Aphelical place*; as in the page before quoted. For when he allows the Ascendant in *Cromwell's* Nativity, the power of *Hileg*, and the *Sun* at the same time within 12 degrees of the *Cusp*, and locally in it, seems to me a substantial piece of Nonsence, quite contradictory to the most approved Authors in being, who allow all of them, that the Ascendant is the second place in power to entertain the *Prorogator*; and that the *Sun* there is also certainly *Hileg*, if the *Moon* is not above the Earth. So that should I insist on no other reason but this, it would be sufficient to prove the Figure and Time of his Nativity false; and this because he makes that imaginary Direction of the Ascendant to the *Square* of *Mars*, the only one to prove the truth of the whole Calculation. For if we should allow such a Direction in that Figure, as the *Sun* to the *Square* of *Mars* (which indeed there is none before he should be Ninety one years of Age) yet it is wholly misapplied, and a power given to it quite distinct from the Order of Nature, and the Authority of Authors: the Ascendant not having power to kill when the *Sun* is in the *Horoscope*, or any other place, giver of Life. I have been the plainer and fuller in this point, because it is the Principal Foundation of Nativities, and the only thing first to be known in the Directions and Predictions about Life and Sickness, and the only thing neglected and forgotten at this time among the Professors, both old and young; they having only the Name of it, but nothing of its Power and Use; but I have spoken enough if understood; and more will be to no purpose if not understood.

But again. In this Nativity that he hath published and asserted for truth, there is another *Notorious Error*, and that is, he lets the *Sun* pass by the *Square* of *Mars*, the *Square* of *Saturn*, and body of *Jupiter*, Lord of the eighth House in the fourth, that fatal place as they call it; and kills him with the Ascendant to one single Direction only. Now, if we should allow that the Ascendant had power, and did kill by Direction to the *Square* of *Mars*; Why should not the *Sun* to those three fatal Directions beforementioned, give the Native the same effect of Death long before, as they did now? I know no reason to the contrary, according to that sort of Astrology which is common among most of the Professors, but especially used by this our Famous and most Renowned *Nativity-Maker*; as may appear by those Ingenious and

Learned

Learned Treatises that he hath befriended the World with, being filled with abundance of Errors and Contradictions. But to return to our Business again; at the time of this great Hero's death, besides the Directions mentioned as the true Natural Causes thereof; there were other things worth our consideration that did concur as Concomitants to the same; and the first was his Revolution for that year, and indeed a very remarkable one it was, if we consider it well and fully. And seeing I have mentioned something of Revolutions, I will also speak a word or two of their use and abuse. The Professors of this Age make a great bustle about the exact time of a Revolution, that is, to find the exact Minute and Second when the *Sun* comes to his Radical Place, for which purpose they have invented a great many Fooleries, and to little purpose; but when this exact and critical Time is obtained, and a Figure set, they gravely tell us of strange and prodigious Effects that the Planets have by being in particular Houses therein; that the *Horoscope* and *Midheaven* of a Revolutional Figure, is of a great signification both to the Native's Life and Reputation. Nay, they are now grown to that perfection in their Trade of this kind, that they work Directions in that Figure like as they do in the *Radix*; to which purpose also they have made us a measure of Time, with other kinds of Tables to compleat their Folly, and render their Art ridiculous. When indeed the Ancient and more Authentick Authors have taken no notice of such things as these; and *Ptolomy* himself hath not above four Lines in his four Books that have any relation to the Revolutions in Nativities; and therefore how they came by all these whims, it would be worth while to consider, (for we have not one word about them in *Firmicus*, one of the oldest Astrologers we have, that came after *Ptolomey*), and perhaps may find a spare sheet in my next Treatise, to unriddle the Juggles that they have jumbled together to cheat themselves, and the rest of Mankind. For I do assure you, There is nothing in *their* method of Revolution, neither can they fetch their Authority further back than *Origanus*, *Argol*, *Schoner*, *Hispalensis*, *Junctine*; and two or three more of them that have taken it up upon very slender Authority, and they that still follow, do every one endeavour to improve the Errors of him that went before. For I will now soberly ask one question; and that is, to tell me what they have found in the Revolutional Directions, that was not as plainly discovered by the Transits

Opus Reformatum.

in the Revolution, and the Returns? If so, what should we go to make abundance of Confusion when it may be done with less trouble? And to be plain with you; The truth and mystery of Revolutions doth really consist in nothing else but the Transits and Returns of the Planets to the Radical Points and Parts of the Nativity, and to the places of Direction. And to this end there is no need of abundance of labour to gain the exact time of the *Suns* return to his Radical places; if you miss ten Minutes of it in time, it will be no great matter of Error in your Judgement, if you understand your Business. And to say the truth, the Radical Figure may very well serve for every Revolution throughout the Native's whole Life, placing the Planets in the degrees of those Signs that they shall be found in at the time of the *Suns* return to his Radical place, or near it. And after this manner I will give the Figure of this great Native's final Revolution; and it is as followeth,

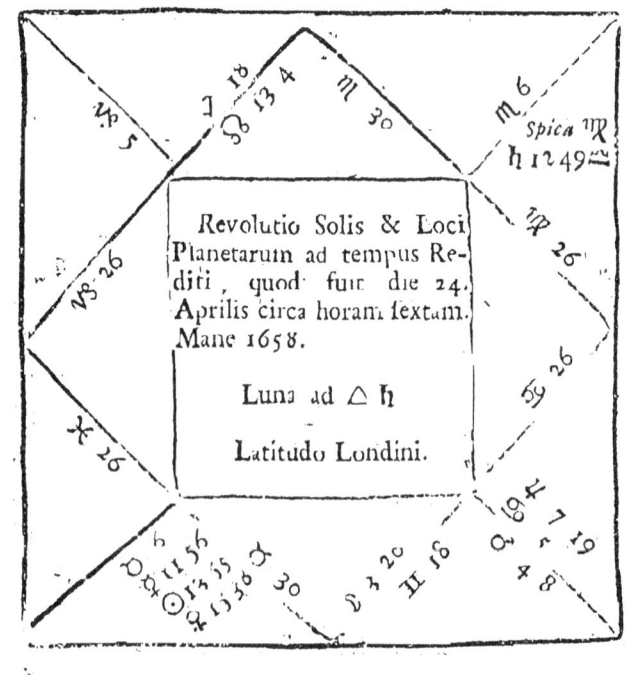

Latitud Planitar.			
♄	2	46	No
♃	0	14	No
♂	1	24	No
♀	3	40	So
☿	0	52	So
☽	0	38	No

Revolutio Solis & Loci Planetarum ad tempus Rediti, quod fuit die 24. Aprilis circa horam sextam. Mane 1658.

Luna ad △ ♄

Latitudo Londini.

Having considered the Directions, and also the Point or Part of the Ecliptick the *Moon*, who is giver of Life, is arrived at in this year by direct Direction in *Zodiaco*; and that is about 14 degrees

grees of *Sagitary*, the exact Square to her own Radical Place, and at the time of the *Suns* return, going to the opposite point of that place, and to the Square of her own place in the *Radix*; *Saturn* and *Jupiter* are both return'd to their own Radical Places; and so is *Mars* and the *Moon* to the Square of theirs; *Mercury* and *Venus* are in *Taurus*, where they were in the *Radix*, and not far from their own Radical Places. So that you see all the Planets are returned to their own places except *Mars* and the *Moon*, and they are in Square to them. Now, the use I shall make of the Revolution is this; The *Moon*, *Mars*, and *Saturn*, are all of them Promittors by direction; *Mars* is in Square to *Saturn*, Lord of the Radical Horoscope, who is return'd to his Radical Place; and the *Moon*, tho *Hilig*, yet she is here a Promittor also, and is going to the direct Opposition of the place of Direction, and to the Square of her own place; and besides this, *Mars* is going to the Mundane Parallel of the *Sun*. And to sum up all, we find both the *Moon* and *Mars* in violent Constellations, the *Moon* being with the *Aldebaran* of the Nature of *Mars*, and *Mars* is with those Stars in the beginning of *Cancer*, called *Castor & Pollux*, of the nature of *Saturn*. So that we may from the *Suns* return, and the then Configurations compared with the Directions, conclude, That according to second Causes, it could be no less then mortal. When I have done this, I always consider Secondary Directions, and Progressions, and also observe if they help on the Work; for if all concur, we may certainly judge that nothing but a Miracle can save; and therefore under this Revolution, we find that the Ascendant by Secondary Motion was directed to the *Opposition* of *Jupiter*, the *Sun* under the *Square* of *Saturn*, and had been so about six Months, and the *Moon* to the *Opposition* of *Mars*, and that just toucheth about the time of his Sickness, all which are ill, and shew a bad year. The Progression began *January* the 2d, about six of the Clock in the Morning, *Anno* 160¾. and was but an indifferent one; you may if you please call it bad, for the *Moon* was on the *Suns* Radical place, *Saturn* and *Jupiter* on the place of Direction, in Square to the *Moon's* Radical place, and *Mars* in *Opposition* to his own place; but *Venus* is on the Radical Ascendant in *Conjunction* with the *Sun*, and that is all that may be called good in this Progressive Lunation. But above all, the *Ingresses* and *Transits* of the Planets at the time of the beginning of his Sickness, and of his

Death

Opus Reformatum.

Death, are very remarkable; for about the time that he was taken Sick, which was *August* the 26th, there was a Transit and Ingress of the *Sun* on the *Moon's* Radical Place, in Square to the place of Direction; and a little before that, there was a *Conjunction* of the *Moon, Mars*, and *Mercury*, on, or near the same degree, and so configurated as before; and the very day of his Death, the *Moon* did Transit the Radical Place of *Mars's* Body, and *Saturn's* Opposition, and also in *Opposition* to *Saturn* that very day of his Death; and the *Sun* in an exact Zodiacal Parallel with *Saturn*, and going to the Zodiacal Parallel of *Mars*, and to his *Conjunction* also. Thus I have endeavoured to shew you, how I understand the method and manner of judging Death by *Primary* and *Converse Directions*, *Revolutions*, *Secondary Directions*, *Progressions*, *Transits*, and *Ingresses*; which if rightly understood and practised, would give the Students in this Science more satisfaction than all those Whims published by our Modern Authors, and stollen from them by our *Popish Oracle*. And I hope by this time, I have given the Professors and Students in this Art full satisfaction, in proving that the Nativity which *Gadbury* printed, was notoriously false; and grounded upon Principles next to none; and that the Reasons and Rules given to assert its Truth, are no ways becoming a Man of Skill or Ingenuity; especially one that pretends to be the Master and Head of the whole Tribe, and endued with the advantage of Twenty five years Experience, and more; when he wrote and published *Cromwell's* Nativity last in the year 1685. And so I come in the next place to give you my General Judgement on the whole Figure, after the manner that the rest of our Profession do on the Twelve Houses; and perhaps too, I may follow the same Order in my Judgment, but not in their Rules and Principles of Judgment.

A Judgment on the preceding Nativity, after the manner of the Twelve Houses.

THE first thing I shall consider, is the length or shortness of the Native's Life; and from the Positions in general, what time may be probably assigned for the number of his years: yet I know very well there can be no positive Judgment given on that point, because the number of his years depends on the distance between the giver of Life, and the Anaretick point, as to the certainty of their number, and the time of Expiration; but yet give me leave to tell you there must be Arguments of a long Life in the Position, or else I shall be very sparing in his number of years; and to be yet more plain with you, the Arguments of Long Life are such good Rays and Positions, that roborate and fortify the Giver of Life; and this the more when the *Hileg* is naturally strong, and well-placed in the Figure. *Length of Life.*

And in this Nativity we find the *Hileg* Angular, in *Trine* to the Sun and Mercury, in *Sextile* to *Jupiter*, and also in Reception with Mercury; and besides these, we find the *Sun* and *Mercury* in *Sextile* to the *Ascendant*, and in *Sextile* to *Jupiter* likewise, and he in his Exaltation in *Cancer*; and no ill Rays of *Saturn* and *Mars* any ways afflicting either *Sun*, *Moon*, or *Ascendant*; so that we may rationally conclude the Native was designed by Nature for a considerable long Life; and not only long, but also a healthy one. I know there are some according to the usual Cant, would tell you, That the Square of the three Superiors from those Cardinal Signs should give him bad *Lungs*, with pains in his Head, the *Vertigo*, *Lethargy*, &c. imperfections in his *Reins*, *Gravel*, *Stone*, and abundance more of these things, had they seen his Nativity before he had been grown to years of Ripeness. But I dare venture to say, That he had none of these, the *Gravel* excepted; but they that would know more of these things, let them read carefully the 17th Chapter of the 3d Book of *Ptolomy*'s Quadripartite, *De Læsionibus & morbis Corporum*. *The Moon is Hileg.*

The Native's Understanding, Judgment, with all the other Faculties of the Soul, depending on the Position and Configurations of *Mercury*, as one well says, *Qualitates animæ, quæ propriæ sunt* *Understanding and Judgment, &c.*

sunt mentis, & ratiocinationis, sumuntur in singulis ex Mercurii conditione. Which if true, then hath our Native a most excellent Position for intellectual Abilities; for his *Mercury* is as strong as in any Figure I have seen. For here is *Mercury* just past the *Conjunction* of the *Sun*, and in his *Oriental Occidentality*, increasing in Light and Motion, in Reception with the *Moon*; but that which is the greatest, and most to be observed, is, that the *Moon* beholds him with a *Trine*, and *Jupiter* with a *Sextile*; and what is more, *Jupiter* also beholds him by a Mundane Square, so that they are really configurated both in *Zodiaco & Mundo*; and besides we find him in a fixed Sign the House of *Venus*, and in a Zodiacal Parallel with *Venus*, in *Sextile* to the *Ascendant*. These Positions must be allowed to give all the great and excellent Qualifications that are requisite to make a Counsellor, a States-man, and a Soldier; here is no Rashness, but Resolution upon deliberate Consideration; here is no Timidity, nor yet unstedinefs in Judgment: here is no Dulness nor Stolidity, but a Natural and Native Sharpness of Fancy at all times, fit either for Inquiry or Council. In a word, The *Moon* in *Virgo* in *Trine* to *Mercury* in *Taurus*, is without doubt the most agreeable Position to give a good, quick apprehensive Fancy and Judgment. *Multum enim ad animæ proprietates signa conferunt, in quibus Mercurius & Luna versantur, multum & stellarum adspectus id solem & ad Cardines, & natura cujuslibet planetæ Congruens certis Inclinationibus animæ.* Quadripartite *Ptolomæi*, Lib. 3. Cap. 18.

Of his Riches, &c. I shall consider his Riches from the part of Fortune, as the general Significator of Wealth; but yet before I begin my Judgment thereon, give me leave to premise a word or two. I would not have you think, because that he arrived to the Government of a Nation, and had the use and command of the Kingdoms Money and Treasure, that I call him Rich, for I look on that to be but the common Attendant of his Honour and Grandeur, and not the excellence of his Fortune to Riches. For a King may have vast Sums of Money, and yet be no rich Man, as we have seen in K. C. 2. and a King may have far lesser Sums than ever he had, and yet be a very rich Man, and lay by him a great Treasure for his own Use and Posterity, distinct from the Interest of the Nation and People, as was K. H. 7. Therefore I would not be thought to build his Honour upon his Riches, which is indeed no such thing, but that kind of his Wealth was really founded on his

Honour

Honour and Grandeur; for the Sword was the Anvil upon which he wrote out his Fortune, his Honour, &c. And as that always brings a certain Charge, so it usually brings a Supply of Fortune to defray it. And therefore I shall consider his Fortune distinctly and separately, from that which came by his Honour; and what it might have been, had he continued in that Station in which he was Born and Bred. *Ad rem vero*, the part of Fortune (as I said before) is the only Significator allowed by *Ptolomy*, for Riches and Fortune in the World; and that we find about 2 degrees distant from the Cusp of the Sixth House in *Cancer*, in Sextile to *Venus*, and disposed of by the Moon and *Jupiter*; all which are strong and potent, and do certainly promise (whoever hath such a Position) Riches and Plenty of the things of Fortune; and this by various ways and means. And I am of Opinion, that it being in *Cancer*, a Tropical Sign, doth not add a little to the Advantage. *Ptolomy* says, Lib. 4. *Caput de Facultatibus*. *Jupiter per fidelitatem, præfecturas,* &c. That which *Jupiter* gives his Assistance to the Natives Fortune, he doth it by Places and Offices of Trust, Command and Rule in the Government, &c. And tho he doth not say it, yet I judge the Moon in Trine to the Sun and *Mercury*, gives the same things as relate to Dominion; and therefore from these and such like things, we may judge He should grow Rich, and increase his Estate. But then we find the *pars fortunæ* is in an exact Zodiacal Parallel with *Mars*, and is also going to his Mundane Parallel; this gives damage and loss to his Estate, and why may not this be the Expence and Wasting of his Estate and Fortune in Military Service at the Beginning of the Wars, and afterward too I believe? And indeed it is in *Ptolomy*'s own words, *Mars ex Militia & Gubernatione Exercituum*. And tho I think he did increase his Fortune, as he did advance in Honour; yet I think some men would have got more, for I could never hear that he left any large Sums at his Death, unless they were Debts. I do therefore conclude, that the Parallels of *Mars* had their Effects also as well as the other Rays; but besides these, we find *Mars* in the Second strong, and also Lord of the Second, but in Opposition to *Saturn*, and Square to *Jupiter*; this shewed he would gain much, and advance mightily, but it would be by Violence, Force, and with Opposition too. But wherever you find *Mars* strong in the Second, that Native always gets much, *per fas, aut*

H *nefas*,

nefas; he cares not which, and seldom parts with it again as long as he lives.

The old way and custom is to judge these things from the Third House. But *Ptolomy* teacheth us another Doctrine, and that is, to judge of Brothers and Sisters by the Tenth and Eleventh Houses, with *Venus* by Day, and the *Moon* by Night; and this he doth not do dogmatically and positively without rendring you a reason for it, *Lib. 3. Cap. 5.* from which Principles and Method I do here form and collect my Judgment. The Sign *Sagitary* doth possess both the Tenth and Eleventh Houses, and *Jupiter* Lord of it is in *Cancer*, a fruitfull Sign, and in *Sextile* to the *Sun* and *Moon*, but in *Square* to *Saturn* and *Mars*, and both *Saturn* and *Mars* are in Opposition, and casting their Squares to the Cusp of the Eleventh House. These Positions seem plainly to shew he had Brothers, but not above one Sister, if any; but not many, if any, of both Sexes should live to years of Discretion and riper Age; and do think the *Sextile* of the *Sun* and *Jupiter* should give one that might live to some considerable Age.

But the Square of *Jupiter* to *Mars* and *Saturn*, and their Squares also to the Eleventh House, should also shew, that their Agreement was but indifferent, and that the rest of his Consanguineal Relations (Children excepted) and he, should not have an extraordinary Intimacy and Kindness the one for the other, neither indeed should they very well agree in reality, tho in his Post and Quality his Power commanded it; and therefore his more inferior Relations durst do no less than shew him the Respect due to his Quality, and for which reason I shall omit all further discourse thereof. But before I make an end of this Paragraph, lest I should be questioned, because I have overturn'd the old custom of the Third House, it will not be amiss if I give you *Ptolomy*'s own words, and perhaps that may stop a more violent Inquiry from the short-sighted *Caprico*, that thinks himself able to call me to an account; and his words are these, *De fratribus vero, siquis generali Investigatione contentus erit, nec supra quam possibile est, numerum & particularia Exacte quæret, Physica ratione de Germanis, & ex eadem matre natis sumet Judicium, ex signo M. C. & materno loco: Excipiente Venerem Interdiu & Noctu Lunam. Cum enim id signum & succedens significent matrem, & ejus Liberos, erit idem fratrum Locus.* And at last he concludes thus, *Cæterum siquis particularia curiosius scrutari*

Opus Reformatum.

scrutari volet, Patricem stellam collocet in Horoscopo, falso themate, ut in Genesi. Lib. 3. Cap. 5.

The usual way of judging these matters among the Professors of this Science in general, is from the Fourth and Tenth Houses, of the Native's Father and as they do Brothers, Sisters, and Relations, from the Third Mother. House. But the Great *Ptolomy* takes his Judgment from the *Sun* and *Saturn* for the Father, and the *Moon* and *Venus* for the Mother. And according to their Positions, Strength, Weakness, and Configurations to the other Stars, with respect to the Parts of Heaven, where they are all placed; so he judgeth of their Condition, Original, Health, Riches, Length or Shortness of Life, &c. Yet I think it is not altogether amiss to take notice of those Houses, as well as the other Bodies that he mentions; and this the rather, because I find he calls the Tenth House, *Locus Maternus*, in another place; and therefore I shall consider them together.

In this Native's Radical Figure, we find both the *Sun* and *Moon* most excellently fortified by the good Beams of the benefick *Jupiter*; and besides, they also in *Trine* to each other from *Taurus* and *Virgo*; the *Moon* is the stronger of the two, as being Angular, increasing in Light, and in Parallel as well as *Sextile* with *Jupiter*, who is in *Cancer*, his Exaltation, direct, and increasing in Motion. But the *Sun* is in *Taurus*, among violent Stars, Cadent, slow in Motion, and only in *Sextile* to *Jupiter* in the Zodiack, but in Square in *Mundo*. And if we add to these Significators, the Lords of the Fourth and Tenth Houses, which are *Jupiter* and *Mercury*, we shall not find any thing considerable to alter the Judgment from the former Determination of the *Moon*, *Venus*, and *Jupiter*, being far stronger than the *Sun*, *Mercury*, and *Saturn*: from whence it is natural to judge, that the Natives Parents were moderately healthy, and long liv'd; and that they might live till the Native was arrived to a perfect Age, and to a considerable number of years; yet I shall judge the Father to be the more healthy, but the Mother the more durable and longer Liver; that she was subject to the Spleen and Vapors, because the *Moon* is in Parallel with *Mars*, and *Jupiter* in Square to *Saturn* and *Mars*: that she was subject to Obstructions of her Lungs, Hypochonders and Stomack, because of the former Square of *Saturn* and *Jupiter*. And tho' I have been so favourable to their old *Mumpsimus* of the Third and Fourth Houses, as not to condemn it; yet I do

H 2 say,

say, That this Doctrine of the Great *Ptolomy* is most rational and consentaneous to Nature; and what I can experimentally justify in some hundreds of Nativities.

Seeing all People are subject to some Distemper of Body or other, it is not amiss to say something to this point also. And before I begin it, I will ask *J. G.* what Disease or Diseases the *Protector* had that, were fixed, chronick and durable, because he hath placed *Saturn* (in the Nativity, he hath made him) on the Cusp of the Seventh, a little towards the Sixth House, in *Opposition* to *Mars* on the Cusp of the *Ascendant*, the only two points in the whole Scheme, to give broken Bones, dislocated Joynts, and Chronick Diseases, and yet I do not remember that it was ever said he was subject to either of them; [*perhaps now and then a Wound, the honourable Mark of a Soldier*] but a Brave, Lusty, Jolly Gentleman, as I my self can testify, having seen him some scores of times. And to this purpose, I will give you *Ptolomy's* own words in the Case; as you will find it; Lib. 3. Cap. 17 *De Læsionibus & morbis Corporum*. And he begins with these words following, when he comes to inquire into the Hurts and Diseases of the Body. *Universalis vero regula hæc est. Duo Cardines Horizontis Inspiciantur, videlicet is, qui est in ortu, & alter, qui est in occasu Præcipua vero consideretur is, qui est in occasu, & Locus Antecedens, qui prorsus non est Copulatus Ascendenti. Et observetur quomodo maleficæ Planetæ ea Loca adspiciunt. Si enim gradibus qui Ascendunt in dictis Locis, juncti sunt Corpore, aut adspiciunt eos quadrato adspectu, vel ex opposito; seu alter planeta maleficus, seu uterque: Læsiones, & morbi natis accident.* Thus you see, in the Nativity that *J. G.* made, for the Protector, this very Rule of *Ptolomy* takes place positively; for there we find *Saturn* upon the Cusp of the Seventh, in direct *Opposition* to *Mars* on the Cusp of the Ascendant. And, you see also both the Angles of the Horizon in that Figure, are afflicted, which by *Ptolomy's* Rule [which I suppose they do not dare deny] ought to give Hurts and Diseases to his Body. But on the contrary, he was a Brave, Bold, Healthy, Fortunate Man, and none more free from Wounds, Hurts, or Diseases of Body than himself. So that this is another strong Argument to prove that Figure false, and that the *Figure-maker* did not know any thing of the matter he pretended to give the World an accout of. And yet to add more, neither *J. G.* nor any Man else can shew me a true Nativity where the two Infortunes were in Opposition from the Tenth

and

and Fourth, or First and Seventh, and that Native prove a Fortunate Man or Woman throughout their whole Life, as did this Gentleman. And so I came to consider the Figure of his Nativity, [which I call the true one] and to see what Disease or Injuries to his Body are predictable, according to the Doctrine and Principles of the forementioned Author.

Both the Angles of the *East* and *West*, are free from the Malefick Beams of *Saturn* and *Mars*, and the Sixth House, which is his *Locus Antecedens* is possest by the benign Planet *Jupiter*, and there is no ill Ray cast to the Cusp of the First and Seventh Houses, but the Square of *Venus* from the Cusp of the Fourth; and besides, the *Moon* who is Lady of the Seventh, is in *Sextile* to *Jupiter* in the Sixth House, and the *Sun* in *Sextile* to him also. Which Positions are no ways likely to give any Chronick Disease or Hurts, and Accidents of detriment to his Body; neither indeed had he any that was remarkable and visible; and for those that are not so, I think they are inconsiderable, especially, if we consider that all Men are subject to some little defects in Nature, which may be Impediments, but not Diseases in *Ptolomy*'s sence and meaning; for in the Chapter beforementioned, he doth thus distinguish between Hurts and Diseases. *Differunt enim hæc interse. Læsio semel corrumpit membrum aliquod, nec adfert postea Cruciatus Intensionem: morbus vero, aut assidue, aut per Intervalla correptos excruciat.*

But to consider what he might be subject to, let us consider *Mars*, and *Saturn* in *Opposition*, and both in Square to *Jupiter*; these might give him something of the *Gravel* in the *Kidnies*; with a hear in, or about those parts; he might also be subject to the *Head-ach*, or some little disorder there, coming from the *Stomack* and *Spleen*, for we find both the Maleficks in Square to *Jupiter* in *Cancer*; and besides this, he might also be liable to some Obstructions of his *Lungs* either by *Colds*, &c. but none of these continual, but accidental, and only happening upon bad Directions, Transits, Returns, &c.

The *Sun* and *Moon* both in *Sextile* to *Jupiter*, and in *Trine* to each other from *Taurus* and *Virgo*, and the *Moon* and *Jupiter* applying to a Mundane Parallel; the *Sun* is in *Sextile* to the Ascendant, and *Venus* in Square to it, and *Saturn* no ways afflicting the Significator of Marriage, are indubitable Signs that the Native should Marry. The *Moon* in *Virgo*, a barren Sign, and a Sign of one shape, and in Aspect to no Oriental Planet, and but to one Occidental

Of the Native's Marriage, &c.

dental, besides the *Sun* and *Mercury*, which in this case are all one, should allow him but one Wife, nor is there any Rule here that allows two: the time of his Marriage should neither be early nor late, but between both; and therefore, I judge, he might Marry about the Twenty fifth or Twenty sixth year of his Age; for in Mens Marriages, I esteem Eighteen years of Age early, and Thirty years of Age late; but in Women, I count Fifteen early, and Twenty five late. And as to the Description of his Wife, I shall take a method quite opposite and contrary to the common way in Practice; and therefore I do say positively, That the *Sun* and *Jupiter* are Significators of this Gentleman's Wife, with a little mixture of *Mercury*, but that concerns her Intellect more than her Body. These Positions describes her to be a Woman well descended, of a middle Stature, fleshy Body'd, and when in years Fat, her Hair brown, or rather brightish: a Woman of a high Spirit, a generous Temper, a healthy Constitution, Ambitious, Long-liv'd, and one of much Ingenuity and Sence.

But if honest *J. G*'s Figure were true, she should be one of the worst humoured Women in the World for Passion and Pride, for they describe the Wife always by the Seventh House, and the Planets therein placed, and there we shall find *Saturn* in *Opposition* to *Mars*, and Square to *Jupiter*; and besides, according to their own Rules, *Saturn* on her Ascendant in *Opposition* to *Mars*, should give the Native a Wife, but short-liv'd; tho I confess, I know no reason why those two Stars so placed and configurated, should give the Woman a shorter Life than the Man. But I confess they are not to be asked Reasons, for if any one doth give them that trouble, it will be without satisfaction to him for his pains, for their Notions are Apodictical, and their Rules without Reason.

Of the Native's Children, &c. — In considering the Native's Children, and their Qualification, we must have recourse to the Tenth and Eleventh Houses, and the Planets placed therein, or in the Houses opposite to them; but in this Figure we find none in either but *Venus*, and therefore let us consider her with the Lord of the Tenth and Eleventh, and the *Moon*; and we find *Jupiter* Lord of those Houses in *Cancer*, a Prolifick Sign, and his own Dignities, in *Sextile* to the *Sun* in the House of *Venus*, and in *Sextile* to the *Moon* in the Seventh, and also in Parallel with her applying. These Positions shew, that the Native should have many Children; and as *Venus* was on the

Cusp

Opus Reformatum.

Cusp of the Fourth, and the *Moon* also Angular, I should conclude, that the major part of them were Females; and because *Venus* is free from all manner of Affliction; and *Jupiter* Cadent in the Sixth, in Square both to *Saturn* and *Mars*, so I judge there were some of the Males died before they came to Ripeness of years, or Maturity. That his Children should advance to a considerable Quality or Station, is visible; because *Jupiter*, who is their Significator, is in *Cancer* his Exaltation, In *Sextile* to the *Sun* and *Moon*, the Fountains of Promotion and Honour; but perhaps some may object and say, You might have spared your labour in that point, *Object.* and not pretended to give a reason for it by the Stars, seeing their Father was advanced to a degree to make his Children as Great as himself, and leave them in Possession of such a Power, as to be able to defend themselves when he was gone. To this I answer, That there is no Man riseth to any great and remarkable *Ansiv.* Post or Station; but he must have great and illustrious Positions for so doing and acting; and it is very probable, that some of those Stars that give him his Honour, may be also Significators of his Children, and so gives an Illustrious Issue, as well as an honourable Parent. But besides, we find *Jupiter* in Square both to *Mars* and *Saturn*, as well as in *Sextile* to the *Sun* and *Moon*, which did also shew Rubs and Misfortunes in their Lives, which I shall leave to the Reader to judge, whether it was verified or not. And observe, that a poor Man as well as a rich Man, may have famous and eminent Children; and a rich Man as well as a poor Man, may have poor, dejected, and infamous Children, and this from Principles in Nature, and Rules in Astrology, without any Injury to true Divinity, or the Great Being. But to conclude this Paragraph, I desire all those who are Angry with my Method in judging on this Subject, as well as the whole Figure besides, that they would forbear Quarrelling with me, and fall upon *Ptolomy*; but first let me advise them to understand him.

By long Journies, we commonly understand those of the Sea, *Of the Na-* in going into other Kingdoms or Nations, which our common *tive's Long* Trade Astrologers judge from the Ninth House, and his Lord; *Journeys* but I pass by that, and say, that the Significator of long Journeys *&c.* in this Figure is the *Moon*, [as *she that pleaseth may read more at large*, Lib. 4. Cap. 9. Quadripar.] and as she is in *Trine* to the *Sun*, in *Trine* to *Mercury*, her Dispositor, and in *Sextile* to *Jupiter*;

So

so his Journeys should be about great and eminent Actions and Business; and the Issue of them should be Great, Famous, and Fortunate; for you see the *Moon* is no ways afflicted, neither were his Undertakings beyond Sea in his own Person without Success and Glory, he always coming home Victor and Conqueror. But if we should accept and judge by *J. G*'s Figure, and take either *Jupiter* or *Saturn*, they having both of them Dominion in the Ninth House, but *Jupiter* the most Power, his long Journeys would have been [by that Position] full of Labour, Toil, Trouble, and generally without Success; but if that should have given success, it would have been attended with much difficulty and doubtfulness.

How, and to what degree of Greatness this Gentleman did arrive, is known to the whole World; and therefore I shall directly examine the Causes of it Astrologically, without any further inquiry into the *Modus Acquirendi*; seeing he was really possest of the greatest Power that the Dominion of *England* was able to give him.

In his Radical Figure we find Six of the Seven Planets essentially fortified, according to the Dignities allowed them by *Ptolomy*'s *Lib. I.* for *Saturn* and *Jupiter* are in their Exaltations, *Mars* in his own House, *Venus* in her own House; *Mercury* in *Taurus* in Reception with the *Moon* in *Virgo*; and what is yet more, the *Moon*, who is the *Lumen Conditionarium*, is Oriental from the *Sun*, is Angular in *Sextile* to *Jupiter*, and in *Trine* to the *Sun* and *Mercury*, her Dispositor; and what is yet more, the Position of *Saturn*, *Jupiter*, and *Mars*, are perhaps the most considerable of all; they all casting their Benefick Beams to the Tenth House, the Angle of Honour and Preferment, and they also in those Signs which we call Cardinal, and are in the Zodiack, equal to those points that we call Angles in the Figure. And these are the reasons that I give for this Native's Rising and Advancement; and as the Three Superiors are in the Cardinal Signs, in Square and Opposition one to another, so you see he attained his Grandeur by a kind of Violence, Force, and Labour, joyned and assisted with Power; and by that means and method he maintained it all his times.

The Birth is Nocturnal, and the *Moon* is Light of the Time in an Angle, and her *Satellites*, or *Stupatores*, according to *Ptolomy*, are the *Sun*, *Mercury*, *Jupiter*, and *Venus*, she being in *Trine* and

Sextile

Sextile to them all; nay, and we may reckon *Saturn*, and *Mars* too, for she is in a Zodiacal Parallel with them also applying; and the Three Superiors, according to his Rule, are, two of them in *Trine*, and one in *Sextile* to the Mid-heaven, and all of them applying likewise; and *Jupiter* Lord of the Tenth, the Angle of Honour. To which I will add this Observation, That neither *Sun* nor *Moon* is in any ill Aspect with any of the Planets, nor any of the Planets placed to his disadvantage in the Figure. The *Sun* who is always the Significator of Honour, Glory, and Reputation, is likewise free from all ill Circumstances, and in *Trine* to the *Moon*, *Sextile* of *Jupiter*, and Conjunction with *Mercury*, and *Mars* just rising before him. Which if compared and considered with the following Chapter of *Ptolomy*, shews, That Arms and Armies would be the Practice of his Life, the Delight of his Soul; and by these things he would raise his Honour and Fortunes.

The great *Conjunction* of *Saturn* and *Jupiter*, in the Year 1623. in the 7th degree of *Leo*, near the Cusp of his Seventh House, in *Trine* to *Mars* in his Second, and in *Sextile* to *Saturn* in his Eighth, was none of the smallest Causes of his Greatness and Promotion; neither was that *Conjunction* in the Year 1643. which was on the Cusp of his Second, in exact *Trine* to his Tenth House, and in *Sextile* to *Venus*.

But perhaps it may seem strange to some, why he was so Old before he began to appear upon the Stage of Mundane Affairs; which thing is not indeed very strange; because all the Planets are in Occidental parts of Heaven, *Jupiter* and *Venus* excepted; and none Angular but *Venus* and the *Moon*, all the rest being either in Cadent or Succedent Houses, which always give what they promise in the latter part of the Life; and this is the more confirmed too, if we observe, that all but the *Moon* and *Saturn* are under the Earth. So that if the Positions are but really perpended, it will seem no strange thing that this Native did not Advance and Rise sooner. But if *J. G*'s Figure should be allowed, all the Planets are Angular but the *Moon*, which must without doubt give the Native his Honour and Preferment early; even in His younger Years; which 'tis plain he had not, I confess, I have no Authority from *Ptolomy* for this Judgment of the Time and Age, when the Native shall receive those things of Honour promised him in his *Radix*; he only speaking to the thing in general, *Si dignitatem, vel*

Why so long before he began to rise and appear in the World.

non

non habeat. But my Experience in many Nativities, and the method by which we judge early and late Marriages, which is much after the same manner, with some other things that I have formerly remarked in the same Case, is sufficient for me to believe that this method is not improper to be followed and practiced in judging this, and things of this Nature.

Ptolomy makes a distinction between Friends and Friends, and Enemies and Enemies; for he calls nothing Friendship, but what is durable and intirely real; and all the rest of it he calls Familiarity, and the effect of Conversation and Society. By Enemies and Enmity, he understands a perfect Radical and perpetual Hate. All the other things of Difference, Debate, and Controversy, he looks upon it to be nothing more than little Accidents or Casualties in Conversation. And to consider and judge of these, he doth not make use of the Eleventh House as the manner is; but considers the *Sun, Moon, Part of Fortune,* and *Horoscope*; and his reason is, because he judgeth *Friendship* and *Amity* among Men, to be either for *Council, Pleasure,* or *Profit*; and indeed upon some or all of these Principles, Men do generally love and support, or differ and destroy one another, and therefore *his Judgment* is founded upon reason.

In the Radical Figure we find the *Sun, Moon,* and Ascendant, well befriended by the Rays of the other Stars, but the Part of Fortune is in Parallel both to *Saturn* and *Mars,* both in *Zodiaco,* and *Mundo,* and *Mars,* who comes very near *Ptolomy's* Rule, who is in his own House, and not much above 17 degrees distant from the *Sun* (ascending) by the Oblique Ascention, is in *Square* to *Jupiter,* and *Opposition* with *Saturn*; the *Moon* is in Reception with *Mercury,* and all the rest of the Planets in their own Dignities, except the *Sun.* Hence it is reasonable to judge, That this Native should have both many Friends, and many Enemies; and as the Part of Fortune is afflicted most of the four, so I judge the hatred of his Enemies was real, and the cause of it was, because of his Profit and Advantage he received with his Power and Honour. Besides, *Venus* is in Square to the Ascendant, which might raise him some Enemies that did envy him for the Pleasure and Ease of his Life, and other things that were the advantagious Circumstances of his Station he was in, at the latter end of his days. While he was in the Army he had many Enemies, and they none of the Ordinary People; but the Parliament was his Friend at all times.

Opus Reformatum

times. When he came to be Protector, he had Enemies always plotting against him; but at the same time all Nations were his Friends, either for Love or Fear; and what is more, it was his own *Prudence, Courage, Council,* and *Conduct,* that carried him through and above all these things; and this is aptly signified by *Ptolomy's* own Rule and Words, which are these, *Cum Lumina congruunt, erit amicitia adjuncta consilio optima & utilissima.* Which in this Figure and Nativity takes place, for the Lights are in *Trine* to each other; the one in *Conjunction,* and the other in *Trine* and Reception with *Mercury,* and all these assisted by the Beams of *Jupiter,* who is in *Cancer,* and in *Trine* to the Mid-heaven; By which means he is doubly concern'd in giving and supporting his Honour and Friendship, which were indeed really inseparable. In a word therefore, this Valiant and Fortunate Native had many Enemies, and those great and considerable in their Quality, and this judgeable by this Position; but he had more Friends, and those more powerful to support his Interest, which is the usual and natural Effect of so good and fortunate a Position, as he was blest with. Thus you see the best and most Ancient Astrologers, had other ways to judge of Friends and Friendship, Enemies and Injuries by them, without making use of the Seventh House, the Eleventh, and Twelfth; with their Lords and Governors, and Planets placed therein, which method is indeed absurd and ridiculous, if compared with *Ptolomy's,* which is founded on better Principles of Philosophy and Reason. But more of those Fooleries you shall have in my *Defectio Genituarum,* now ready for the Press.

It is not very material to our work in hand to take notice of this part of Judgment in this Nativity, because he was not liable to the Fate and Accidents of private Men; for Princes seldom know their Servants, [some few excepted], and by that means are not liable to any Differences and Discord with them, nor are their Servants admitted to any intimate Familiarity with their Masters; for when they are put into an Employment, the Service expected from them in that Imploy, is Diligence and Faithfulness in their Duty to their Master. But we may certainly conclude, That all Princes have Servants of both sorts, good and bad; for according as those Ministers of State are affected, that put in, and imploy the Inferior Servants, so must that Prince expect to be served or be Betrayed; and I could wish we had no Examples of this kind in *England.*

Of the Native's Servants

I 2   But

But for the Readers satisfaction, I will also give the Judgment of this matter with the rest. *Ptolomy* doth allow the Twelfth House, and Planets placed therein, to signify the Native's Servants; but if there are none in that House, to take those placed in the Sixth; but most chiefly to observe how the Lord of the Twelfth House doth agree, or disagree with the chief and most principal parts of the Figure, and from thence make your Judgment of the matter in hand. In the Nativity now under consideration, we find *Saturn* Lord of the Twelfth House in *Libra*, his Exaltation, but in no Aspect, either good or bad, to the Mid-heaven, Ascendant, *Sun*, *Moon*, or part of Fortune, only in Parallel with the last of them, which should indeed shew the Native's Servants to be none of the best; but if we consider that *Jupiter* is in the Sixth House, and there in a Zodiacal Square, but a Mundane *Sextile* to *Saturn*, I should judge that his Servants were Moderate, Trusty and Just; and this the rather, because *Venus* beholds the Cusp of the Twelfth, with an exact *Trine*, but this last I speak of my self, there being nothing of that in the Rule. Upon the whole matter, I do judge, had this Native been of the Common Quality, and liable to those Accidents that Subjects must meet with in such Affairs, that his Servants would have been just in their Duty, but stubborn and head-strong, and that the Native and they would have agreed moderately well; some little differences there would have happened, but yet true and trusty in the main.

I am now come to the last part of Judgment, that is to be given on the Nativity of any Person, *Nam ultra mortem nihil*; but the most confused part of the whole Art, as it is now understood and practised by all those that pretend to understand the Language of the Stars, and have just skill enough in hard Words, to make the rest of Mankind believe that they are really what they confidently call themselves; that is, *Astrologers*. And therefore I shall be a little the larger on this Paragraph. *First*, To shew the World their Mistakes: And *Secondly*, To give a few Directions in order to set them right; but in this I shall be very short and concise, and that for several Reasons, which perhaps you may find elsewhere mentioned in this Treatise. For I am now handling a Nativity, not giving General Rules so to do; which perhaps I may perform at a more convenient time; for I really believe I have taken as much pains in that part of Astrology that concerns Sickness and Death, as any Man; and for that reason, I think I ought to understand

Opus Reformatum.

stand it as well. However, when time shall serve, I will give the World what I have prepared and intended, and let them that are more skilful and knowing Correct it; for which I will give them thanks, if I am convinced that they have done it. But I shall divide my Discourse on this matter into Three Parts, and bring all under three distinct Heads.

First. The Cause of Death.
Secondly, The Quality of Death. I mean of a natural Death, I not intending here to run into a Discourse of Violent ones, because it would be too long, and also not suitable to my present purpose.
Thrdly, To compare the Cause with the Quality. And, è contra, from whence will arise some Queries.

The Cause of Death is variously asserted; some laying the Cause of it on a bad Revolution. So one served my Friend Mr. *R. B.* whom they said lay under a bad Revolution four years succesive; and kill'd him at last, for which they could never give any other reason, and yet had his Nativity to consider in the thing. Some lay the stress on Eclipses of the Luminaries, and these they tell you do mighty things, especially in Death. Nay, many of them to my knowledg have no other Cause to alledg for the late Abdication, but a poor small Eclipse of the *Sun*, on the *Sun's* Radical Place, and day of his Birth, *October* 14. 1688. *Mane.* Which if they please to consider, there was an Eclipse of the *Moon*, *April* 15. 1660. near that place, and that a very great Eclipse, and yet did him no harm. Also in 1669. *October* 14. at which time the *Sun* on his Radical Place was Eclipsed in 2 degrees of *Scorpio*, the very place of the *Dragons Tail*, and yet I do not remember that it did him any harm, nor yet kill'd him; but any thing serves when better Reasons are not in their Power. Sometimes they tell us, that great *Conjunctions* kill, and yet that shall not happen in divers Years after the *Conjunction* is over and past. And this I have often heard alledged as the Cause of Death, when such a *Conjunction* hath happened on the Mid-heaven, Ascendant, *Sun*, or *Moon*, &c. of a Nativity, in which they could find out no other reason more substantial. They likewise say, That Comets oftentimes kill when they begin, or expire, on the chief Points and Parts of the Nativity. But this as well as all the

The Cause of Death.

Reasons

Reasons beforementioned, are false and groundless; and I do positively say, cannot Kill, nor ever did, *per se*, at any time. How far such things as these are concerned in Death, I am sensible, and may sometime or other give a more particular account thereof; but to say these Kill, is nothing else but a Refuge for Ignorance, and let them bring me one Example where these, or any of them have killed, and I will bring them twenty where they have not done it, and yet attended with as much violence as the other.

But notwithstanding they have these Back-doors to let in Excuses and Shams, to cheat and delude themselves and others; and also to Baffle and Banter a more serious Inquiry after Truth, which they pretend is their Standard; I say, these very Men do also own, and allow, that violent Directions to the *Hilegiack* points, give *Sickness*, *Death*, and other *Misfortunes*. In which I do agree with them, and do assert that these are the *only*, *real*, and *principal Causes* of *Death*, and that all the others are but *Subsequents* and *Collaterals*. And these Directions are nothing else but Bodies and Rays, carried and conveyed from one part of Heaven to another by the perpetual Flux of Motion. And about these Directions there hath been a great, and a long Contest, one being of this Persuasion, and another of that, how to contrive their Operations, to bring the Significator and Promittor together, according to the true design and Intent of Nature; in which point I find they are not yet well agreed, neither is it certain when they will; tho' in the Angles it is certain there can be no mistake, nor indeed any where else, if they would but observe, and pursue Truth in that Tract that Nature hath made. But in this point we do all agree, that Directions of a violent Nature give Death; and in this I do agree with them, and that it was Directions that was the cause of this Native's (the Protector's) Death; and yet I am not unsensible, that he had in that year an ill Revolution, and an Eclipse of the Sun in May 1658. in exact Square to the Moon, in the *Radix*, who is Giver of Life. And that the Comet of 1652. had its beginning in or about the 10th degree of *Gemini*, in Square to the *Moon's* Radical Place, and the *Moon* in his last Revolution on that very place in *Gemini*, or near it; with some other things, which I do no ways allow to be the cause of his Death, but those Directions only in the preceding Table, and they are, as I remember, Seven in number.

This

Opus Reformatum.

This being granted, That Directions are the Astrological *The Quali-* Causes of Death; the next thing is to inquire into the Quality *ty of Death* of it, and how to judge this according to the Method and Directions of our Authors, would puzzle a far stronger Brain than I have to imploy in it; as I believe you will conclude, and readily judge, when you have heard the Cause opened, and the Matter fairly stated, according to the usual Method and Practice now in use among those Men called Astrologers, or such as pretend to it.

In any Nativity, when they come to consider Death, they tell us, That the Native's Death will be by such Means, Ways, or Disease, as is agreeable to the Lord of the Eighth House, his Nature, Position, and Configuration. And to colour the Foolery of this Delusion, they tell us, That the Lord of the Eighth House is the *Anareta*, or killing Planet, when there is not one in Twenty or Thirty that dye by the Direction of the Giver of Life, to the Lord of the Eighth House. If so, then there is nothing more plain than the Contradictions in their very Rules, laid down to instruct those that are more Ignorant than themselves, if any such are to be found. For is it not a plain piece of Nonsence to say, That this or that Direction is the cause of Death; and at the same time tell us likewise, that the Disease by which he must expire, will be of the Nature of the Lord of the Eighth House, &c. when perhaps *Venus* may be Lady of the Eighth, in *Trine* to the *Moon*, or *Sextile* to *Jupiter*; but perhaps the Direction may be the *Sun* or *Moon*, Giver of Life, to the *Squares* or *Oppositions* of *Saturn* and *Mars*, and one of them Lord of the *Horoscope*. And it is impossible to reconcile these two Rules together, to make them either agree, or serve for a Cloak to hide their Errors, for there cannot be two Causes to specificate one and the same Disease; and those Causes so Antithetically opposite, and yet the Disease shall partake but of one of them when all is done, and that is the Direction or Directions, that the Giver of Life is then directed to; and according to the Nature of that Star or Stars, so shall the Distemper or Disease be. And indeed, this is the only rational method, and the other altogether improbable; for it is the occasion of the Directions touching at that time, that gives the Sickness, which if so, it is reasonable to think that should give the Quality of the Disease also, and not the Lord of the Eighth. But I will end all in a word or two about this matter, and if I can, put it out of doubt; let *Jupiter* be Lord of the Eighth, and in it, in *Pisces*, or where you please, in *Trine* or *Sextile* to the *Sun* or *Moon*, and the Giver of Life be directed to the Bodies of *Saturn*, *Venus*, and *Mercury*, in *Aries*, *Scorpio*, *Capricorn*, or *Aquary*; especially near any violent fixed Stars, or to the Body of *Saturn* or *Mars*, and the Squares of the other two, and that Native shall either be poysoned, or intoxicated with poysonous Physick, and this in defiance to *Jupiter*, Lord of the Eighth, who I am sure gives no such thing. And so I come to the third thing, and that is to compare the Cause with the Quality or Effect, which is the Disease, &c.

The way to compare these things, is to examine such Nativities as the chiefest of the Professors have published to the World, and to see how they make their Rules, and the Death of the Patient agree; if the Disease be from the *Sun* or *Mars*, it is a *Fever*, a *Hectick*, or such like; if it is from *Saturn*, it is a Cold Distemper, as *Coughs*, *Defluxions*, *Agues*, &c. if from *Jupiter*, *Apoplexies*, *Imposthumes*, diseases of the *Lungs*, &c. if from *Venus*, *Dysenteries*, diseases of the *Stomack* and *Liver*, *Fistula's*, and diseases of *Repletion*; if from *Mercury*, *Deliriums*, *Madness*, *Convulsions*, *Coughs*, and diseases of the *Breast*, with all those Infirmities that rise from an excess of *Driness*; if from the *Moon*, *Diarrheas*, and other *Fluxes* of the *Bowels*, *Convulsions*, *Obstructions* in young Women, diseases of the *Womb*, and such like. Then again, they give variety of Diseases, according to the Mixture and Complication of their Rays, which is no very hard thing to examine, if you are but willing to take a little pains. And the reason why I advise you to compare the Disease and its Quality, with that which you call the Cause of it, is for you to observe, how they do agree one with another, and how all of them together do agree and correspond, to the Rules laid down for that purpose. *Doctr. of Nativ.* page 142. sect. 1. page 261. sect. 8. And to consider when any Native or Patient is dead, whose Nativity is known to be true and certain; whether had you been to have given your Judgment thereon before Death, you would have predicted that Disease of which he died, or some one very like it in Nature and Quality, [for I know there are none can be absolutely particular] by the Position of the Lord of the Eighth House, having respect to that Angle it self, the Planets in it, and those Configurations with which the Lord of it is affected. I say, a few Trials of this Nature, in a little time will

will soon shew you, to which side Truth casteth a favourable Aspect; whether to the Power of those Directions at Death, or to the Power and Position of the Lord of the Eighth at Birth. To which purpose let us make a search and inquiry into some Nativities that are known and allowed.

Query 1. Who would have judged by the Position of the Lord of the Eighth, that King *James* I. should have been poysoned; for *Jupiter* Lord of it, was in *Sextile* to the *Moon*, and in *Square* to the *Sun* and *Mercury*, which should rather have given a *Cough*, distemper of the *Lungs*, and a *Hectick Fever*, than an *Ague* and *Poyson*. But the Directions that kill'd him do naturally give Poyson, for it was the *Sun*, *Hileg*, to the Body of *Mars*, Square of *Venus*, and Body of *Saturn*.

Query 2. What Artist skill'd in that Learned Doctrine of the Lord of the Eighth, would have judged *Charles* II. should have died by Violence, when *Mars* Lord of the Eighth was in *Sextile* to the *Sun*, and Lord of the Ascendant, and in no ill Ray with any, but the Square of the *Moon*? And yet the Directions that kill'd him were Violent, and might give Death by a sort of Violence, among which, that he died by was one kind.

Query 3. Who would have judged that the Earl of *Essex* should have been Beheaded, when *Jupiter* Lord of the Eighth was in *Libra*, and free from all Malefick Rays? *Collec. Genit.* p. 45.

Query 4. The Case of Duke *Hamilton*; why he should dye in that manner, when *Jupiter* and *Mars* were no ways afflicted, the former being in *Sextile* to *Saturn*, and in *Trine* to the *Sun*; and the latter in no Aspect with any, but the *Opposition* to *Venus*? *Collec. Genit.* p. 67.

Query 5 Why *George* Duke of *Albemarle* should dye of a *Dropsy*, when *Mars*, Lord of the Eighth, was in *Square* to the *Sun*, and in *Sextile* to *Venus*; which cannot be allowed to give a *Dropsy* in my Opinion. *Collec. Genit.* p. 70.

Query 6. Why Sir *Robert Hilburn* did not dye a violent Death, seeing *Mars* and the *Sun* is in *Conjunction* in the Eighth, among violent fixed Stars; and *Saturn* going to the *Square* of *Jupiter*, Lord of that House, from Cardinal Signs; which is indeed a very violent Position. *Collec. Genit.* p. 124.

Query 7. Why Mr. *Massianiello* should not expire by a Natural Death, seeing that the *Moon*, Lady of the Eighth, was no ways afflicted, but going to the *Trine* of *Mars*, *Trine* of *Saturn*, and *Trine* of the *Sun. Collec. Genit.* p. 155. But I suppose this is one of Mr. *John*'s made Nativities, and therefore ought not to questioned.

Query 8. Why Sir *Frech-Holles* should dye by so violent a Death, as being shot to pieces, when the *Moon*, Lady of the Eighth, was seperating from the *Trine* of *Venus*, Lady of the Tenth, and going to the Body of *Jupiter*, Lord of the Atcendant in *Pisces*, for the *Moon* was not full 16 degrees in *Pisces* by her Latitude; and *Jupiter* was almost 19 degrees by his *Collect. Genit.* p. 159. This is the Gentleman that was to live some decades of Years, (by *J. Gad.*s Prediction) but was kill'd within six Months after he had printed it.

Query 9. In that Nativity printed for *Oliver Cromwell*'s, *Collect. Genit.* p. 145. Why *Jupiter* in *Square* to *Mars* and *Saturn* should give an *Ague* and *Fever*, and as they say, *Poyson*, when at the same time, *Jupiter* is in *Sextile* to the *Moon* in *Sextile* to the *Sun*, to *Mercury*, and *Venus*, which Positions do not use to give such Accidents, but rather a *Consumption*, or some other Disease of the *Lungs*. But besides that, even in this Figure here before us, and by me now corrected, why should *Mercury* that governs the Culp of the Eighth, and is in *Sextile* to *Jupiter*, and *Trine* to the *Moon*; or *Venus* who governs the rest of that House, being in no ill Aspect with any of them, but in her own House, and free as well from Benefick, as Malefick Beams, give any Disease of the Nature of that he died of? Whence it is plain, that none of these Rays, either of *Mercury* or *Venus* can be allowed by any Rule I have read in that method of Judgment, from the Lord of the Eighth House, to give either a *Fever*, *Ague*, or *Poyson*, &c. And indeed to examine it rationally, it will appear a very lame, empty sort of a Rule, that the Lord of a House should give so considerable an Accident to Man's Life, as the Quality of the Disease of which he must dye, and that House but an imaginary Point or Part of Heaven, that he is called the Lord of; and because he is Lord of that House, he must kill and destroy; nay, and give Death by such a kind of Disease as is not usual to his Nature, Position, or any other Qualification: which if they would but consider, renders their Art [by their own Rules] a very uncertain, falacious Inquiry, as doth appear by their Authors compared with those Queries preceding. And so I come to give the true Cause of his Death, that in all Nativities shall hold Good and Authentick, the Rule being well understood, and then well observed.

Lastly,

Lastly, He that will come to the true knowledg of Astrology, in this thing of Death, he must in the first place throw by all these Shams and Fooleries, that are kept in use without any Approbation of truth, or any other Authority but that which some call Antiquity. And I have been somewhat the longer on this matter, to shew how idle a thing it is in it self, and yet how much magnified by those that pretend to Astrology. Not a Nativity done without the use of this Rule; and not one Nativity in forty, where the Rule takes place, unless it is by chance; for till they can prove to me, that they have a better foundation for their Houses, than any I can yet learn, I must beg their pardon, for my not believing this, and a great many Fooleries more in the Art of Nativities. Of which I will give a fuller Account shortly in my *Defect. Gen.* There is no other thing can share in the Cause of Death, and the Nature and Qualification of the Disease, but the Direction or Directions that are then in force and operation, by Direction to the Giver of Life. I do acknowledg, that *Revolutions, Secondary Directions*, with *Transits, Returns, Eclipses*, &c. may increase the Arguments of the certainty of Death, but all of them together cannot give Death, or specificate the Disease that leads to it. but the Directions only: As I could shew you in some of those Nativities mentioned in the former Queries, where the Diseases did exactly correspond to the Directions, that gave them, *Sensu Astrologico*, And to this purpose, there may sometimes be three or four Planets concerned in the matter, sometimes but one, but rarely less then two serve to give the Disease and Death. To this purpose, in the Nativity of *Charles* II. it was the *Moon* that gave the Disease, but it was *Mars* that kill'd him, altho there were divers Directions, I am sure six or seven in force and operation when he died, and help'd to compleat the Work of Mortality. Likewise in this Case of the Protector *Cromwell*, it was not *Mercury* or *Venus*, Lord or Lady of the Eighth House, that gave him either an *Ague*, Fever, or *Poyson*, no nor *Saturn*, Lord of the Ascendant in the Eighth, in *Opposition* to *Mars*; but it was the Directions of *Saturn*, and the *Moon* her self, that gave his Disease, but that of *Mars* kill'd him. And that I do assert to be the true Cause of his Death, and shall have a proportional Effect in all other Nativities; where the *Moon* is *Hileg*, and in that part of Heaven; that is, it shall give Death, but perhaps it may not be by the same Disease. but it shall be of the same Nature, violent and quick, as indeed are most of those

Directions

Directions where *Mars* and the *Moon* are concerned, but especially where they sway and govern. And that you may be the more satisfied, do but examine the Nature of the Promittors in Direction, and compare them with the Nature and Circumstances of his Disease by which he expired. Both which being throughly considered, in the next place consult the Text of *Ptolomy* in his Fourth Book, Chap. 10. *De genere Mortis*, and you will (I believe) be soon satisfied about the truth of that matter. And so I will conclude my Discourse on the Nativity of this Great *General*, *Statesman*, and *Politician*; whom Mr. *Dreyden* in his Panegyrick on his Death, commends for his great Labour, Toil, and Industry, by endeavouring to the utmost to shorten the Kingdoms Miseries, and put an end to the War, which other Men made their Trade and Profit, and made it their business also to protract it. His words are these,

Our former Chiefs, like Sticklers of the War;
   First sought t'enflame the Parties, then to poise;
The Quarrel lov'd, but did the Cause abhor,
   And did not strike to hurt, but make a noise.

War, our Consumption, was their gainful Trade;
   We inward Bled, while they prolong'd our Pain.
He fought to end our fighting, and essay'd
   To stanch the Blood by breathing of a Vein.

THE SECOND PART.

The Argument that induced me to it.

Having finished this Great Man's Nativity, corrected the Figure, and refuted those absurd Errors, which others have built thereon, under the Notions of Rules and Directions for the Young Students to Steer by; I am directly led to examine a Book not less fill'd with Errors, than *Cromwell*'s Nativity [printed by the Gentleman you have heard mentioned in this Treatise] was with falshood and shams. A Book written to introduce a new and imaginary Whim, that *J. G.* did believe the Power of his then Interest, was able to put upon the World. A Book, that the Arguments which are brought to prove the thing there propounded, and his Principle asserted, are either false, misapplied, or else lugg'd in by head and shoulders. A Book, not written to do the Artists of *England* any Service, but rather an opportunity made use of, to shew how plaguely he was abused, and his Reputation curtailed, by being called and esteemed a Papist, from the Popish-Plot to that time; and yet at the same time, with a side-long, skew-whiff Argument, to ridicule the Objections against the Cheats, Fooleries, and Absurdities in his Popish Religion, as I shall have occasion to shew anon more at large. A Book, written to justify and maintain the Errors of his Youth, [I had almost said the Sins too] which were great enough then, and might have sav'd him this labour of Painting and Hanging up a Sign, to have them the easier seen and discovered; and to shew you he had no more skill in Astrology at Sixty years of Age, than he had at Thirty. For in the Year of our Lord, 1660, and 1661, he made a Collection of Nativities, and most of them false ones, as shall ere long

long appear. From these Nativities thus made, he form'd a hundred Aphorisms; and most of them as false as his Nativities. I say from these false Nativities, he form'd those choice Aphorisms, a quarter of which, I am confident, to this day he never prov'd to be true. And from two of these Nativities, [and I am certain they are both false, for I have made one appear so already, and will do so by the other before I conclude this Treatise] namely *Charles Gustavus*, King of *Sweden*, and *Oliver Cromwell* he form'd the Eighteenth Aphorism, which was this, *Cardinal Signs possessing the Angles of a Nativity, makes the Native* [of any Condition or Capacity] *most Eminent and Famous in his Generation, and to do such Acts as After-ages shall admire him.* And from this Aphorism made in the Year 1661. he writes a Book in the Year 1684. to justify and promote the thing which he calls, *Cardines Cœli*, which is my present business to inquire into.

An Inquiry into J. G's Cardinal Errors.

THere are a sort of Men in the World, that whether they write or talk, do pretend it is for nothing else but Truth, of this Stamp and Noise, is the Author of our *Cardines Cœli*; as you may see in his fawning Epistle to the Learned Sir *E. D.* who, as he there confesseth, sav'd him from the Gallows. And indeed the whole Treatise is nothing else but a heap of Words and Jingle; nothing at all relating either to Truth in general, or that of Astrology in particular. It is like the common Dialect of his Discourse, Evasive and Treacherous. And for the first Eighteen Paragraphs in his Book, there is not a word to the purpose, and matter of the Treatise. And therefore I shall pass by all, till I come to that part of it, where he discourseth about *Cardinal Signs* on *Angles*, &c. which is the only thing I have undertaken to refute, according as he hath asserted it; for whatever the mystery of Cardinal Signs is, I am sure he hath a wrong Notion about the matter, and that not only the Nativities he builds his Aphorisms upon, but also those he brings to prove his Theory, are false. But before I begin to examine that Book, it will not be amiss for me

to

to lay down my Opinion, as an Axiom concerning the Power of Cardinal Signs.

Cardinal Signs signify nothing on the Angles of any Nativity, &c. But Cardinal Signs on the Angles of a Nativity, and some of the Superiors placed therein, do certainly make Men Famous and Prodigious in their Generation. And so they do in those Signs, tho not in the Angles.

Whoever he is that pretends to Astrology, and denies the Power of Cardinal Signs, not only in Nativities, but in other general Affairs of the World, makes too much haste to discover his Ignorance and Folly; and whoever he be that placeth more Power in them, than Authors and Experience allows and justifies, makes too much haste to discover his Confidence; which indeed hath been in divers other things in this Art, the Practice of too many Professors of Astrology; by which means we are at this day in such a Labyrinth of Errors and Confusion. For most of the Modern Authors [I call them Modern that have been within One or Two hundred years] have dispersed Errors, and according to their Interest, so they were believed and promoted. Take an Instance in one: and that is the Learned Treatise of *Naibod* on *Alcabitius*, which hath made such noise among some very Learned and Judicious Men. Concerning which Book, if I were to speak my plain Opinion, perhaps it might not be convenient in this place; for I have a very ordinary Opinion of the Book, altho Learnedly done; and this for some reasons of my own, distinct from the Opinion of others. And besides, I could point out their Errors, and some of their Authors too, but that it is not my business in this place to meddle with those things; but all in good time.

Why Cardinal Signs should give those stupendious and amazing Effects in Nativities, &c. that this Gentleman speaks of, and yet not known to the Ancients, is a thing I cannot easily believe; neither is it at this day asserted by any but himself, and those of our Nation, who were deluded into the belief of this idle Assertion. For the Cardinal Signs without Planets in them, are but empty Spaces in Heaven; and what reason there is, that those empty Spaces should be allowed so great and mighty a Power,

if

if they have any such thing, must in my Opinion depend on one of these three Reasons, according to their Assertion. *First*, It must either reside in the Name, Power, and Virtue of the Sign. Or, *Secondly*, In the Nature and Power of the fixed Stars that are in those parts of Heaven. Or, *Thirdly*, As being the Medium, and two extreams of the Ecliptick. As to the first, I disown it wholly, not allowing any Mystick Power to the Name of *Aries*, *Cancer*, *Libra*, or *Capricorn*, nor any more Power and Virtue to that part of Heaven so called, than to any of the parts of the Zodiack besides; for we all know, that the Names of the Twelve Signs, are but what the first Inventers imagined those Constellations to be like, and have therefore called them by these Names. And what is more, those Constellations and Parts of Heaven that did possess those points at the time when these Signs were so named, are either by the Precession of the fixed Stars, or Retrocession of the Equinox, divolved from those Points, near a whole Sign; as in the Sign *Aries*, which takes its Name from the *Ram*, the Figure of which Creature is described in that part of Heaven, and I judge at that time was in, or near the Point of the Equinox; but now the first Star in that Constellation, and known by the name of the first Star in the *Ram's Horn*, is in 28 degrees of *Aries*, and about 30 or 40 minutes. So that if the Figure of this Creature gave a name to the Sign, and a power to the Part of Heaven, then the Precession of the fixed Stars hath quite altered the Case, and it is slipped away into that part and space then called *Taurus*; and so of the rest; niether do I care by what Names you call the Signs, so I can but tell what you intend by them, and that we may by those Names know now, and where to find the Seven Planets by their motions disperfed throughout the Zodiack. But besides, the empty Spaces of Heaven were never yet pretended by any Man, to have any the least Power imaginable, without the presence of the Planets or fixed Stars to illustrate them; and so far I do allow them, and no further.

Secondly, As to the power of the fixed Stars in those Signs, I think no Man will lay the stress there, because there are no such thing in two or three of them, unless they will make such Stars as have great *North* or *South*-Latitude useful in this Case, which I am very unwilling to allow in Nativities; for the fixed Stars that have great Latitude, can have but little force in the Angles of a Nativity; and I hope no Man will deny, that the point they

call

call the Cusp of the House, must be in the Ecliptick, whether in the Horoscope, or Mid-heaven, or the opposite Points. In the Sign *Aries*, there is not a Star of the first Magnitude, nor any of the second, but the *Head* and *Girdle* of *Andromeda*, and they having *North* Latitude, about 26 degrees; however, if they were nearer I should not look upon those Stars able to illustrate a Space of Heaven, sufficient to give it such a Power, seeing there are Stars far more considerable to that purpose in the Zodiack, tho' not in Cardinal Signs. In *Cancer* we find none of the first Magnitude, but *Syrius*, or the *Greater Dog*, and that Star is about 40 degrees from the Ecliptick with *South*-Latitude; which is a little too far to have this power here pretended. The rest are all of the second Magnitude, and they are the *Bright-Foot* of the *Twins* in the beginning of *Cancer*, with 6 degrees 50 minutes of *South* Latitude; and the Star called *Hercules*, with the *Lesser Dog*, having about 16 degrees of *South*-Latitude; there are others also, but, I think less serviceable to their purpose than these are, if they depend on the Power of fixed Stars. In *Libra* there are two of the first Magnitude, the *Virgins Spike* and *Arcturus*; yet none but the *Virgins Spike* serviceable in this Work, as being near the Ecliptick, and hath but little Latitude; but *Arcturus* hath above 30 degrees of *North*-Latitude, and doth rise with the middle of *Virgo*. And when the beginning of *Libra* ascends, that Star is a considerable distance above the Horizon, and not to be said in the Ascendant; and besides, it culminates with the beginning of *Scorpio*, and for those reasons no ways serviceable. In *Capricorn* there is also but one Star of the first Magnitude, the bright Star in the *Harp*, called *Lyra*, which hath above 60 degrees of *North*-Latitude; and tho in *Capricorn*, yet it riseth with the latter part of *Libra*; there are divers Stars more in that Sign, but all of the third Magnitude, and less, except that in the *Vulture*, called the *Bright Star*, which hath almost 30 degrees of *North*-Latitude. Thus you see there is but one Sign of the four, that hath an eminent fixed Star near the Ecliptick, which is the *Virgins Spike* in *Libra*; and tho it riseth with the 21st degree of that Sign, yet it sets with the very beginning. Hence, these things have no sway with me to believe that the fixed Stars are able to make these Signs so famous and powerful, as my Virtuous Adversary doth assert, and endeavour to make us believe. For it is plain, That other Signs are endowed with famous and eminent

nent fixed Stars, near the Ecliptick, and yet not taken notice of, in this case.

Thirdly, If they will say, That their Eminence and Power lieth in being the Medium and Extreams of the Ecliptick, it is possible I may have some faith to believe that reason, and upon very good grounds too; but yet I wholly deny, That this reason can be allowed to prove the empty Spaces of Heaven to have any Power when on the Angles of a Nativity, as, perhaps, I may shew by example before I conclude this discourse. But the true Reason is, because when the Planets arrive at the two Tropical Points, they then reach to their utmost bounds Northward or Southward, and this is made the more remarkable if they happen to have great Latitude, *North* in *Cancer*, and *South* in *Capricorn*: by which means they exceed the Ecliptick, and obtain a greater degree of Declination; and for that reason, must have a larger course to run in our sight, if in *Cancer*, because they have a greater Diurnal Ark; if in *Capricorn*, the same to our Antipodes; and therefore a truly Regular Position in this Nature, is a Figure wherein the beginning of *Cancer* is on the Tenth, and the beginning of *Libra* ascending, otherwise it is but an Oblique Position; for if *Cancer* happen to ascend, it riseth *North-East* almost; and *Capricorn* its opposite Point, sets almost *South-West*. But the other Figure is not so irregular nor confused, but hath the four Angles with Cardinal Signs, the Ascendant directly *East*, and the Seventh directly *West*, as the other two Angles are *North* and *South*; and yet all this is but an empty Bubble and Rattle, without the Planets are in those Signs to animate and illustrate the Figure. Nay, I will allow any Man to have those Signs on the Angles, and let but the Planets be in abject Signs and Houses, and see what sort of Figure that Man will make in the World, and how famous he will be in his Generation. The Equator, or the two Signs *Aries* and *Libra*, for no other part of it is or can be conceived in our Astrologick-way in the Ecliptick, but those two Points, because there the Ecliptick cuts that Line at opposite Parts; and there are none but those two Points of Heaven where the Planets can be, and yet at the same time be visible to the whole Earth: for the *Sun* in the Equator is visible to those [if any such are] that Inhabit within the *Artick* and *Antartick Circles*, and have the Poles in their Zenith; and so of the rest of the Planets, which no other part of Heaven can perform, but those only, which doth intitle

those

those Points to something more Eminent and Remarkable in their Position and being, then the rest of the Twelve Signs. With this likewise we may consider, That even by God's appointment, *Aries*, or *Abib*, was the beginning of the Year, in the *Jews* Ecclesiastical Account. But in their Civil Account, they began the Year in *Autumn* in the Month *Tisri* or *Ethanim*, so that both those Points of Heaven were made then the Standards for Time, and the Measures of their Years, before the Astronomers were able to tell the World, that their Year did contain 365 days, 5 hours, and about 50 minutes. There might be many more Arguments raised of this nature, to prove, that these Signs and Points of the Equator are both Eminent and Remarkable, as that of their primary Power and Precedence in Mensuration and Trigonometrical Problems in the Doctrine of the Sphere. Their Primacy and Authority in giving that motion that is the measure of Time in Directions. Their Primacy and Supereminence in admitting no Parallel, and being the only Standards of Equity to the whole World, as being the peculiar Points that gives equal Day and Night to all the Inhabitants of the Earthly Globe. Likewise their Fertility and prolifick Endowments to all those Places that are Situate under that Line, and have those two Points in their *Zenith*; yet I do not attribute that fertile Power to those Signs of Heaven, and those individual Points of the Ecliptick and Equator; but to the Rays of the *Sun* who is the Author of all Generation and Production, and always brooding in, or near their *Zenith*; from whose heat [by which the Terrene Menstruum is fermented] the fertile Earth sends forth its Emergent Product, and also hastens their Maturity; and not only the Parts of the Earth that lies near, or under this Line, but all the World over, even to the Poles also; for when the *Sun* returns from *Capricorn*, and approacheth the Equator, it puts a Generative Ferment into all the Seeds of Nature, exciting Animals to Procreation, and the Earth to Production, as *Quercetanus* well observes. Lastly, That which is as remarkable as any thing I have yet mentioned, is, that as these Points are the Standards of Time, so they are of distance also; for all Zodiacal Parallels are measured from the Equator, and from no other point, nor part of Heaven, but of what use they are in Astrology, few understand, either their Nature or the Operation in the Mechanical part; therefore I shall say no more thereof.

Thus you see our Ancestors had some reason for believing the Cardinal Signs, so considerable in their Astrological Observations, and Judgments on Nativities, &c. when they found Planets therein placed, which according to their Positions did, and always will give things remarkable according to their Nature. As for example, In the Inclinations and Qualifications of the Mind, which is the Rudder to steer the Body with. *Ptolomy* tells us, That the Signs add much to the Temperature of the Mind; but how? Why they are those Signs wherein *Mercury* and the *Moon* are placed. And then he tells you of Tropical, Fixed, Bicorporeal, &c. *Lib.* 2. *Cap.* 18. And the same things are preached also by *Campanella, Lib.* 4. *Cap.* 7. *Artic.* 1 & 2. So says *Junctine* likewise, *Pro qualitate animi igitur, considera Locum Mercurii & Lunæ quæ signa occupent.* Specul. Astr. fol. 50. Col. 4. Neither is *Cardan* silent altogether in this thing, but speaking almost the same words, *Duode Exam. Genitur. in tertia, in Octava, in Nona & aliis Nativitatibus.* Secondly, In Diseases, if those that signify their Infirmities are in Cardinal Signs, they certainly give the more violent sort of Diseases, and such as are hard to be cured, as the *Leprosy*, and other Leprous and Cutaneous Diseases that spread the whole Body over, and sometimes Cancerous Accidents. But all these must be either when the Luminaries, or Significator of the Disease, are in those Signs and Parts of Heaven, *Vide Ptolomeum in Lib.* 3 *Cap* 17. And of the same Opinion is *Albubater*, That it is the presence of the Planets in the Signs, not the Signs themselves, that give the Disease or Diseases, *De Nativita, Cap.* 63. But Thirdly and Lastly, That which is more to my Business, and will point to the Matter in hand, is that thing of Dignity and Preferment; in which Case no Man ever laid the Cause and Ground of it yet in the Signs of Heaven, but the Planets and their Positions, till my Worthy Friend J. G. begun to set it on foot. Neither *Junctine*, nor *Omar*, nor *Ptolomy*, nor *Campanella*, nor *Cardan*, nor *Albohali*, nor *Guido Bonatus*, or any other of them that have come to my hand, have given any countenance to such a kind of Judgment as this is beforementioned. And to give one Text for all, from one of their oldest Authors that they so much admire, [I having spoken enough of *Ptolomy* before, one whom he talks of, but knows nothing of the Man, nor his Matter] and that is *Albohali*, De Judi. Nativit. Cap. 30. de dignitate, *Aspice decimum & dominum ejus & partem Regni cum suo domino, & solem in Nativitatibus diurnis, Lunam in Nocturnis: &*

scias

scias quis ex eis habeat plures dignitates, quia si fuerit inter illum, qui plures dignitates habuerit, & dominum Ascendentis Alictisal, vel Commixtio aut Configuratio, erit Natus homo Regius, & ex regno ditescet & summum honorem consequetur. Observe (says he) the Sign of the Tenth and his Lord and the Part of Dignity and his Lord, with the Sun in Diurnal Nativities, but the *Moon* in Nocturnal; for if there were Commixtion or Configuration between that Planet that hath most Dignities, and the Lord of the Ascendant; he that is then born shall advance to some Power in Government, and shall grow Rich thereby. And to tell you the truth, this Author doth speak the same Language that they all generally give out for Doctrine in this Case; tho some may make little Additions of their own, yet none ever denied this, neither do I believe that Mr. *J. G.* will directly oppose it, tho I judge he thinks this discovery of his more excellent than that, but not so generally useful; for the former is to be considered in all Nativities, especially in Mens, but this of his in none but those having Cardinal Signs on all the Angles, which may amount to one or two in Twenty. However that is nothing against it, neither doth it impair the Invention, were the Aphorism it self true; which is plain to me, that it is not. But let every one believe as he likes. And so I come to his Arguments and Reasons, by which he endeavours to prove and enforce the belief of that idle Opinion about Cardinal Signs, &c. to be of themselves able to make any Native great and famous in his Generation. The first Eighteen Paragraphs of the Book being spent only in Words and Noise, without any Relation to the matter in hand, he comes at last to lay his Principle and Thesis in the Nineteenth Paragraph; he tells us there in plain words, that it is so famous and remarkable, that it wants nothing but *Belief* and *Proof.* Pray, what do the most absurd Errors want besides, or stand more in need of than those two things; nay, let Errors be but believed, and a little proof will serve turn among those Converts. And to say the truth, he doth as good as tell us in those words, That Antiquity doth not in the least own or protect it, and whether the Modern Astrologers would own and believe it, or not, he was in some doubt. For it is certain, that which wants the *Attestation* of *Antiquity*, and the *Consent* of *Modern Astrologers*, is a perfect Innovation, and wholly strange to those of that Profession. And the very words of this Paragraph puts the whole matter into doubt.

Neither

Neither is the twentieth any ways to the purpose; for the Moveable Feasts of the *Church*, the *Jewish-Passover*, Feasts of *Tabernacles*, and *Unleavened Bread*, that he there talks of, are no more to his *Cardinal Signs*, than the Mist before *Adam* that went up from the Earth, was to the last wet *Summer*, or the Children of *Israel's* going through the *Red Sea*, to the most Renowned *Salisbury-Race* in 1688. But when he talks of our Blessed Saviour's coming into the World, and also suffering under Cardinal Signs, 'tis a sort of Cant that I do not well understand. If he means by that, a Conjunction of the Superiors, *that is false*; for the Conjunction that preceded the Birth of our Saviour, was in *Gemini*, *Alsted. Thesau. Chron. Cap. 54.* If he means that he had Cardinal Signs on the Angles of his Nativity, at Birth, *that I deny*; for *Cardan* and *Morinus* have no more sway on my Faith in that thing, than *John's* Arguments have for Cardinal Signs; and besides, a Learned Divine of our own Nation, did once believe that Position of *Cardan's* having *Libra* ascending, but he altered his Opinion afterward, and made it *Sagitary*. However, it is my Opinion, That if the Angels in Heaven do not know when he will come, poor Mortals on Earth do not know when he did come; and 'tis a thing better let alone than medled with. For let any man but consider how we are put to it sometimes to gain the true time of a Birth of a Man or Woman, born in the same Parish where we live, and perhaps not forty years before; nay, and it may be not find it neither in the Conclusion, tho the time may be given as certain [and perhaps more too] as that of our *Saviour*, *Alexander* the Great, *Nero*, *Julius Cæsar*, and abundance of the old Popes, that they pretend to have by them, but most of them false; for the distance in time, the faults in Chronology, the obscurity of their Births, and the impossibility of having them transmitted [if they were then known] down to us true at this distance, are Arguments sufficiently rational to believe all those, or at least most of them are false and fictitious. And by the same Rule, his Confident Adventure [in his 1st Paragr.] that he tells you of, illustrated more fully on the Geniture of his Immortal Arch-bishop of ever Pious Memory, &c. was but a Delusion and Falsity put upon Mankind; and those in particular that are Studious in that Science; and that brings me to his Reasons grounded on Authority.

And, the first he gives us, is from *Cardan*, Seg. 5. Aphoris. 129. *Absis solis, ab Ariete ad Cancrum, Inhabitabilem reddit Austrinam partem.*
Borealem

Borealem autem habitare facit. A Cancro ad Libram, bene habitabitur Borealis & Australi dominabitur. A Libre ad Capricornum, Austrina habitabitur, sed boreali parti minime imperabit. A Capricorno ad Arietem, imperabunt Australes Borealibus quasi desolatis. In *English* thus, When the *Sun's Apogæon* moves from *Aries* to *Cancer*, it depopulates the *South* part of the World, and renders the *North* habitable. From *Cancer* to *Libra*, the *North* shall be well peopled, and govern the *South*. From *Libra* to *Capricorn*, the *South* shall be well peopled, but not govern or command the *North*. From *Capricorn* to *Aries*, the Inhabitants of the *South* shall have the Dominion over the Northern Countrys, they being as it were desolate. I think I shall have no great need to say any great matter to this reason in his twenty second Paragraph; neither would any Man but he, have brought this to prove Cardinal Signs on the Angles as he endeavours. And all that any Man can pretend from this Aphorism, is, that *Cardan* did believe the Cardinal Signs to have a great share in the Affairs of the World in general, and of the dividing and distinguishing the Parts of the World, to the times of their Rise and Ruin in particular. But that it hath any relation to Nativities, he that hath but half an Eye, may see the contrary; and he may as well assert from the same Aphorism, that every time the *Sun* passeth any of these Cardinal Points, there must be some great Action done in the World, and also Men born to do great things for the Foundations or overthrow of Government; and indeed the Aphorism seems to favour these, rather than the other of his; but to be plain, it concerns neither of them. But suppose I should deny the Authority of the Aphorism, as being a thing grounded on Supposition, the World being as yet too short-liv'd to prove one quarter of it; I believe it will much weaken *John's* dependance on it; and to this purpose, pray consider whether the *Aphelions* are fixt or moveable, for our Authors are at a difference about that point, which is the main thing that *Cardan* hath grounded it on. Now, if the *Aphelions* are movable, then that of the *Sun* compleats its Periodical Revolution in almost 23000 years; but if they are fixt, then it hath no other motion than the Precession of the Equinox, which will compleat its Revolution in almost 25000 years; and the World at this time, according to the best Account from *Helvicus* and *Alstedius*, &c. hath not seen yet the number of 6000 so that we have above 19000 years to run through, before we shall be able [or others for us] to set their hands to the truth

of

of this Aphorism. A fine large Tract of time to compleat and prove the truth of an Aphorism, when we [I suppose] shall have no occasion to quote or use it: And shews *Cardan* as well imploy'd at the writing of it, as *J. G.* was, when he brought it to prove Cardinal Signs on the Angles of a Nativity, *&c.* and I think no Man that hath his Sences intire, will conclude the Arguments thence derived to have any sway to make impartial Men believe it. And for his discourse there of Baking and Brewing, it seems to me more remote from the matter, than what he said before, it doth indeed shew the power and force of Fermentation at the time of the Vernal Equinox; and yet I dare say *John* did never try the Experiment in the use of an Election to that purpose, tho he commends it to others. Nor did ever any Man yet say, That the Beer brewed at the *Suns* entrance into the Signs *Cancer*, *Libra*, and *Capricorn*, obtained any singular Approbation for Strength and Virtue, before that brewed at other times in the year.

The Text he hath quoted from *Ludovicus de Regiis* in his Twenty fourth Paragraph, is no more to his designed matter, than the Text of *Cardan*. And now I see, whereever he finds an Aphorism with the words *Equinoctial* and *Tropick* in it, he presently takes it by the Lugs, and presseth it into his Service right or wrong; and for those two words sake only, hath he brought that Aphorism to prove the foolery of his own imagination, when there is not one word in the Text to encourage it. And therefore I shall not dwell on these things that are so obvious and plain, but proceed to those things that are more idle, and more ridiculous.

I will put his 26th and 27th Paragraphs together, for the proof of which, pray observe what Aphorisms he useth, and consider with your self, what force there is in them to his end and purpose. *Quando Saturnus in Libra & Jupiter in Cancro fuerit, tunc magnæ in Mundo Mutationes contingent.* That there shall happen great Mutations in the World, when *Saturn* shall be in *Libra*, and *Jupiter* in *Cancer*, *Card. Seg.* 7. *Aphor.* 6. And is not this a very swaying Text to prove Cardinal Signs on Angles, to do those mighty things that my dear Joy, Mr *John* pretends to. Is there any one word in the Text, that can be supposed to countenance such a thing? None as I can discern, but those two words, *Libra* and *Cancer*. And then with as good reason and success, he lugs in *Diasipodius* Aph. 79. *Signa Equinoctialia sentiuntur dominum habere superstatum Legum, &c.* That Equinoctial Signs are perceived to have

Power

Power and Dominion over Laws, Religion, Rights, and Ceremonies. And because they have so, then both they and the Tropicks must *per se* on the Angles of a Nativity, do great and strange things, says *J. G.* Why truly he might as well have pitcht on these two Texts to prove the Birth of the little *Prince* of *Wales*, his Master; or his own Marriage at *Wildhouse*. For the word *Equinoctial* put to *Laws* and *Ceremonies*, do in my Opinion point directly at those things, rather than Nativities in his Sense. But because we do allow the *Equinoctial* and *Tropical* Signs, to have great Power in divers Cases, when the Planets are in them, must we therefore allow them to do every thing, and have a share in every Cause in Nature, purely by their own Power without the presence of the Planets? 'Tis a Doctrine that I can neither learn or allow. And I dare be confident, that *J. G.* himself doth not believe the thing that he hath here endeavoured to put upon the World; he did it only to shew his Parts, and how he was arm'd with Arguments, and the Art of Persuasion, on which you may see he did depend in this attempt. But of all the marks of Confidence throughout his whole Book, recommend me to his 28th Paragraph, in which he hath really out-done himself, and not only shewed the World the Authority of his groundless Foundation, but his unskilfulness in *Grammar*, and his Confidence [I had like to have said something else] in affirming a thing, without the least pretence and shew of Authority in the very Aphorism it self. Nay, I will go further, and challenge himself, or any man in the World to prove, that there is one Letter or Tittle in the whole Aphorism, that hath the least pretence imaginable to prove any thing about Cardinal Signs, or any other of the Signs on the Angles, or the Cusps of any of the other Houses; which is a piece of unheard-of Confidence, for a Man to put upon the World at such a rate, and make Authors speak what they never thought or intended; nor will the words in the least favour what he designs.

He quotes only four words of the Aphorism, *i. e.* Cometæ in Cardinibus, Regum mortes, &c. *Comets* (says he) *whenever they appear in Cardinal Signs, they betoken the Death of Emperors, Princes, Potentates,* &c. Cardinal Signs you see, do still carry a Signal of Wonder and Amazement in them. By which you may see he lays the stress of the whole Aphorism on the word *Cardinibus*, which he renders for Cardinal Signs, and therefore pray take the whole Aphorism together, that you may see the Impertinence and Ignorance of the Man

Man. Seg. 3. Aph. 117. *Cardan. Cometæ immobiles Seditiones, mobiles autem Bella indicant ab Externis. In Cardinibus Regum Mortes in nono loco Religionis Jacturam, in Octavo vel Duodecimo loco Pestilentiam, aut Jacturam segetum, in undecimo Nobilium Mortes.* Which is thus in *English*. Immoveable Comets give Seditions; but moveable Comets shew Wars between Nations; in the Angles, death of Kings; in the Ninth House, injury to Religion; in the Eighth and Twelfth Houses, pestilence and damage to the standing Corn; in the Eleventh House, the death of Noblemen. And now where, and by what word of all these we shall get power and room enough to lug in *Cardinal Signs*, I vow it seems to me impossible, unless we were animated with such Souls as honest *J. G.* was, when he wrote it. Oh my dear Joy! that ever thou shouldst translate *Cardinibus* for *Cardinal Signs*, and mistake *Cardinibus* for *Cardinalibus.* For it is plain, that *Cardan* means nothing else by *Cardinibus*, but the Angles of the Figure or Scheme of Heaven delineated in *plano*, because he mentions there also the other four Houses above the Earth, *i. e.* the Ninth, the Eleventh, the Twelfth, and Eighth Houses. Now, if *John* can but tell us, by what Rule in *Grammar*, by what Figure in Writing, or Construction, this word is to be thus understood in favour of his new-invented Principle, *alias*, whim of *Cardinal Signs* on *Angles*, I shall be ready to recant what I have written, and to give him not only the Right hand, but also the Service of my Pen once again to justify him: But I am sure he will save me the labour of both, and plead guilty to the Charge I have here laid before him. This Crime had been pardonable in a young Suckling, that is wantonly playing about the foot of *Parnassus*, and never had time to digest his Instructions and Rules laid down, and given him by his Nursing-Mother: But for an old Bell-weather that boasts his being snatcht from the Breast of *Minerva* at ten years of Age; *And yet for all that, says, he knows most words in* Thomalius *and* Rider; *and that he hath* Mars, *Lord of his Ascendant, and* Saturn *and* Jupiter, Alfhutens *of his Figure, which was so well known to his Adversaries, that like* Snails *they pull in their Horns at the least touch of his Pen, and durst not peep out in their own Vindication.* Say'st thou so *John*? Why then perhaps upon that Presumption you undertook this mighty Work, to unhinge the Principles of *Astrology* with your *Cardines Cœli*, and throw Heaven out at Windows, by help of a New Invention from *Brick-Court*; or perhaps he hath got the *Circulatum majus Paracelsi*, which they say dissolves all Metals, and

may

may, being used and improved by so great a *Virtuoso* as this is, easily dissolve the *Angles* of a *Figure* into their *first Matter*; and from thence to make *Cardinal Signs* at pleasure. Perhaps you will not believe this; why, these are no hard things in *John's* Religion, and I believe the *Priest* with his *Hoc est Corpus*, can do one as well as the other; *Ay by my shoul can be*. Thus you see upon what Authority *John Gad.* hath raised this mighty Structure of his *Cardines Cœli*; and to say the truth, the other parts of his Book are full as false as this is, tho not so obvious and notorious. For to translate *in Cardinibus*, to be meant in *Cardinal Signs*, tells us in plain terms, it shews him to be Egregiously Ignorant, or Audaciously Confident, in offering so boldly to assert a thing without any Authority, that he must needs believe was understood by some body else as well as himself; for otherwise he had been safe. And so I will leave my old Friend Mr. *Cardinibus*, only desiring him to take good notice of two Lines in *Marcel. Palingen.*

Indoctum raro esse probum contigit, & atras
Errorum in tenebras mentem Ignorantia trudit.

In his 29th Paragraph, he fetcheth an Aphorism from *Cardan*, as he says, if he doth not mistake; which tells us, *That He, who is born at Noon, when the Sun enters the Vernal Equinox, will be great and famous, without other Testimonies.* And this Aphorism *John* says, is directly intended by *Cardan* for that very end that he here brings it; and that this puts the matter out of all Controversy, and sways the Balance on his side, because at that time the Cardinal Signs possess the four Angles of the Celestial Figure, and make the thing as plain as a Pike-staff. Now observe, this is as notorious as the other, and the thing alledged by him directly false; by which he hath shewed his accustomed Confidence to a hair again. For if *Cardan* had intended such a Doctrine, as my Friend here brings it to prove, then he would have said thus, *Whosoever is born on this side the Latitude of 54 degr. the day the Sun enters Aries, will be Great,* &c. And to make it more plain to the *English*, he doth exclude *Berwick*, and all Places beyound it out of his intent; that is, he hath writ an Universal Aphorism, and yet hath excepted all *Scotland*, part of *Ireland*, most part of *Sweden* and *Denmark*, and divers other Kingdoms and Dominions out of it, which is indeed a sort of Nonsence in it self, and not to be charged upon *Cardan*, but another Man that

that better deserves it. For *Cardan* lays down his Aphorism in plain words, and makes it both positive and general, which it cannot be in *Gadbury*'s sense that he here useth it for, and this is plain, because in the Latitude of 55 degr. when the first Scruple of *Aries* is on the Cusp of the 10th House, the first degree of *Leo* ascends on the Ascendant, which puts the Aphorism quite out of doors, to all them People in that Latitude, and beyond it, if *J G.* is to be believed; when *Cardan's Aphorism* [if there is such a one] intends nothing else but the *Sun* in the *Equinox* and *Mid-heaven* together. So that the thing is plain to every one that will but consider. That whatsoever he here brings in under the notion of Authority, is all of it strain'd and forced beyond the intent of the Authors; as you may see more plainly in his following 30th and 31st Paragraph.

And here he comes to a close Proof of the Argument, and this he says, is from his noble *Firmicus*, in the Nativities of *Pindar*, *Archilocus*, and *Archimedes*, Fol. 173 & 174. And these three famous Men are but in two Nativities, and those two no ways brought to prove Cardinal Signs, but that the *Conjunction* of *Mars*, *Venus*, and *Mercury* in *Libra* in the Ascendant, in *Opposition* to *Jupiter* in *Aries* in the Seventh, in the Nativities of *Pindar* and *Archilocus*; and the *Conjunction* of *Mars*, *Venus*, and *Mercury* in *Aries*, in *Opposition* to *Mars* in *Libra*, in that of *Archimedes*, do produce great Men, and those of excellent Parts; but this was not from the Cardinal Signs, [tho I do allow the Positions to be the better for being in those Signs] but from the Planets in those Houses and Parts of Heaven; and on that and that only, doth *Firmicus* lay the Effects of the Position, as you may see, p. 173. But it was pretty odd, that they two should have both one Nativity, i. e. *Pindar* and *Archilocus*, and happen to be born in one and the same Minute, which if true, is a mighty Confirmation to Astrology; and that too confirmed by another example of *Demosthenes* and *Hermodorus*, who were also born together, as *Firmicus* says. But if *John* hath no better Arguments and Authority to prove his Hypothesis by, than these, he had as good give up the Cause; for I believe *Firmicus* knew the Nativities of *Demosthenes*, *Hermodorus*, *Archimedes*, *Pindar* and *Archilocus*, much about so well as *J G.* did Judge *Hales*'s, Sir *Frech. Holles*'s, *Oliver Cromwell*'s, *Charles Gustavus*'s, King of *Sweden*, and the *French King*'s, in his Collection of Genitures, with forty more that I could name, if occasion serv'd. And in his 33d Paragraph; after all these Assertions, he says, *He knows no reason why his Aphorism should not wear the Livery and Character*

Opus Reformatum.

ter of Truth; unless it can be proved, that Persons have been born with Cardinal Signs on the Angles of their Genitures, and lived to years of Maturity, and have not been famous in one kind or other, *i. e.* for Honour or Dishonour, Vice or Virtue, Wealth or Poverty, Learning or Ignorance, Courage or Cowardice; and if so, then the complaint brought against him is unjust.

To this I answer, The Proposition is very unfair, for there is no Man born into the World [or at least ways very few] that keeps the exact Medium of his Birth, but either falls below it, or riseth above it, and so hath more of Honour or Dishonour, in his Generation; and for Learning or Ignorance, I wonder he should talk of that in this Discourse, when he knows that depends wholly on the *Moon* and *Mercury*. And I utterly deny [and he knows it to be true] that any man had ever more of Cowardice or Courage, for his Angles being possessed by Cardinal Signs; for the one depends on the Rays of *Saturn*, and the other on the Beams and Power of *Mars*. And that of Honour and Dishonour, Poverty and Riches, depends on their peculiar Causes, and no ways concerned with the Cardinal Signs on the Angles; yet I grant that the Causers of these things being in those Signs [no matter what House they are in] may make their Effects more remarkable and famous. And so my Friend *John* leaves his Authorities, and falls in with his Antagonists about other things, which I shall over-hale, because there are some things that will yield matter that is worth reading, especially about that of his own Nativity, and the reason of his Imprisonment; as you have it in his 34th Paragraph.

Where he tells us, That he did foresee his being in the Popish Plot in 1679. twenty years before it fell out, and that by his own Nativity. Why really *John* this was a mighty Argument of your Skill; but suppose I should not be able to believe it? Why, then I judg he will rebuke me sharply for it, because he printed it in his Doctrine of Nativities, more than Twenty years before, and thereby it appears to be certainly true, it falling out exactly according to the time there mentioned in the Table of Directions, which was the *Medium Cœli ad quadratum Solis*, falling on the 12th House of his Figure at Birth, which shewed Imprisonment, and the Frowns of Great Persons. Ay, that is to the purpose, falling on the Cusp of the Twelfth, which is a plaguy corner of Heaven. And yet for all this, I do not believe one tittle of it; and I will tell you why, in a very few words; I cannot believe it, because every Square or Quadrate

drate in any Circle, ought to consist of 90 degr. and no more, whether in *Mundo* or *Zodiaco*; but this worthy Gentleman makes this of his to consist of 123 degr. and a few minutes, which seems to me an odd sort of a Square; and indeed I wonder how many such Squares he, or any other of those Philosophers will make in a Circle of 360 degr. For the proof of this, do but observe, They all allow that there are but 90 degr. between the Midheaven and the Ascendant, which makes up the Square, Quadrature, or 4th Part of the Circle; so that the *Sun* must come to the Ascendant, before the Midheaven comes to his Square; but at that time, when my old Friend says the *M. C.* came to the □ of ☉; the *Sun* was 33 degr. and more from the Horoscope; and to say the truth, the Midheaven to the Square of the *Sun* in *J. G's* Nativity will not come up till about 85 or 86 years of Age by his Figure, which is [to be plain with you] false. 2*dly*, I cannot believe it, because the *M. C.* to the □ of ♀ should have been as Malefick, and of as ill import as the □ of the ☉, because he is in ☌ with the ☉, and his Square falls also on the Cusp of the 12th House, and yet no trouble of the Nature and Quality of that in 1679, when he was in the Plot to Murder *Charles* II. Nor did his *M. C.* to the □ of ♀ in 1685. ever give him any thing of the Nature of the Direction at that time. And besides, why should not the Mid-heaven to the □ of ♃, at about 24 or 25 years of Age give Imprisonment, and the Frowns of Great Men, Bishops, and Lawyers, by the same Rule that the ☉ did it afterwards. I know he hath no other Sham to excuse it with, but by saying, it did not fall on the Cusp of the 12th House; a plaguy kind of an Argument, and one would think it is sufficient to convince any man. But 3*dly* and *Lastly*, I cannot believe it, because he lets the Midheaven pass by the Body of ♄, which is a real and visible Direction, and a most fatal one too in all Nativities, either to Life, Liberty, or Reputation; and trumps up an imaginary Direction, which there is no such thing in nature. I know I shall have Enemies in this case, and therefore I will put it fairly to them all. Pray, *Gentlemen*, which do you think is the most proper Direction to throw a man into Prison for betraying the Nation, endeavouring to bring in Popery [this is plain upon him, for he turn'd Papist afterwards] to Murder the King, and such like Crimes; the Mid-heaven to the Body of ♄, or to the □ of the ☉? If the □ of the ☉, then what did ♄ give? if ♄, what did the □ of the ☉ give? For you have not Accidents for both Directions; and at that time, when he makes the *M. C.* to the Body

of

of ♄ to be in force, was he top and top-gallant; then it was every one pull'd in his Horns at the dash of his Pen, not daring to appear in their own Vindication, Prog. to his Alman. 1669. Where it is plain to me, that one of these two Directions is false, they being both expired, and but one Accident, 2*dly*, That his own Nativity is false, and that he never knew yet how to correct it. And 3*dly*, that he did not understand one word of the truth of Astrology more at the writing of his *Cardines Cœli*, than at the printing his Doctrine of Nativities. And for the other part of this 44th Paragraph, that I have not touched on, 'tis all false, and a lye; and I will instance in one thing. *He says he doth esteem it all mens Duty to be Obedient to the Lawful Established Government, both in Church and State.* Here he hath plainly given himself the lye; for in 1690. he was catcht at the Post-Office in sending a Treasonable Letter, in which was a Popish Declaration, and a Scandalous Copy of Verses on the King and Queen, which he promised in his Letter should be printed speedily: In short, there was enough to have hang'd twenty men in the two late Bloody Reigns, and yet this *Gentleman* escaped; and how many of such Letters he did send, that were not catcht, he will not tell us, I suppose; and was this obedience to the lawful Government? Yes, without doubt; and do but call at *John*'s Office of *Sedition*, and there you shall find a Popish Casuist shall make it as plain as the Nose on your Face. But, I suppose, John meant, *that it was all mens Duty to be obedient to the Established Government that would set up Popery.* A very honest, consciencious Fellow, and a true Subject to a Protestant Prince; ha! Mass *John*, is that true? *Vix Credo*. But by this you may easily guess, whether what he says is to be believed, or not, let him fawn and dissemble with the Government in what Language he pleaseth. Nay, I dare be positive he will not take the Oaths to Their Majesties, as appointed by Parliament, he is so good an *Englishman*. But talk about *Charles* the Martyr, and his immortal Arch-bishop, and there you hit him; if you would know the reason, 'tis because their Religion is all of a piece. And yet further, let him but observe his own words in the 56th Paragraph, *Where is our Love to Christianity,* (says he) *or the blessed Author of it, who hath taught us better Lessons, than to injure the Quiet of another, or to cast fiery Bombs at the Innocent, and this without first asking a reason of the Difference, or fairly proclaiming War?* and so on in the following Paragrah. It seems it was an Injury at that time to fall upon *Him*, without giving either warning, or shewing Cause why. But he had forgot that in 1687. when he did be-rebel and

Villain

Villain me in print, when [I solemnly protest] I gave no Cause, nor Occasion; only his Zeal for Popery and the Holy Cause, prompted him on, to abuse me without a Cause, and to shew himself a malicious, envious Fellow. And in that humour I leave him quarrelling with *Gassendus*, and trifling with his Reader, and come down to his 80th Paragraph, where I find him very angry with his Adversary for thinking he was a Papist; which doth indeed shew the strength and excellence of that *Gentleman*'s Judgment; for *Gad.* did really turn Papist afterward.

And here let me beg my Readers pardon for my departing from the Text; tho indeed it is not my fault, for I am still pursuing his matter; by which you may see what shift he makes to leave the Cardinal Signs, and lug in an Argument to shew his Cardinal Errors, his Religion I mean. And for above a dozen Paragraphs together, he doth merrily Ridicule the Enemies to Popery, and those that believe the story of Pope *Joan*. Concerning all which, I shall only make these Remarks following, nor being willing to spend Paper and Time upon so idle and foolish a thing, as *J. C*'s Religion. 1. Then, Let us observe how peevish he is in the 82d Paragraph, and how unwilling to be counted a *Papist*, and what Shrugs, Shams, and Quibbles he uses to evade the Story. And at last, to convince us that he is no Papist, he tells the World they may see him at the *Abby-Church* very often at Divine Service, [not a word of the Sermon] which without doubt is a special way to prove a man a Protestant, as if no Papists came thither; but who hath seen him there in the last four or five years, ever since he used to go to Mass, and was Father *Peters*'s Convert; ever since he told Cap. *C.* that Popery was the only true Religion; and to sum up all, since he was Married by a Popish Priest at *Wildhouse.* 2dly, In all the Paragraphs, where he hath complained of his hard usage, under that report, ridicul'd Popery after a sham sort of a way, his laughing at the story of Pope *Joan*; how *Dangerfield* and *Care* had be-papisted him; how *Coley* had sent him to his Beads; and how he was burnt twice in Effigy with the Pope; yet this is remarkable, in all that ridiculous Stuff, he doth not say, He *is no Papist*, only endeavours to sham a belief upon us, as he would do this of his *Cardinal Signs* 3dly, If he was no Papist, why did he always forget to put in the Fifth of *November*, by the name of *Gunpowder-Treason-day*, which he did many years together; and yet I have heard him swear he forgot it; but I know what he, his Oaths, and his Promises are, especially in all those things, when

and

and where the Popish Cause is concern'd. If he was no Papist, or a Well-willer to it, why did he always herd with the Priests of that Faction, and with others publickly known Papists, and in their Company talk impudently in defence of them and their Church, as I my self have heard? If he were no Papist, why did he endeavour to make so many Converts to that Persuasion? But if I do not name who, I know his faculty of swearing, By Heavens 'tis a lye, will be the answer.

1. Then he endeavoured to Convert Mr. B. a Divine of the Church of *England* to the Popish perswasion, which his puny Parts was not able to do; then he went with him to a Learned Gentleman in the City of that Persuasion, who did his endeavour to convince and convert him, but it would not do; then he went with him to that learned Gentleman, Dr. G. who did [said Mr. B.] say as much for that false lying Religion, as any *Casuist* of them all could do; and after they had exchanged some Sheets of Paper in Controversy, the Doctor let his expected Convert rest in his own Persuasion. At this my Friend J. G. was very angry, and with taunting Language told Mr B. that he did believe he must at last of all be forced to have him to Father *Petre*, and Father *Ellis*, two Notorious and Arch-Traytors, at that time very famous and industrious to destroy the Protestant Religion, and subvert the Laws of the Land. Another *Gentleman*, was one Sir R. P. whom he also did perswade to turn Papist, and told him it was the only rising Religion; and he did foresee by the Stars from the ☌ of ♄ and ♃ in ♌, that it would root out the *Northern Heresy*, and be the Universal Faith over all *Europe*; and therefore did advise him to turn betimes, and be an early Convert, which was the best way to Preferment when the Government came into Catholick Hands; by which you may see on what Topick this worthy *Gentleman* builds his Religion, and what made him at last turn profest Papist; upon the whole, it admits of a seasonable Query, Whether or no this were not down-right Treason, according to the Antient Laws of the Kingdom of *England* ? 4thly, Do but consider, what a bustle he hath made in nine Paragraphs about Pope *Joan*, the Petticoat-Prelate. In which I do observe two things; 1. What a pretty sort of endeavour he useth to put the whole Story into doubt and question; how many shams hath he lug'd in by head and shoulders, to amuse the Reader about it? How many Objections are there raised, to make the thing seem improbable? How many Doubts propounded in reference to her Quality of State, and her pregnant Condition, to render it impossible? How many People hath he there reflected on

N as

as Nonconformists, and others, to abuse them with his Language, and us by the imposition of his Arguments? How many Suppositions hath he put by way of proof to what he intends, when indeed he had no proof for the least tittle of his Objection to the Story, but the Zeal of his Soul for the Popish Cause, and his Malice to Protestants, he at that time believing as the Church believed. I confess, the way he hath taken, is a fine Sham-argument, tho not to convince them, yet to stagger People, and make them believe it was an abuse upon Holy Church. And by this way of argument, I dare to swear, I could perfectly defend, clear, and justify a certain Sinner within a mile of *Colledge-street*; For example, suppose a man hath a good, brisk, comely, gentile Woman to his Wife, what need hath he to go a Whoring? Or, who can believe he would tempt another man's Wife to leave her Husbands bed, and cohabit with him? Who can imagine he should bring a Whore into his House under his Wive's Nose, and get her with Child, and then have her out to Mrs. *Wright*'s to lye in? Who will believe that when the Woman was up again, he should seek to destroy her? Who would judge a man that came to Prayers to the Abby, as a Protestant, should ever Plot to Murder a King, as good a Protestant as himself? And can any man be persuaded, that he who hath made so much Noise about Duty and Allegiance to Kings, should, *be catcht in a Plot* about two year ago, to destroy one of the *best Kings* in the World, only he is a *Protestant*, and that *John* hates. Certainly no man will believe, apprehend, or imagine one word of this to be true, because it doth not seem needful, requisite, or necessary. Thus I think I have cleared that *Gentleman* from his Sins, as well as he hath confuted the Story of Pope *Joan*, only in fewer words. And 2dly, to shew the Papists, that what he did now by a side-long glance as a Protestant, was to let them know, he would undertake any thing bare-fac'd, as a Papist, when they should have courage enough to set up Popery by a Law, and to let them know. That he would Be-heretick the Protestants, and Church of *England* then, as he had heretofore *Be-rebell'd* the Nonconformists. And if you read his *Reply, p. 8.* and divers other places in that Book, you will find his Arguments for so doing; where he doth as good as tell us, That all those who were against setting up Popery, and thwarting that Kings designs, were down-right *Rebels*. *Traytors*, and *Hereticks*, and fit for nothing but *Jayles, Faggot, Gibbet,* and *Ax*. Thus hath *John* vindicated the *Pope* and Chair of *Rome*, from those Aspersions of Temporal Whoredom, which was a good Emblem of

her

her being the Spiritual *Whore* of *Babylon*; that there was no such Creature as Pope *Joan*, and by consequence no Bastard: But I had rather he had spoke something [tho not half so much] about the other *Joan*, he knows who, and to have sworn he had never got her one. But, alas poor man!

At last he is pleased to quit this worthy *Lady Pope*'s Affair, having done like a good dutiful Child to his *Spiritual Father* and *Mother*: *Hic* & *hæc*, *Papa* & *Papissa*, a Pope of the doubtful Gender, the Infallible Father of an unspotted Church, the bountiful Treasurer of the Mercies of God, Master of the Office for Prayers and Benedictions, where none perish but they that are poor, and want Money. It was this Holy Mother that *John* went backward to cover her Nakedness, and discover'd his own; an old Jilt deluded the poor Gentleman into her Quarters, decoy'd him to a tryal of Skill, and then turn'd him up like a ragged Colt on a Common, that is fit for nothing but the Pound when he breaks Hedges. But he is never long to seek, either a new Mistriss, or Religion, being always assisted with a grave Gentlewoman for the one, and a large Conscience for the other. Whip, says he, in the 93d Paragraph, like a Munkey in a Crab-tree, he takes a swindging leap from his Holy Mother, Pope *Joan*, to his dear and beloved *Urania*, and at once he throws himself both into her Bosom and Acquaintance; when perhaps, if the truth was known, the poor Gentlewoman never heard of him in her days before; but no matter for that; he says he is a Retainer and Domestick in her Family; and if you will believe him, can take upon him what Office and place of Trust he pleaseth; sometimes he is her *Secratary*; by and by he is one of her *Privy Councellors*; sometimes a *Porter* at her Gate; and sometimes you shall find he is one of her *Bullies*, for in what shape soever you see him in, you must be sure to construe him a Servant, and a Man of mighty Power in the Court of the *Divine Urania*, the *Glorious Urania*, his *Dear Urania*, that will deny him nothing. Now, if I were in *Urania*'s place, and should hear him *Cant*, *Flatter*, and *Fawn*, as generally he doth, I should judge him come to *Beg*, *Pick my Pocket*, *Rob* or *Cut my Throat*, because such Language is always useful and necessary, before the Perpetration of those private Villanies. But in the 95th Paragraph he tells us, That *Urania* is a *Virgin* and *Spotless*, which is the greatest wonder of all, *And he acquainted with her so long, and so intimate as he says he was*. And so I leave him in the Embraces and Enjoyments of his Spiritual and Cœlestial Ladies; and come to the next

N 2   thing

thing remarkable, and that is, he tells the Readers those *Aphorisms*, called the *Centiloquium* of *Ptolomy*, are really owned to be *Ptolomy*'s; which I positively deny, and will do my endeavour to make my Assertion good; and this for two Reasons 1 To shew the young Students how they may shun the common gross Errors. And 2*dly*, to let the World know I do not dissent from the common Practice and Method, without good Reason and Authority.

Every Textuary Author, that writes upon any Science, Art, or Subject whatsoever, doth generally take care that his Matter be all of a piece, and not one place or Text to thwart another, one Principle directly opposite to another, and a general incoherence throughout his whole matter, for if so, then no man will be able either to understand him, or receive any Benefit or Information by his writings. And whosoever reads the *Quadripartite* of *Ptolomy*, will soon judge that he was not a man likely to be guilty of such an Absurdity, or weakness in his Judgment and Reason. And therefore for the better clearing of the matter, I will take the pains to compare some of those Aphorisms, with some of the Texts in his *Quadripartite*. And before I begin, let me take the liberty to make this Observation upon that great man, and those Aphorisms said to be his. In those 100 Aphorisms, we find 16 that do in particular refer to, and concern Elections, divers Horary Questions, and some Decumbitures, &c. yet [notwithstanding the Aphorisms seem to be written with a sort of Authority] *Ptolomy* hath not written one word of any of those parts of Astrology, nor given the least countenance to them in any of his Writings, which to me seems very strange, that he hath not throughout his *Quadripartite*, made the least mention of any such thing, nor any reference to any such Book, which we may suppose a man so well skill'd as he was, would have done, if he had designed to have wrote any thing of the like nature; and therefore to give some broken, imperfect Sentences about any Science, that we know he was Master of, is to tell the World, that either he knew no more, or at leastwise if he did, was maliciously resolved to hide it from Posterity; which uncharitable Opinion I cannot be induced to believe, no more than that they are his Aphorisms, and by him penn'd; which I dare be bold to say, they were not. But perhaps some may say, That he may have written something of that nature, which might be lost; 'tis true, such a thing might be, but then there would have been some Reference to it in some of his Writings, as he hath in Chap. 6. of Book II. in his *Quadripartite*, *De genere Eventuum*, where

he

he hath made mention of a Book that is lost, *i.e. Liber Magnæ Compositionis*; but not a word of any else, as I could meet with. And so I come to consider the Aphorisms themselves.

In the 37th Aphorism, 'tis said, *That they who have ♈ or ♎ ascending, shall be the cause of their own Death.* Which is directly repugnant to the Doctrine delivered in the Chapter, *De genere Mortis*, Book 4th, of his *Quadripartite*, where he makes no use of any of the Houses in his Judgment about Death, but the *Midheaven*; neither doth he take notice of the *8th House* in any thing that relates to *Death*; and it is upon the mystick Power of that House, the 37th *Aphorism* is founded. Now, if he had thought the obscure Houses had any power in that thing of Death when he wrote his *Aphorisms*, he would have certainly made some discovery of his Opinion, when he was writing that Chapter, *De Morte*. But neither in that, nor the other of Diseases, doth he take any notice of it in the least. But the reason of this Aphorism is, Because, when ♈ ascends, then ♂ is Lord both of the Ascendant and Eighth Houses; and when ♎ ascends, then ♀ is Lady of both those Houses. So that the Lord of the Ascendant, being Lord of the 8th House, makes the Native some way or other, the Cause and Author of his own Death, which is an absurd thing to believe; and that the Houses should give a power to the Stars, because the Signs [appointed them for their Houses] happen to be upon those empty Spaces in the Heavens, which they call Houses, the whole Scheam being divided into twelve equal parts; and do you think this is not a very likely story, and that *Ptolomy* doth agree with *Ptolomy* very well? What say you? I should also have observed, that in the same Aphorism, it is said, *He that hath ♍ or ♓ ascending on the Horoscope, shall be the cause and author of his own Preferment and Advantage*; and the reason is, because the same Star is Lord of the First and Tenth Houses, which is directly opposite to *Ptolomy*'s Doctrine in the Chapter, *De Dignitate*. And so is the 46th Aphorism.

The 76th Aphorism discourseth about violent Deaths and lays the cause of the violence to the charge of ♄ in the Tenth; and yet the Native [forsooth] must dye of such a Death, as the Sign on the Cusp of the Fourth signifies. If it be an *Earthly Sign, he shall be knocked on the Head by the fall of a House. If a Watery Sign, he shall be drowned.* But if a *Humane Sign, he shall be Hanged.* And at last tells us in the end of the Aphorism, *That if a Fortune shall be in the Eighth House, he shall be near these dangers, but shall not dye by them.* Which overthrows the whole Doctrine of *Ptolomy* concerning violent Deaths, and natural too.

too. For he lays no stress on any of the Houses for violent Deaths, but the Position of the Luminaries, &c. and for the Eighth House, he doth not so much as take notice of it throughout his whole Book, as I remember; but for the Midheaven, he mentions it twice in the Chapter of Death, and no more; and then no ways favouring this Aphorism, if you understand *Ptolomy* and his Principles. Whence it is plain, that the Aphorism is directly repugnant to the Doctrine of *Ptolomy* in his *Quadripartite*.

In the 58th and 66th Aphorisms, you find the word Profection used, both in the *English* and *Latin*, not only in the Translation of *Trapezuntius*, but in that of *Jovianus Pontanus* also; but *Trapezuntius*'s Commenting on the *Centiloquium*, gives us a strange Explication of the 58th Aphorism; and tells us of a confused motion, which he fathers on this Aphorism, and endeavours to prove it by his own Nativity, which he calls an *Aphetical Profection*, [of which more anon] and I believe thinks it is a confused motion himself, because he uses terms in his Discourse, that are really doubtful and suspicious in themselves; as, *Tamen propter varios Circulorum multiplicesque anfractus, & stellarum loca, non ita præcise nobis Cognita ut res flagitat*. But when he comes to Comment on the 66th, he inverts this word Profection, and makes it signify another sort of Doctrine, of which *Ptolomy* hath spoken more fully in Chap. 16. of Book III. about Addition and Substraction in a killing Direction; a thing known to very few of our Age, either Theorically or Practically. I say he inverts this word *Profection* to quite another thing, wholly remote from the former, and yet the word in the Text is the same in both, i. e. Περίπατ⊙ and why they should have two such different significations, I know not. However, that I will pass by, it being not to my present purpose. Now, if we do allow this word Profection, as *Trapezuntius* hath translated it, and given the meaning of it in the first Aphorism; we shall not find one tittle in the four Books of *Ptolomy*, to give any colour or shew to such a Notion; no, not in the last Chapter of his Fourth Book, where they would insinuate a ground for that, and some other Innovations. And as he hath given us the meaning of the word in the other Aphorism, the Text is much darker, and far more abstruse than that Text in Book III. and Chap. 14. where *Ptolomy* doth lay down that Rule plain and easy. Whence it is visible, that the *Centiloquium*, and the *Quadripartite*, were the products of two Heads, and bespeaks them also men of different Parts and Abilities. But besides, this word *Profection*, or Περίπατ⊙, περιπατος, doth refer to Motion, and that too of the Hilegicals, as they all own: and I do not remember, That I ever found that word in either of his two last Books, where he discourseth of Nativities alone; but when he makes mention of the Hilegical Points, he always useth these words, Αφέτικος τόπος. *Per omnes casus veriata*, As you may see in his 11th, 13th, & 14th Chapters of his 3d Book; and in the 11th of his Fourth. And to tell you the truth, I really think that word περιπατος is ill translated, for it truly signifies, *Ambulatio, aut via in qua aliquis ambulat*. And therefore is referable to Direction. Lastly, As to this thing of Profections, as now understood, I look on it as a confused groundless thing, and inconsentaneous both to Nature and its Motions; for the Order of Nature is regular, but this is wholly irregular. For Example, They make each House to move a whole Sign every Year; and if you have the first degree of ♒ ascending at Birth, the next year you must have the first degree of ♓ there; when you know by Oblique Ascention there is ♓ intercepted, and you will then find your whole Figure perfectly in disorder, and no ways agreeing to any Figure in our Table of Houses. For when you come to have 1 degr. of ♓ ascending, you ought by rule and order to have 19 degr. of ♐ on the Tenth, but in the profectional Figure you must have 2 degr. of ♑ culminating, and so forward every Year; by which way you will have no regular Figure again, till ♒ comes to be on the Ascendant, as at Birth. Hence you may see, if you please, what a confusion we are brought to by following Authors without Authority, and what pretty Inventions have been found out to kick Truth out of doors. And after all this, They render περιπατος in the 77th Aphorism, to signify Directions, as *Trapezuntius* allows in his Commentary thereon; and yet with it, because he will not lose his Opinion, jumbles in a lame Discourse of Profections likewise, but to as little purpose as the former. And I do declare, I know no use of the thing, nor any Authority for the name, if they insinuate any other Motion by that name, than the real and natural Motion of the Significator in Direction, of which let every man judge as he finds himself inform'd by his Reading, instructed by his Reason, and inclin'd in his Practice. But there are divers other things that I could take notice of under this consideration, were it wholly needful, as the 78th, and 88th Aphorisms, which do not want a deficiency sufficient for Objections of this nature; but I judge this enough to shew what ought to be considered, and to excite abler Pens to expatiate

patiate thereon for the benefit of those that may come after us; and to let them know, all is not truth that is Printed and Published to the World under the name and notion of Astrology; and also, that I care not a rush whether they believe me or no.

I hope no man that hath common sense, and hath also read the *Quadripartite*, will ever believe the 95th Aphorism was penn'd by *Ptolomy*, where it is said, *That the Images and forms of things, &c. that rise with every distinct decanate in the Ascendant of Nativities, shall shew what Trade, Art, or Imployment the Native will chuse to live by.* Which, if you please to compare with the Doctrine delivered in the 4th Chapter of the 4th Book, where he discourseth at large. *De Magisterio*; you will find, that two things were never writ more opposite and contrary than they two are. For *Ptolomy* makes no use either of the Ascendant, or the Faces of the Signs, or the Images and Forms of men or things therein rising; which is so absurd a Doctrine to father upon *Ptolomy*, if but compared with his own words in his *Quadripartite*, that no man can assert it to be his, without blushing the same moment. His words are these, *Magisterii dominus sumitur ex duobus modis, à sole & signo Medii Cœli.* Which in my Opinion have no Relation, Proportion, or Likeness to the words in the Aphoristical Text, and yet both believed to be our Authors words, when there is nothing more unlike in the very ground and principle it self, and for that reason I cannot believe it to be the Doctrine of the Great *Ptolomy*.

Lastly, And to mention no more, pray look into the 56th Aphorism, in which you find a lame account of the *Moon*'s nature in her several distances from the *Sun*; where he tells you from the New to the Full [for so I understand it] the Humidity and Humour of Natural Bodies doth increase, but from the Full to the New it decreaseth; which in general terms I believe may be true enough. But then, to what purpose should *Ptolomy* give us an Aphorism here about a thing of this nature, and leave it so imperfect as he hath in the *Centiloquium*, [if his] when he had long before given it us in plainer words, and more intelligible terms to be understood [for I suppose these Aphorisms were writ last] in the 6th Chapter of his 1st Book, where he plainly tells us, *Luna enim à Conjunctione, donec apparet dimidiata, magis est rigatrix. Inde usque ad plenilunium calefacit. A plenilunio, donec iterum dimidiata apparet, desiccat. Ab eo tempore, donec occultatur, frigifacit.* Which is in plain words and terms, easy to be apprehended. Then what need had *Ptolomy* after this, to give us another Aphorism imperfect and lame, unless he lived to forget what

Opus Reformatum.

what he had writ himself, and so in his doating, fumbling days, did that which was next to nothing; which I judg this, and a great many more of those Aphorisms in the *Centiloquium* to be; nay, there are some of them seem to me to be very idle or imperfectly given to us, as the 16, 50, 65, 78, 87, and divers others of them, that may be justly called in question. Thus I have given you my Opinion, why I think the *Hundred Aphorisms*, called, the *Centiloquium* of *Ptolomy*, are indeed and in truth not his. And thus far have I gone also to inform Mr. *J. G.* and his *Antagonist*, in the 168th Paragraph, That those Aphorisms are mistaken as to their Author, and that they were not his whom they believe, and affirm them to be; and therefore, if they will have them to be his, and that they can prove it too, they will very much impair the Authority of *Ptolomy* in my Judgment and Opinion; and the only reason is, because the Text in the *Quadripartite* is never to be reconciled to those in the Aphorisms, unless some witty Moderator can unite their Principles by the Mystery of Language in a Learned Comment upon both of them. In a word, this is not the only time that *J. G.* hath affirmed those Aphorisms to be *Ptolomy's*; and therefore I am of opinion, that either he never read the *Quadripartite*, or if he hath, he never understood it beyond the bare words, knowing nothing of the principles, nor design of the Author, as to the Phylosophick, Astrological Practice thereof; but if these two should happen to be true [which I am sure they are not], I am confident he never did compare one Principle with another; and to be plain with you, I am partly sure he cannot; but I hope he will endeavour to learn [being a man of such mighty Parts and Ingenuity, as he himself in divers of his Writings tells us he is], if the Holy *Harlot* of *Rome* hath not made him as perfect and infallible as her self, which accomplishment most of her Babes reach to, and arrive at; and seeing he hath been of that Sacred Persuasion so many years, it would be strange if he should not have attained something of her mighty Qualifications and Virtues; both in Morality and Religion, and to have arrived at the unerring Principle of positive Perfection. Which if he be, then farewel all hopes of Reformation in my old Friend, for where that sort of truth hath once prevailed, there is seldom any admittance or entrance for *Heretical* Persuasions and Instructions, either to reform his Errors in Science, or his Hobby-horse Religion. Lord! *that ever a fellow should turn Papist, after having gone twenty years to St. Peters Westminster, as a Protestant!*

Q   Having

Having run over that part of his proof that depends on Authorities and Reasons; I am now come to the Second part of his proof, and that is his *Train of Experience*, as he hath entitled it, and propounded to do it in Ten Nativities, which I shall distinctly examine by themselves, and prove the major part of them false, as well as the *Protector Cromwell's* was. And for those few that are true, I will shew that they depended upon other and more probable Causes, than that of Cardinal Signs on Angles, and in the examining of them, I shall consider the possibility of their Truth, by the probability of their Accidents that did attend them both in their Lives, and at the times of Death. For I will not take them upon trust from him, as he hath from others, and so take it for granted, because he says it; and whosoever shall examine his Collection of Genitures, shall certainly find the major number of them to be false, because taken upon trust, as he hath done the rest he hath published, for the most part, by which means the Readers are abused. And the first Nativity he begins with, is that of *Charles Gustavus*, King of *Sweden*, whom he tells us, was born at the time inscribed in the Figure following, set *Ptolemaically*.

The King of Swedeland.

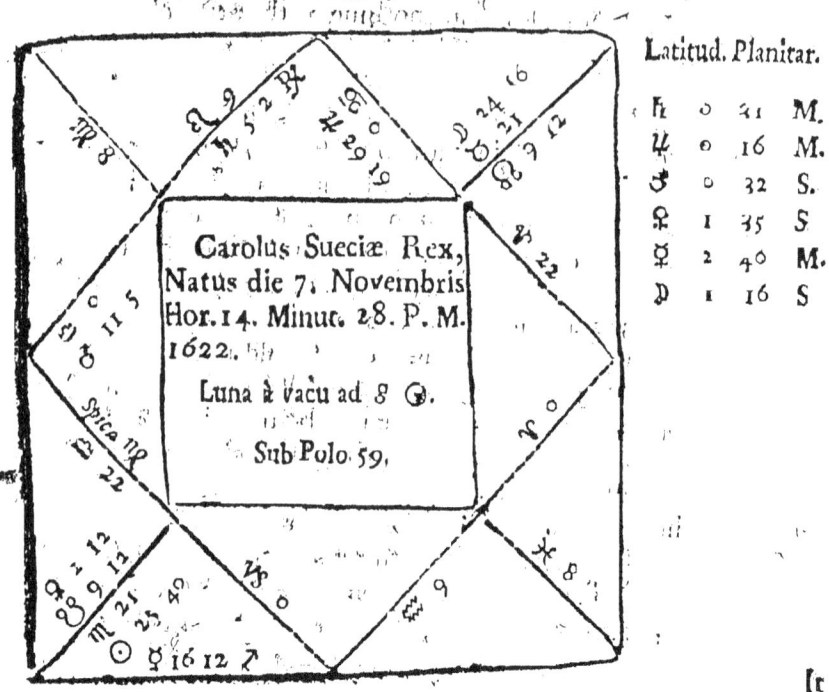

Opus Reformatum.

It would have been very convenient, if my worthy good Friend would have been so kind as to have given us the estimate time of this Great Prince's Birth, but seeing we have it not, I must make the best use of that he hath here afforded us; and this Nativity, he says, in his Collection he corrected by the M. C. ad Corpus ♃, at which time Queen *Christina* surrendred, and he was crowned, being then about 32 years of Age, and at 37 he dyed, which without further trouble to the Reader, I will accept for truth, and ask him if he doth really believe that the M. C. ad ☌ ♄ kill'd him, which he affirms did do it in his Collection of Genitures; and if he still says he doth, I would have him tell us by what Rule it must do it here, and miss in 20 or 30 besides. For I lay this down as an Axiom, that the M. C. ad Corpus ♄, may ruin and destroy the *Honour*, *Estate*, and *Reputation* of the Native, but never kill him, if the ☉ or ☽ happen to be in any Aphetical Place, which in this Nativity you see the ☽ is in; and therefore I question the *whole Figure*; for the ☽, who is *Hileg*, could come at that time to no ill Direction of the Lord of the 4th, 6th, 8th, or 12th, but on the contrary, was very near the Zodiacal △ of ♀ without Latitude, and free from all ill Rays. But if the Body of ♄ had such a mighty influence [as he says] at that time to kill, being directed to the Midheaven; why did not the Ascendant to the Body of ♂ in his detriment, and the Midheaven to his Square kill him when he was young, between the Age of 12 and 15; for I dare be certain that two Directions have more force than one, whether good or bad. But I will descend to Examples in other Nativities, and the first shall be his own, which if true, as he hath printed it in his *Doctrine of Nativities*, and owned it twenty five years after in his *Cardines Cœli*, that his M. C. ad □ ☉ came up in the year 1679, which if so, then the Midheaven to the Body of ♄ came up in the year 1670, or beginning of 1671, and was so far from killing him, or destroying his Reputation, that he was then in the top of his *Grandeur*, growing in his Reputation, ruffling any one whom he pleased, and no ways Sick, or in danger of Death. The second is the Nativity of *Gustavus Adolphus*, printed by my Friend likewise, *Vide Collect. Gen. p. 31.* where he lets him pass the Midheaven to the Body of *Mars*, and Square of *Saturn*, from violent parts of Heaven, as smoothly as could be; and kills him about three years after, with the *Sun* to the *Square* of *Mars*, and *Opposition* of *Saturn.* But then, say I, why did not those two other Directions kill him three years before, as well as one kill this than? Perhaps

he

he will say, because the *Sun* is *Hileg*, and in the *Ascendant*; why, then by the same Rule, is not the *Moon Hileg* here in the Ninth House, and so of the same force with the other? But I suppose, if he had not found the *Sun* complying with his skill readily, it had been but altering the *Midheaven* and *Ascendant* two or three degrees, and then the other should have done the feat as currently as in this man's. With this also, consider the Nativity of *Nostradamus*, where the *Sun* is placed on the Cusp of the Midheaven, and yet he outlived the *Midheaven*, and *Sun* to the Body of *Mercury*, *Opposition* of *Mars*, *Opposition* of *Saturn*, and *Opposition* of *Jupiter*, Lord of the *Eighth House*, and the three latter all in *Conjunction* in *Cancer*. Now, is not this a very strange story, that the Stars should be so plaguy partial in their Influence, to kill *Charles Gustavus*, because he was a fighting King; and let *Nostradamus* live, because he was a Popish Prophet? 'Tis very strange! one single Direction kill'd *Charles Gustavus*, two would not kill *Gustavus Adolphus*, nor four *Nostradamus*, and yet all to the same point and part of the Figure, the Midheaven. Nay, in his own Nativity, it did not so much as make him Sick, nor give the least symptom of danger to his Life, altho the Ascendant was *Giver of Life*.

Doth this worthy Friend of mine believe, that any man can think or judge these irreconcileable Stories can ever be ranked among the truths of Astrology, or that any man shall be so void of Reason and Judgment to believe his Notion in the one, and make his understanding stoop to a lye, and give consent to the truth of the other; being opposite one to another, as to the Notion and Practice. For it is most certain, if the Body of *Saturn* [or *Opposition* either] to the Cusp of the Tenth, did or doth ever kill, I think it must always do it without Rules of Exception, but here he forceth a Notion upon us, which he openly contradicts by permitting the contrary to pass for Doctrine in other Nativities, as you may see in Mr. *Stepkin's* Nativity for one, where *Saturn* is in *Sagitary* in *Opposition* to the *Sun*, and yet the Mid-heaven to the Opposition of one, and the Body of the other would not kill. In the Nativity of Mr. *Stephen Rogers*, the Midheaven to the Body of *Mars* did not kill, p. 138. Mr. *Gataker* passed the Midheaven to the Body of *Saturn* and *Mars*, without doing him any injury to his Health; and so did Dr. *Morton*, p. 92. pass and out-live the *M. C.* to the Body of *Saturn*; and yet this great Prince must fall by a Direction, that either would or could not kill any Body else. *A very hard Fate!*

I can-

Opus Reformatum. 101

I cannot deny the Midheaven to the Body of *Jupiter*, to be a Direction suitable enough to signify that of his Coronation; yet do not believe it was that which gave him that Promotion. But for the Body of *Saturn* for his Death, I do declare it is a thing impossible, and never to be allowed by any man that pretends to understand Astrology; unless it is for a sham to serve a turn when nothing else will do, the Rule being directly against it; and you see here are several mens Nativities where it did not kill; nay, in his own too; and for that very reason, I think he ought to tell the World why it did not kill. And I am sure those Examples that do, and must prove a new Notion [as this of his is] ought to be unquestionable; and these of his are not, and upon very good Authority too. And I do dare him to shew me an Example in a true-taken Nativity, where the *Sun* or *Moon* were givers of Life, and the Directions to the Midheaven kill'd, and the *Apheta* at the same time free from all Malefick Rays by Direction, as in this of *Charles Gustavus*'s, the Illustrious King of *Sweden*. I say, If he can shew me a true-taken Nativity [that I can be satisfied is true, and no trick or sham upon me] where such a Direction kill'd under the circumstantial Qualifications beforementioned, I will disown my *Diana*, the Great *Ptolomy*, for I do think I partly understand him, and am partly sure he, nor no man else can shew such a one, if the Doctrine of *Ptolomy* [which of all is the most rational] is true; and I can also assure you, that it is not every one that says he knows and understands him, that speaks truth. And to convince you, I could, if need were, give Example sufficient. Now, to sum up all, there is but one Direction to prove this Nativity to be true, according to *John Gad.*'s Correction, and that is the M.C. ad *Corpus Jovis* for his Coronation; and for this Accident by altering the Figure a little, I can give you three or four Directions, that are as probable as that he gives, if not more; and the first is, the Midheaven to the ✶ of ♂; The second is, the M.C. to the △ of ♀; The third is, the Midheaven to the ✶ of the ☽, and △ of the ☉; But the fourth, and the most probable, was the ☽ to the Mundane Parrallel of ♃, and this suddenly followed with the ☉ to the like Mundane Parrallel of ♃; and then the ☉ and ☽ will come to the Mundane Parallel of ♄ for his Death direct and convers; and also to the Zodiacal Parallel of ♀, yet I confess this last Direction is something an improper one, because they are, when the Direction is finished, both out of the Ecliptick; and for that reason, I do not look on that as a Cause, but a Concomitant. The ☉ and ♀ in the Revolution

in

102 *Opus Reformatum.*

in ☌ and ☍ to the ☽'s Radical place, and the ☽ in direct □ to ♂ his Radical place, and the ☽ by secondary motion in ☐ to the ☉; and this is the most proper Position that I can think rational to select for this great Man's Birth, not having the estimate time; and the Figure agreeing to this time, will be about six degrees of *Gemini* on the Tenth, and about the middle of *Virgo* ascending, which doth precede his time above an hour. And I know no reason, but that he may be as far out in this, as he was in the *French King's*, that he printed at the same time, and would still have justified it [no doubt] had not *Morinus* long ago convinced him. And to conclude, I am not sure this Figure that I have supposed for the King of *Sweden's* Birth is true; but I am confident his is not, and therefore it will but *meanly plead for the Honour and Power of Cardinal Signs on the Angles of a Nativity.*

The next he makes use of to prove his wild Notion, is the Nativity of the Duke of *Guise*, and it is the Position following; the Planets places from *Origanus*.

The Duke of Guise.

Natus die 4 Aprilis horæ 5. min. 27. Mane die ♀, 1614.

☽ △ ✶ ☉ ad ✶ ☿.

Latitud. *Paris*.

	Latitud. Planitar.	
♄	1 39	So
♃	2 3	No
♂	0 21	So
♀	4 35	No
☿	0 30	So
☽	4 50	So

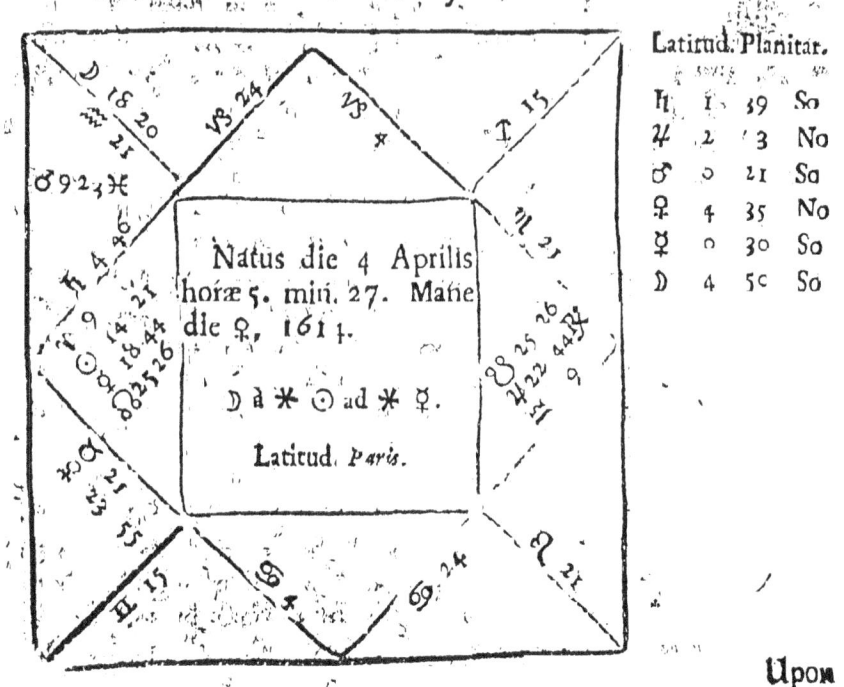

Upon

Opus Reformatum. 103

Upon this Position, *John* would also build his imaginary Whim of *Cardinal Signs*, which he hath here, by what Authority I know not, placed on the four Angles. He neither tells us his estimate time, how, or by what means he came by it, nor by what Directions and Accidents he hath corrected it; but with a sort of Confident Imposition puts it upon us, as if we were bound to believe it because he says it. And for that very reason, I do mistrust the truth of it, well-knowing that all he ever did in Nativities, was for the most part attended with little else but Ignorance and Error to an extraordinary degree; and for those things that he hath befriended the World with, they were all either borrowed or stolen [as I shall prove hereafter] the method being only his. But as for this Nativity, it may be true as to its Effects, and not have Cardinal Signs on the four Angles, as you may observe by making it a little sooner, and yet the Position every way as forcible with ♐ on the 10th, and ♓ on the Ascendant, as by having these Signs that he hath placed there; or it may have Cardinal Signs on the four Angles, and not a rush the better for that, excepting the four Planets that ♈ and ♎ carries along with them. For it is the Planets, not the Signs that do, in the Opinion of the most Sober Astrologers, that were Masters of what they professed, Influence the Affairs of Mortals, and give the variety of Fortune, good or bad, to the Sons of Men. For whenever *Ptolomy* makes use of the Signs in his Judgment on *Diseases, Marriage, Qualities of the Mind, Dignity, Riches,* and *Death*; It is for no other reason, but because the Planets are there, as I can illustrate in all those things beforementioned, if it were really necessary to this my present business, and that it would not swell this Treatise too big. But I suppose the Quotation is sufficient, and therefore let those that are willing to know more of the matter, read the Text, and see whether I speak truth or not. Before my worthy good Friend *J. G.* had arrived at this mighty Mystery of *Cardinal Signs*, there were other Causes that did do as well as these, as you may see in his *Doctrine* of *Nativities, p.* 163 where he hath given you the Positions as Arguments for *Kingly Genitures*, in all which the Planets only are considered; and sometimes with them, their Domal Dignities, but never that, without the Planet, but often the Planet without that. Why should not the *Lord* of the *Tenth*, In ☌ with the ☉ in the *Ascendant* in his *Exaltation*, give considerable Preferment, and raise a Man above the degree of his Birth? Why should not four Planets in the two Equinoctial Signs, give a man a Fame and
Reputation

Reputation in the World, and make him popular in his Generation? Why should not the ☉ [who is Light of the Time] in ✶ to the Midheaven, and in △ to ♃ in the 7th, with the *Virgins Spike*, give a main the Favour of his Prince, and the Love of the People, and these for some remarkable Actions and Services to his Country? Why should not ♀ in exact △ to the Midheaven, applying in ♂ her own House, be allowed to give *Honour, Preferment, Renown*, and *Reputation* in his Generation? I say, Why should not all these popular Positions and Configurations, give the Duke of *Guise* that *Honour, Preferment*, and *Popularity*, that he enjoyed in his time, without crowding in the Cardinal Signs to give that, which the other were fully able to perform. And to this purpose, pray observe but my Friends own Rules in his Doctrine of Nativities, [that take place in this Position] p 46. *The ☉ in the Ascendant in his Exaltation, He will Rule over others; He will acquire Authority, Honour, and Dignity from Princes; He will have great Increase of Riches; He will be of Long-life, and Powerful.* And in p. 55. he says, *Jupiter in the 7th declares the Native to be Victorious over his publick Enemies*, &c. In p. 164. he says, *When the Lord of the 10th shall be posited in the Ascendant, it gives great Authority to the Native over Vulgar Persons; He will be Beloved and Honoured of Great Persons, and shall be imployed in Offices of Concernment, Administrations, &c. and the great things and business of the Kingdom; He also receives Honour and Profit from his Employment and Profession.* Now, if these Rules [all which take place in this Figure that he hath printed] were ever true, why should they not be so still? And if they are so now, we have Astrological Reasons enough to prove the probability of his Grandeur and Fortune, without flying to this silly sham of Cardinal Signs, invented for no othe reason, but to shew his Skill in the managing a bad Cause, and to try his Interest among the Astrological Students, how far they would dance after his Pipe, in complying with those Errors that he thought fit to impose on the World. Or else it was to out-brave his then Adversary with a canting Notion that he had never heard of, nor read in any Astrological Author, before this Learned Answer that he was pleased to give him, called *Cardines Cœli*.

But after all this noise and talk, Let us compare this Position with some other Aphorisms of *John's*, in his Doctrine of Nativities, and you shall see how he doth besiave him, and by his *Rules*, what a Knave he makes him to be. And first, in p. 46. he says, *When Saturn shall be in the Ascendant, he gives many Troubles and Difficulties, melancholly*

melancholly Perturbations, both of Mind and Body; his Life shall be full of Dolours, Griefs, and Troubles; and it will be a Terror for him to live. In p. 106. he tells us, *That when the Lord of the Ascendant shall be in the Twelfth, it gives the Native many Enemies; and much Evil, and many Oppositions from them; he will be in danger of much Imprisonment, and many Molestations and Infortunacies from Malicious Persons.* Pray let me desire the Reader not to be surprised at these Contradictions, when he compares these Aphorisms with them just now mentioned; for you see (according to *John's* Principles and Practice in Astrology) we do as Gamesters in their Pastime at Nine-pins, set up a whole Family by the power of the Stars, and immediately kick them down again. But to proceed, in p. 95. *Doctr. Nativ.* he says, Saturn *Significator of Manners, and ill dignified.* [*as in this Nativity*] *it makes him Envious, Covetous, Timerous, a Lyar, and a perfect Hypocrite.* And a little after he says, *The Sun Significator of Manners, as here, makes a Proud, Restless, turbulent, Domineering Fellow; one whose Promises shall end in smoak.* In the Collect. Genit. Aph. 12. *The Sun in the Ascendant, makes eminent Boasters, and very proud Persons; and by the same rule that Mars there makes Lyars,* Saturn *there with him must make very deceitful, perfidious Men and Hypocrites.* And there is one Aphorism more among those in his Collection, which [if true] overthrows this whole Figure it self; and we know Aphorisms ought to be undeniable Rules, and next to infallible; for their very Name tells us, That they are Rules separated from the rest, to be observed as Maxims of truth. And that is the 25th Aphorism, where he says, That *the Lord of the Ascendant stronger than the Lord of the Seventh, the Native always overcomes his Enemies; and the contrary.* But in the Figure of this great Duke, we find ♃ in the Seventh in ♎ to the ☽; and ♀ Lady of the Seventh in ♉ her own House. So that the Seventh House, and his Lord, are far stronger than the Ascendant and his Lord; by which Rule he should be always overcome by his Enemies, that is, he should be unfortunate. But on the contrary, he always overcame his Enemies, and was very Fortunate, and did great things in his time, as may be seen by those that please to read that Book called his *Memoirs*. For I do not intend to give the History of his Life, and suppose you do not expect it.

But the great and principal Objection that I have against the truth of the Figure, said to be his Nativity, *is that of his Death in the year* 1664. for which I am confident, my good Friend *J. G.* can give no reason, nor assign no cause directional from that Figure and Position.

tion. I say again, They cannot give any Direction for his Death, let them make what point they please *Giver* of *Life*, or *Hileg*; and I hope if my good Friend will allow the *Cardinal Signs* to have such power [with the good Positions here present] to give such stupendious Effects in the Affairs and Actions of his Life, he will undoubtedly give us some accout also of the Direction, or other myftick Cause of his Death. For if *Oliver Cromwell*, *Charles Guftavus*, and *William Laud*, had significant Causes in nature to forethew their Deaths; I hope he will not deny that Authority and Aftrological Demonftration in the Nativity of this great and illuftrious Duke of *Guife*, and therefore, if there is no cause to be affigned for his Death by my Friend *John*, or any of his Admirers; the argument refolves it felf into this *Dilemma*, i. e. Either *Aftrology is deficient, and not able to give an account of the matter; or elfe the Figure given by my Friend is falfe and fictitious, and induftriously made to ferve a turn as occafion did require*; as I fhall make appear by what follows. The ☉, who is in this Figure fet to the time inferibed the true Giver of Life, and is directed to no bad or malefick Rays at the time of the Duke's death, for he paft the ☉ to the □ of ♂, at almoft 34 years of Age, *Ark* 33 deg and to the △ of the ☽ at 40 years of Age, *Ark* 39 d. 33 m. and to the △ of ♃ at 47 years of Age, *Ark* 46 d. 11 m. nor were there any Antifcion in their way, to be pretended to in many years before nor after. The Afcendant, which according to their Principles may alfo kill, if directed to ill Rays, for all the ☉ is in the fame Houfe [as he hath given us an Example in *Oliver Cromwell*] but that alfo is free from all Malefick Beams by direction; for the Horofcope paffed the □ of ♂ [*modo Communi*] at 36 years of Age, *Ark* 35 d. 41 m. and the △ of the ☽ at 42. *Ark* 41 d. 53 m. and the △ of ♃ at 49. *Ark* 48 d. 31 m. which was in full force and power at the time of his Death. The ☽ was under no ill Rays at that time neither, for fhe had about a year and a half before paffed by the body of ♀ without Latitude, and fhe doth nor govern either 4th, 6th, 8th, or 12th Houfes, [a thing of mighty ufe among them all] therefore fhe cannot do any mifchief. But the Midheaven paffed the □ of ♀ much about that time; yet I can hardly believe they will lay any ftrefs upon that neither, and that for the reafons beforementioned. And yet fhe is an odd fort of a Gentlewoman, and being among violent fixed Stars, fhe might give him a plaguy lift at that time, by the fame rule that the M. C. to the Body of ♄ kill'd *Charles Guftavus*; perhaps he might dye of a Love-fick fit, becaufe fhe is Lady of the Seventh; or elfe for want of Money, becaufe fhe is Lady of the Second. Ha, ha, ha!
Now

Opus Reformatum 107

Now, under these considerations I will refer the whole matter to any impartial Artist for Judgment [provided he doth not change his Religion too often] whether he really thinks this to be the true Nativity of the Duke of *Guise*, and that he had the *Cardinal Signs* on the *four Angles*, which is the only thing I have undertaken to refute, which I think naturally follows, if the Nativity is false. And lastly, whether it is not far more probable, that he had ♒ ascending about 8 or 10 degrees; and then there is cause enough for his Death, and for his Grandeur too; the ☽ and ♂ in the Ascendant; the ☉, ♄, and ♀ in △, and ♃ in ✶ to the Midheaven. However this is but guess, yet I dare aver it is as near the mark as his, for you may be sure of some hours of Error in the time; and 'tis well, if there are not some days also, for they are small faults in his Practice.

The next *Cardinal* Example is that of *William Laud*, who he compares to *Jesus Christ*, and says, He was murdered, tho he died in a Parliamentary way; but I believe he will not own that expression in the sufferings of the late good People, who were Martyrs indeed for opposing of Popery. The Scheam is as followeth, says *J. G.*

William Laud.

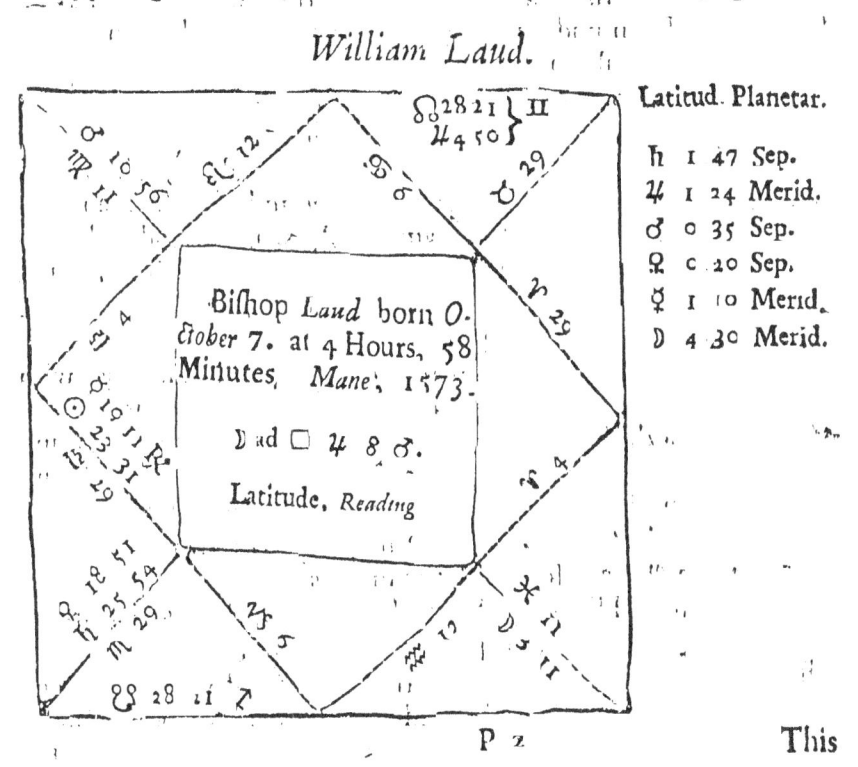

Bishop *Laud* born October 7. at 4 Hours, 58 Minutes, *Mane*, 1573.
☽ ad □ ♃ 8 ♂.
Latitude, *Reading*

Latitud. Planetar.

♄	1	47	Sep.
♃	1	24	Merid.
♂	0	35	Sep.
♀	0	20	Sep.
☿	1	10	Merid.
☽	4	30	Merid.

This

This Bishop's Nativity is brought also by my Friend, to prove what he hath a mind the World should believe, but it is as false as any of the other before going, as to the time and truth of his Birth, as I shall make appear before I leave it, and this with as much plainess as possible I can. As to the Planets places, it matters not whether they are true or false, tho the place of ♀ here differs from his place, given by *Leovitius* about ⅚ degr. but it is not the exact manner of Operation I question; but the misapplying the Rules for Practice, laid down by our approved Authors, and the bringing in of Innovations.

This man, I am informed, was born of mean Parentage in the Town of *Reading*, and from thence brought up at the Hospital fit for the University, to which he was sent, and spent his time for divers years among those men of Learning, after which he was preferred in the Church, where he advanced by degrees, till he came to be Bishop of *Canterbury*; and as I remember, he was 40 years of Age before he grew into any publick fame and repute. Now, it is something strange that his Nativity and Time of Birth should be known to any man, because he was born of obscure Parents, then brought up among Strangers that never mind or inquire into these Curiosities, having so many Children under their Tuition; which would be an endless work, if they should make that their Study, which is very rare. But besides, the Births of men are seldom minded, till they begin to advance in preferment; no, nor then neither, till they come to a degree of considerable height above the Horizon of their Birth; and 'tis well known, that he was towards 50 years of Age before he made any considerable Figure in his Imployment. All which considered together, makes me much doubt and mistrust the truth of the Figure, when I find it so difficult to gain a Nativity in the Parish where I live, tho born not above 24 or 25 years before.

2*dly*, If you please to compare this Figure and Nativity, with that of the famous Sir *Theodore Miyerne* following, you will find the Horoscopes both the same in 4 degr. of ♎, the Planets places being nearly the same in both, the principal difference being in the ☉ and ☽; the ☉ here is in 23 degr. and a half in ♎, and there 14 degr. and a half in the same Sign, the ☽ here is 3 degr. in ♓, but there in 7 degr. in ♏; all the rest of the Planets are not considerably different in either. The ☉ is Giver of Life in both Figures, as being in the Ascendant, and yet ♂ [whom my Friend says] is *Ahareta* in the one, doth not fall out to be so in the other, of which Mystery I know nothing, nor I believe he neither, if he were to be asked about

the

the business. But in *January*, in the year 164¾ he was Beheaded at *Westminster*; and this my Friend tells us was begun by the Midheaven, directed to the Body of ♂ in 11 degr. of ♍ on the Cusp of the 12th House [which no doubt is something the worse for that] which gave his Imprisonment, *Anno* 1641. and about four years after the Ascendant to the body of ♄ with Latitude, put an end to his Life. Now, if this should happen to be true, why did not Sir *Theo. Mayerne* suffer Imprisonment five or six years before him, and also dye a year sooner ! because ♂ in his Nativity was but 5 degr. and a half in ♍, and ♄ but 25 degr. in ♏; and this last was the more violent Nativity of the two, because ♃ who is with the *Aldebaran*, is in exact □ to ♂, and the ☽ and ♀ are in the *Via Combusta*, going to the body of ♄ in ♏, and ♀ Lady of the 8th House, an Argument of much violence with *John*; but instead of dying sooner than the Bishop, these plaguy partial Stars let him live longer by ten years ! and besides, when he did dye, it was a natural Death, and he of a great Age. Now I do confess, it seems a Paradox to me, why the Ascendant to the body of ♄ should not kill the *Doctor* as well as the *Bishop*, and the Midheaven to the Body of ♂ give Imprisonment to the one as well as to the other; for ♂ and ♄ have as good a title to their power in Doctor *Mayerne's* Nativity, as they have in the Bishop of *Canterbury's*, nay, and I think more too; for they say, and indeed it is commonly believed, That *good and holy Men live* above the Power and Influence of the Stars; and if the Clergy-men [the Shepherds] are not good and holy, the Lord be merciful to the rest of the Flock. Therefore, if this be true, and that the Influence of the Stars carries so absolute a fate in its power to spare neither good nor bad, I hope it may serve for an Argument to convince our Enemies of that Profession; or at leastwise take off the heat of their Passion against that, which but few of them understand, how pertly soever they talk of it.

But is it not very strange, That the Ascendant to the Body of ♄ should prove so cruel in the one, and so favourable in the other; and what is more strange, seeing he died a violent Death, why should not the Midheaven to the Body of ♂ kill him, as well as the *M. C. ad Corpus* ♄ did the King of *Sweden*, [beforementioned] pursuant to the 92d Aphorism in his Collection of Genitures. Nor do I know, That there is any Reason to be given, why the Midheaven [in the Bishops] to the □ of ♄ should not be as remarkably fatal to him, as the Body of ♂ was; nor why the ☉ to the Body of ♄, and □ of ♂ [he being *Hileg*] should not kill in both, as well as the Ascendant to the Body of ♄ in the one, and to the □ of ♂ in the other. I say, these things being well considered, carry with them a visible Contradiction one to another, and will without doubt at the first sight only, convince any rational, thinking man, that those Nativities are really fictitious, and not the true Natural ones as pretended; for it is certain, if they were true, there would without doubt have been some effect in the Doctors, like that of the Bishop, on the Midheaven to the Body of ♂, and as sure had the Doctor died as the Bishop, on the Ascendant to the Body of ♄. But, seeing it was not so, I do desire that worthy Person, the Author of those Fooleries, to give us the reason why it hit in the one, and mist in the other; which I am confident would be a great Service to all, but especially to me his most humble Servant. And also, That he would be pleased to permit that Treatise promised in his *Collect. Genit. p. 90.* to be printed; where he says, he will give us a Treatise at large to demonstrate the Correction and Truth of the Nativity of this his *Immortal Bishop and Martyr.*

Lastly, The very same Arguments he gives to prove, That the Bishop should Astrologically dye a violent Death, are the same in the Doctor's, the ☽ excepted, who is not in ☍ to ♂, but in the Combust way going to the Body of ♄ [and if he understood it] in a Mundane Square with ♂, tho' not exact. And therefore I would now ask any man that understands these things, and hath considered and compared them together, Whether these two Nativities are not hard to be believed by any one that is not used to believe Lies, Nonsence, and Contradictions, for it is most certain they cannot be both true, if either of them is; and to tell you the truth, I think neither of them is, and shall rest in that Opinion, till I see my Friend hath in Print made it plainer to me and the whole World, than he hath already done, or I believe is able to do. And when that is done, I will tell him my further Opinion and Judgment in the thing, and assure him, that this speaks but very little to the purpose for *Cardinal Signs* on Angles, according to his Notion and Aphorism. But there is one thing more as remarkable as any of the rest to prove the Figure notoriously false, which I forgot before; and that is in the year 1626. when he was coming into Favour at Court, and learning to be an Instrument for their use, in order to be Bishop of *Canterbury*, [good Bishop *Abbot* being then to be turn'd out, because he would not License Knavish Books] a Privy Counsellor, and a Judge in the Star-Chamber Affairs, he had then his

Midheaven

Opus Reformatum

Midheaven directed to the Square of *Saturn* in *Leo*; and the *Sun* to the Square of *Mars* in *Sagittary*; two as violent and dangerous Directions, as any in the whole Figure; not only in my Opinion, but allowed to be so by all the Ancient and Famous Authors and Modern Professors. By the first of these, in the Nativity of the Duke of *Monmorancy*, he was beheaded, as saith *Morinus*, *Astrol. Gall. p.* 401. And in *p.* 402. the same Author kills Duke *Albert*, the Emperors General, with the Midheaven to the *Square* of *Mars*. And my Friend *John*, himself, kills Judge *Reeves* with nothing but the *Sun* to the *Square* of *Saturn*, *Collect. p.* 121. which is less able than the Body in my Opinion. And he sends Dr *Gouge* out of the World upon the *Sun* to the *Square* of *Mars*; but I must needs say, there was something more, and that was the *Ascendant* to the *Dragons Tail*, a plaguy kind of a thing, *p.* 107. And he hath let the Great *French* Officer dye on the *Sun* to his own *Square*, without any thing else to assist it. As also on Judge *Reeve's*, the single *Square* did the like. Now, what man of Sense can believe this to be *William Laud's* Nativity; and at the same time believe there is any Credit to be given to the Art of Astrology, when the Contradictions in it are so visible, nay, I may say palpable, as my Adversary so ingeniously makes appear.

The next Eminent Nativity that my Worthy Friend makes use of, as an Example to prove his Project by, is that of my Lord *Thomas Clifford*, sometime Lord Treasurer of *England*; and it is as followeth. He hath not told us, what was the Elevation of the Pole; but I think he hath set his Figure for the Latitude of 53 and a half, or thereabouts.

Lord

Lord Clifford.

	Latitud	Planetar
♄	2 23	S.
♃	0 15	M.
♂	17	S.
☊	1 50	M.
☿	2 40	M.
☽	4 46	S.

Natus die primo Augusti, Hor. 10. Minut. 15 Mane, 1630.

♍ ☽ ☌ ☌ ad ✶ ☿ □ ♀.

Lat. 53. and a half.

This Gentleman being not one of the greatest Births in this Nation, was advanced to one of the greatest places that a Subject can enjoy, which was Lord Treasurer, to which he was preferred the 28th of *November*, in the year 1672. and did not continue in it a full year, but resigned his Staff, retired into the Country, and died. Hence we are to inquire what Astrological Causes there were, 1*st*. For his Advancement to that great and eminent Post. 2*dly*. What gave the loss of his Honour. And *Lastly*, The Cause of his Death. For if the Art of Astrology is true, we must expect from a true Nativity, some rational and probable Cause for each of these.

1*st*, As to his preferment there is not one thing to signify it, for none of the Hilegiack Points are directed to any remarkable Body or Aspect at that time; especially, that is any way adequate to his Honour; the ☉ was within a degree and a half of the Body of ♂ at that time, which I am sure could not give either Honour or Content of Mind. The Midheaven was then got into 4 degr. of ♍, where the ✶ of ♀ falls; and I suppose 'tis that Direction that he

hath

Opus Reformatum.

hath corrected this Figure by for his Advancement. But let him not cheat himself with that Notion, for I do assure him, That the M. C. to the ✶ of ♀ comes not up in this Figure, till 58 or 60 years of Age, however, I guess 'tis that which he depends on at this time, notwithstanding the ☽ is in Square to her, both in *Zodiaco*, and *Mundo* applying, and is very unlikely in that Condition to give such Honour. But suppose I should allow this as most of them will do in their Practice, there is nothing else to assist It, for the ☽ is then very near the Body of ♄, and the Square of ♀, therefore 'tis strange it should do it when the two Luminaries were so near ill Rays by Direction; and that of the ✶ of ♀ so weak a Ray, and in ♍ her fall, near the opposite point to ♃.

2*dly*, The loss of his Honour can be attributed to no Direction, but that which gave his Death, and that was at least a degree from touching, which must give at least a year; but this will appear more plain in the last of the three.

3*dly*, For his Death, which was about *August* or *September*, in the year 1673, and they have no Direction to pretend to in that Case, but the ☉ to the Body of ♂; and therefore let us see how that will agree to the time of his Death, he being then just 43 years of Age. The ☉ is distant from the 10th, about 26 degrees, which gives his Pole of Position 24 degrees and a few minutes. The ☉'s Oblique Ascention under that Pole, is 133 d. 50 m. The Ascention of ♂ is 177 d. 5 m. from whence the Ark of Direction is 43 deg. 15 min. which turn'd into time according to *Naibods* Measure in the *Doctrine of Nativities*, gives 43 years, and 322 days, that is, within a Month and a few days of 44 years; but this Native died when he was 43, almost a whole year before the direction of ♂ toucht. And how he will or can reconcile this, I should be glad to see, without his old custom of shamming and shifting.

The truth is, The ☉ to the Body of ♂, did kill this Gentleman, and it did touch exactly at the time of Death, or a little before; but he had not Cardinal Signs on the Angles, as he foolishly and fondly imagines; and I dare venture a Wager with him, if his word could be believed or trusted, that the estimate time, if carefully taken, was after 11 a Clock that Morning, ♌ on the 10th House, and the Ark of Direction that kill'd him, was 39 degr. 10 m. And a Figure set according to that Projection, will shew his Honour and its Greatness, its short Duration, and the shortness of his Life, &c. For the first of which, he had the ☉ to the Mundane Parallel of ♃, which

Q

which is a great and a glorious Direction, he being in his own Dignities in Trine and Reception with ♀, and also in exact *Trine* to the Ascendant. For its short continuance, he had the ☉ in the 10th, in an exact Mundane Square to ♄; and for his Death, the Direction before alledged, which is far more like his Nativity, than that he hath here given him; and I dare almost be positive, that he hath the Sign ♌ on the 10th.

But if this, which he hath given for his Nativity was true, let him but tell us why, according to the Rules of his Practice, the Ascendant to the Body of ♄, Lord of the 4th House, that fatal Corner of Heaven [as they say] and to the Sqaure of ☿, who is Lord of the 12th, and hath Dignities in the 8th House, did not kill this Native, as well as it did his Bishop *Laud*, who had by his Calculation nothing but the single Body of ♄, without any thing to assist it, and yet the ☉ Giver of Life, as here. And *Ann* Queen of *Hungary*, who died upon no other direction but the Ascendant to the Body of ♄, and with that the ✱ of ♀, or Mr. *Gataker* that he says died on the Ascendant to the ☍ of ♄, only the *Bulls Eye* to assist it. Or *Peter Bembus* upon the same Aspect, and nothing else with it, which he says there, is naturally a killing direction. Or the Lord *Francis Villiers* to the body of ♂; and yet the ☽ in the 10th Giver of Life. Or In *Henry* the *Third* of *France*, the Ascendant to the ☍ of ♄, and the ☽ likewise *Hileg*. Or in *Christiernus* King of *Denmark*, where the body of ♄ kill'd of it self, with a little assistance from an unlucky Climacterical Year. And [to name no more, lest it should be burthensom and nauseous to the Reader] That *Excellent young Prince* Edward *the 6th*, *King of* England, who also died on the Asceendant to the body of ♄, and yet the Trine of ♃ falls just after it in ♍. I could mention many more in his *Learned Collection*, that would be serviceable to make good what I pretend to, and give the Lye fairly to his own Inartificial Calculation of this Nativity; which he says he had the honour to perform, and I suppose by that Lord's Command; but the Lord knows what it was, for we must only take his own account of it, which without doubt will be sparingly given. Now pray consider, Is it not very strange, that all these Great, Excellent and Learned men should die on these directions, and yet this honourable Native should so be favour'd by the Stars to out-live and survive those two Directions, when a single one hath done it to others, whom you see here named, and all of them printed by himself in his Collection, to shew the *Truth* of *Astrology*; but *these Nativities*

printed

printed in his *Cardines Cœli* were not for that End; but to shew the wonderful power of *Cardinal Signs* on *Angles*; and yet when it comes to the Conclusion, I dare say you will not find one true Figure among all the Ten that this *worthy Gentleman* hath printed to that purpose. For you see by comparing them one with the other, they carry with them plain Contradictions; thwarts the design he intends them for, and fairly tells the Author to his face, that he is either a very *Ignorant* man, or a *Confident Impostor*; for no man will deny [*J. G.* excepted] that Like Causes ought to have Like Effects, or else *Rules* of *Exception* laid down to let us know when they will, and when they will not give those Effects they talk of, seeing they miss so often; which I am sure he will not undertake to do, the inside of his *Cranium* being not lin'd with matter sufficient for that great Work. And yet what his so long promised Body of Tautology may bring forth, I know not; and I believe a Blind man would be glad to see it; I judge it may be full of words, and to as little purpose as the rest of the things he hath wrote, he hath, I confess, the *Form*, but not the *Power*; the *Words* and *Jingle*, but not the *Matter*; that we wants. We have been served up long enough with abundance of emptiness, mistaken Examples, and unprofitable Rules in the Art of Nativities. But I will take your Authors of the best Authority into my consideration, dissect their Doctrine, and fairly lay before your eyes their palpable Contradictions; so that every one that is not blind, nay, wilfully blind, shall and must confess, that the Astrology now in use is nothing else but Sham and Noise: for if one Direction in 40 or 50 hits, it is more than they sometimes find; and if one Astrologer in an Age happens to make a fair and a famous Prediction before-hand that is answer'd by the Effect, it serves the next Age to boast of: For if they had not *Paris* of *Mantua* about *Cardinal Farnesius*, afterward *Pope Paul* III. *Sixtus ab Heminga*, who predicted the Death of *Don John* of *Austria* to a few days, and *Lucius Belantius*, about the Death of *Mirandula* by him predicted, with some few others; they would be hard put to it to give the World Examples of their Skill, and Proofs of the truth of their Art.

The fifth lie he brings for an Example among the rest, is the Learned and Famous Mr. *Thomas Hobbs* of *Malmsbury*, one that hath given sufficient proofs of his Abilities by his many Learned Treatises that he hath befriended the world with; and tho' descended of mean Parentage; was qualified with natural and acquir'd Parts fit for the greatest Employments Learning can plead

Q 2   for;

for; and therefore I do not blame *John* for bringing so famous a Man's Birth to prove his Assertion, if he is able to justify the Truth of it; which is my next business to inquire.

Mr. *Hobbs*.

```
Natus die 5 Aprilis
horæ 5. min. 2. Mane
1588.

☽ △ ♃ ad △ ⊙.

Latitud. Malmsbury 51.
```

Latitud. Planetar.

♄	1	51	So
♃	0	55	No
♂	0	0	
♀	0	19	No
☿	1	12	No
☽	5	0	No

That this learned Man had a time to be born, I do not in the least question; but that this is the true time of his Birth, I do really doubt and question, and that for these three reasons. 1*st*, The length of Time, a hundred years almost before my Friend *John* did print it, at which time there were few or none could remember the thing particularly; and he himself, if he ever knew it, he was then old enough to have forgot it; and I am of the opinion, that Mr. *Hobbs* himself never gave him his Nativity; so that at the best, it is but hear-say, and indeed I am apt to believe this is the real ground of his knowledg in the matter. And upon the same Authority of *hear-say*, he confidently printed Judge *Hales*'s Nativity, and gave the World as much assurance of it, as if he had been by his Mothers Bed-side when she was delivered of him; when there was nothing more certainly a Lye, than the time he printed for that good mans Birth; and to convince you of the truth of this matter, the very same

Gentleman,

Opus Reformatum.

Gentleman, upon whose report only he printed it, and corrected it likewise; told me above a Twelve-month afterward, That the time he had given to Mr. *Gadbury* for Sir *Matthew Hales*'s Nativity, was a mistake of twelve hours, and yet it happily agreed with the *Animodor* of *Ptolomy*, p.26. of the *Just and Pious Scorpionist.* And to prove this Figure, he printed, true, he tells you the Astrological Cause of his Death, was the Ascendant to the Square of ♀, *in dignitatibus Saturni*, one of the most nonsensical reasons for the Death of a man, that ever was given; *Venus kill!* and yet at the same time, he owns the *Sun giver of Life*, p.18. Nay, there is not a page in that little Treatise, but abounds with Errors or Noise, all which to name in this place would be too tedious; but I will give you some, to shew I do not charge him without a Cause. The Epistle is nothing else but a great many noisy words, to shew us how able he was to manage a false and lying argument; first to assert that Sir *Matthew* had ♏ ascending; and then to vindicate that which was not so, as if he had a Patent to impose upon, and abuse Mankind as he pleases. P. 6. he says, *That Honourable Native had ☿ fortunate in earnest, tho in ♐*. And yet in his *Collect. of Genit.* Aphorism 36. he tells us, ☿ *in* ♓ *or* ♐, *makes a man confident without reason; and pretends to things he understands not.* But this is a small matter, only a Contradiction; and I think it implies, that one of them must be a lye. P. 8. *The* ☉ [says he] *in the Ascendant shews the Native to be of excellent Prudence, Judgment, and Honour;* —— *an observer of his Promises, and a hater of all sordid, base and dishonourable things. All which Excellencies did shine in this our Pious Scorpionist.* It was well he was a *Scorpionist,* or else the 12th Aphorism in his Collection had fell to his share; where he says, *That the* ☉ *in the Ascendant makes eminent Boasters, and very proud Persons.* But because ♏ is a *Chast, Vertuous, Modest,* and an *Humble* Sign, therefore the ☉ in that space of Heaven gives mighty good People. P.18. he tells us, *That* ♂ *is Lord of the* Alchocoden, *and gives his greatest years, which* Ptolomy *tells us are* Sixty six. This is a plain lye fathered upon *Ptolomy* by my Friend *John*; for in the whole *Quadripartite,* no, not in his last Chapter, *De Divisione Temporum,* he never useth any Expression like that, nor gives any countenance to their *Alchocoden* in any thing I have read of his; and my Friend would have done well, if he had quoted the Chapter and Book where he had found it, and to have saved me the labour of Inquiry. In p. 19. he talks of an *Afissor vitæ,* and that is [forsooth] ♃, because he happens to be in that Angle and Space of Heaven, called

the

the 8th House; and yet the Square of ♀ kills, being directed to the Ascendant; now, pray, consider what use they make of their *Hileg* and *Anareta*; for he says, The ☉ is *giver of Life*, & *giver of Years*, ♃ is the destroyer of *Life*, and yet the Ascendant to the Square of ♀ kill'd this Learned Native. Pray, why should not the ☉, who is *Hileg* to the Square of ♀ in *dignitatibus Saturni*, kill as well as the Ascendant to that point; this is Nonsence with a witness, if I understand him, and the greater, because it came from him. But suppose all these things that he says were true in a man, that had such a Figure as he hath printed for the Birth-time of Sir *Matthew*, yet here it is all Folly and Impertinence [I had almost said Impudence] because it is publickly owned, that he was born 12 hours distance from that time; and for ought he and I know, it may be 12 days. Such is his Confidence in taking Nativities on trust, and by hear-say, and then imposing them on the World for truth, which he hath been often catch't in, but how often they have passed undetected, is to me yet unknown. And upon this very Authority of *hear-say*, I certainly believe, he hath trumpt up this Nativity of Mr. *Hobbs* to prove his notion of Cardinal Signs to be true, as he did that of Judg *Hales*, to prove ♏ a virtuous Sign, and without doubt both a like true.

2*dly*, The meaness of his Parentage, considered with the part of *England* where he was born, may render it dubious, there being very few *now* of the meaner and middle sort of People in the remoter parts from *London*, that take any notice, or keep in memory the time when their Children were born; and much less *then*, when Astrology was so little known in this our Nation of *England*; nay, scarce at all known, unless among some Learned Men, who were able to read other Languages besides their own, there being at that time but *little* of Astrology printed in the *English* Tongue, and that *little* very imperfectly known, handled, and understood. Besides the lowness of his Birth obliged him to be abroad betimes from his Parents; and as I hear, he went to the University at 13 years of age; which did prevent him of those frequent opportunities to hear the time of his Birth from his Parents, if they did remember it.

3*dly*, I never heard that he was ever studiously inclined to this Celestial Inquiry; and for that reason, might neglect the taking notice of his Birth, and think it not worth his Memory and Animadversion; by which means, if he did ever know the day when he was young, I dare be positive he did not know, or at leastwise remember the time of the day, in which you know there is 24 hours, and every

every one of those will make a great alteration in a Nativity, especially in one that hath Signs of short Ascentions in the Ascendant; and indeed many aged People do remember the Year and Day of their Birth, but very few of them can give you the absolute time of the day when it was. Whence I conclude, when he had got the day and year, he made him such a Nativity as he thought agreeable to the Life, Actions, and Learning of the Gentleman. And tho I do conclude it possible for him to get the day, yet I do not allow the Figure to be true; but perhaps he hath made this Position to abuse him, as you may see by the 12th and 86th Aphorisms in his Collection, where he gives all such Persons as have the ☉ and ♂ in the Ascendant, a very bad Character, making them *Lyars, Boasters, Proud, Perjured, Contrivers of Mischief,* and *Inventers of Fables*; and more such-like ill Names he bestows upon them; how well they deserve them, I know not. However, those Names do not at all agree with the Character he gives him in his *Cardines Cœli*, which shews my Friend *John* can make the Stars give and act what he pleaseth; cool his Broth, and warm his Fingers, and all with the same Breath.

But to put all out of doubt, let us come nearer and closer to the matter; for seeing they do allow that Directions are the Causers of Death; or at leastwise, that few or none dye without them; Let us see what they can assign for his death, either to the ☉, ☽, or Ascendant, for they are all alike to them, tho I do affirm the ☽ here to be Giver of Life, according to the Position printed. This Gentleman died in *December*, in the year 1679. being then 91 years and 10 months old; and the Ark of Direction to give that number of years, according to their measure of time, is 90 degr. 31 min. Now observe, The Direction that he concludes kill'd him, was the Ascendant to the Square of ♂, and the ☉ to the Body of ♃, Lord of the 8th House, which to me seems very strange, that the ☉ should pass the Square of ♂, and he out-live it almost three years, and at last dye on the Ascendant to a sham Direction, called the Square of ♂ [for the true one did not come up till about 22 years afterward] and at such a time too, when the ☉ was by Direction within a very little of the Body of ♃, the great and only *Balsamick-Star* in the Heavens, whose ill Rays always saves, and certainly much more his Body in the ascending part of Heaven; but is it not very strange that he should confidently take the Directions to the Horoscope to give Death when the ☉ is so near it; for the Ascendant cannot be Giver of Life, nor can it kill with bad Directions to it, when the ☉

is

Opus Reformatum.

is so near, as in this Example. But is it not more strange [how his Catholick Soul judgeth in the case, I cannot tell] that the Square of ☿ should kill, and the Ascendant to the Square of the ☉ should not at about 82 years of Age; and indeed, by *John's* good leave [if *Ptolomy* is allowed to be true] the Square of ♂ cannot kill, because he is under the *Sun*-beams, but any Tooth good Barber, so we can but make *Cardinal Signs* on the *Angles* of this, or any other Nativity. In short, I judge he will find but few of his own party [I mean as to the Principles of Astrology] that will believe the Ascendant to the Square of the *Sun* should pass by and give nothing; and a few years after, the Square of *Mars* kill; and this at such a time too, when the *Sun* in the Ascendant was directed to the Body of *Jupiter*, —— but indeed he was Lord of the Eighth. —— Oh! —— that alters the case mightily. —— *Ha, ha, ha*.

But to tell you the truth, the *Moon* is *Hileg*, or Giver of Life in his Figure, and for that reason, neither *Sun* nor Ascendant can kill by Direction; and at the time of his Death, she was directed to no ill Aspect or Rays. The first thing she meets, is the ✶ of ♀ in ♓, which would touch at or about 95 years of Age. And so I leave it, till he shall think fit to assign some other Cause for his Death, and tell us what Authority he hath for the time of Birth, and by what Authority he will prove this Figure, or any other true; assuring you, that this is not Mr. *Hobbs's* true Nativity; I will not say it is not the day, but I am sure it is not the hour, only a time pitcht upon, and chosen by his unerring Judgment, to prove one falsity by inventing of another; or to speak more to the purpose, he calls for help to Saddle his Hobby-horse. I could put divers other things to him, which I am sure would puzzle his fertile Brain to find security for their truth; as, who he will conclude to be *Hileg*, and then the Lord of the *Alchocoden*, whom they chuse from the former; and whether the Native lived that number of years designed by that Star, and no more; and whether ♂ [who must be Lord of the *Alchocoden*, according to their notions] being Combust in his detriment, and afflicted by ♄, can give any more than his mean years, which are Forty, tho this Native lived Twenty five years beyond his greatest years, which are Sixty six. With more of this Nature, that I pass by, supposing there is enough mentioned to convince any rational man, that the Figure of Birth by him asserted, is all Sham and Trick.

The

Opus Reformatum. 121

The next he brings, is that of the Famous Mr. *Burton*, Author of *The Anatomy of Melancholly*, to prove his fictitious Notion.

Mr. *Burton*.

Latitud. Planetae.

♄ 0 42 North
♃ 1 37 North
♂ 0 18 South
♀ 1 4 South
☿ 1 42 South
☽ 4 38 South

Natus die 8. Febru.
Hor. 3. Min. 44. Mane,
1577.

Latitude 51. 30.

I do believe he hath taken this Figure of Mr. *Burton*, as near the Account he himself gave of it, as can be; and do therefore judge, if this is not true, it is not Mr. *John's* fault; but the Learned Native himself, who gave it to the World in scattered Sentences in his *Anatomy of Melancholly*; and as I am informed, did also give order when Living, for the inscribing it on his *Tombstone* in *Oxford* after his Death; which did not only shew the Gentleman's Ingenuity, but also his Integrity in letting the World understand how far he was acquainted with his own Nativity, lest some Ingenious Nativity-maker or other, should surreptitiously have trumpt up a spurious one after his Death; which is a thing very common, nor only in our Nation, but in others likewise; and by that means we come to have so many Great mens Births that are really false and imaginary, and yet imposed upon us for absolute truth, which the unskilful, ingenuous men run away with, and believe them to be as reported to them. And to convince you that this is true, take an Example in

R one

one man) and that is the *French* King, whose Nativity was printed by Mr. *Gadbury* in 1681. in which Figure he makes 22 degr. of ♏ ascending, and the time 27 min. after Eleven: and this he affirms to be true by the Probation of three Directions and their Concurrent Accidents, as may be seen in his Collection. *Morinus*, he prints his Nativity in his *Astrologia Gallica*, p. 555. in which he makes almost 15 degr. of ♏ ascend, and the Time 15 minut. after Eleven of the Clock, *Mane*, the same day and year, and proves his also by two or three Directions; to which he addeth another Argument of truth, that the time of the day was known, per *Altitudinem Solis Astrolabio sumptam apud sanctum Germanum*; and this a man would think were very exact, coming from a Learned Pen, and he also a Lover of the Art, as well as a Professor thereof. And, yet after all this, I have had an account from *Adriano*, the great *Mathematician* at *Paris*, that the *French* King was born at 15 minutes after Four of the Clock the same day in the Morning; which is sufficient to acquaint us, that there is a mistake, or a little Knavery in this Account given so variously; and is not only in this man, but others likewise; of which more in my *Defectio Geniturarum*.

But as to Mr. *Burton*'s Nativity, I am not willing to make a search into the truth of it, and that for two Reasons. The 1st is, The Respect I have to that Learned Gentleman, being unwilling to call his Skill in question, because I think he gave it us to the best of his knowledg, without any design of Trick or Interest, either to bubble us, or put a falshood upon the World under the Notion of Astrology. And, the 2d is, Because I have no Accidents that are considerable in the Course of his Life, to try the verity of the Figure by, either of *Sickness*, *Preferment*, or *Death*, which are the only grounds to try and prove a Nativity, whether true or false. And yet, if this is his true Figure, I should look upon it to be very difficult for him to pass the ☽ to the Body of ♄, with and without Latitude in *Zodiaco*; and this the rather, because ♄ hath there almost 1 degree of *North-Latitude*; but for the reasons beforementioned, I shall omit all things of that nature.

But suppose we should allow this Nativity to be true, and that Cardinal Signs on Angles should do those wonders that he says they do; yet I cannot see what ground there is for his bringing this Figure to prove it by. For here is almost 29 degrees of ♈ on the Ascendant, and that a Sign of short Ascension, according to his own Notion, and every ones else, and the most he can make it, it, is not above 36 minutes below the Cusp of the Ascendant, that the Sign ♍ hath to rise; and in *his Figure*, there is the whole Sign ♉, and 6 degrees of ♊ in that part, called the Ascendant or Horoscope. Hence it follows, that he lays the whole stress of the matter on the very Cusp of the Angle, or Line of the Horizon, to prove the Mystery of Cardinal Signs, which if true, I think he puts it upon a very dubious proof, both in this Figure, and also in that of *Charles Gustavus* beforementioned; for if we make this a very few minutes later, and that a very few minutes sooner, you will find ♉ ascending in the one, and ♍ in the other; and in my Opinion, will mightily shake, if not wholly confound the very Principle of his design; for I do not believe every Figure of a Nativity to be true, that he says is so; and therefore, if these should be corrected, what will become of his Notion? And for that of the King of *Sweden*, I am sure it is not true; and that for the Reasons there alledged. But besides all these things, he may have his ♄ in the 10th, and ♃ in his 6th House; nay, and ♂ in ♂ with his *Ascendant*, and for all that have ♉ ascending; and indeed, to my apprehension it seems more probable to be ♉, because of that Expression of Mr *Burton's* quoted by Mr *Gadbury*, *And ♂ principal Significator of my Manners, in partile ♂ with my Ascendant*, &c. And by that word *partile ♂*, I understand exactly on the Ascendant, and if so, ♂ must be ascending, for ♂ is almost 1 degree in that Sign, as *Gad.* well knows; and then pray, what will he do for a shift to tickle the Ears of his Admirers into the belief of Cardinal Signs, and their power in this Nativity? Nay, do but observe how he shuffles, and how he is put to it to make a Nativity [nay, driven to the last degree of ♈] to impose an Error on the World, and to cheat us and himself also into the belief of a lye.

But there is one thing more I observe in the 126th Paragraph, and that is, he went to Dr. *Fisk* to know what the meaning of ♌ in the 6th House was, and this in the year 1650, of whom he says, he learnt that little of Astrology that he hath. Utterly disowning his best Master, Mr *Lilly*, by whose Assistance [he says in the Epistle to his *Doctrine of Nativities*] and Favours, he was enabled to compleat that Book, which was printed in the year 1657. Now do you think that Mr. *Lilly's* Acquaintance had done him no Service, besides the use of Books in that Seven years? Or do you believe his asking Dr. *Fisk* that one question, had set him in a Station above the want of other Instructions? If so, he was the aptest Scholar to one, and

124 *Opus Reformatum.*

the most ungreatful to the other of any man living. But I shall forbear any further Aggravation of that Ingratitude, because the whole Nation is so well acquainted with the thing.

His Seventh Nativity he brings to prove his dreaming Notion, is that of *Michael Nostradamus*, as followeth.

Nostradamus.

Natus die 14 Decembris in Meredie. 1503.

The time of this Gentlemans Nativity, Mr. *Gadbury* had from that short Account of his Life, printed by Monsieur *Garencieres*, in *English*, at the beginning of that Treatise called, *Nostradamus's* Prophecies, where it is said, he was born at *St. Remy*, a Town in *Provence*, the 14th of *December*, on a *Thursday* about Noon, 1503. and that he died of a *Gout* and *Dropsy* at *Salon*, a City in *Provence*, or near it, on *July* 2. Anno 1566. being then Sixty two years of Age, and Six Months. The Latitude of the Place is about 43 degrees; and how our worthy Author will make 2 degrees of ♑ on the 10th House, and 14 degrees of ♎ on the Ascendant in that Elevation, is to me a mystery: for if he makes two of ♑ on the Midheaven, there will be about four of ♈ ascending; but that Error I will pass by, it being not to my business now in hand, be it true

or

or false; nor will it deface or confound his design that the thing is brought to prove; tho the rest of the Houses are likewise Erroneous, and therefore I shall proceed in another method.

I perceive by the Authors Expression *about Noon*, that the Native did not leave a particular Account, at what time in that day he was born; for that *about Noon*, might be about an hour or more before or after it, or else the Stars in this mans Nativity had not the usual force and effect, that Mr. *Gadbury* allows, and asserts they have in other Mens Genitures, of which more anon, when I come to those Objections. The Sign ♈ is well known to be but 1 hour and 5 minutes ascending on the Horoscope in that Elevation, and therefore the error of half an hour in time sooner, and 56 minutes in time later than this Figure, will very much alter the Case, and extreamly shake the Authority both of his Aphorism and Skill, so far as they are both concerned in this Figure and Nativity; and if I mistake not, his *Dedr. Urania* will suffer a deliquium also, by the Confidence and Credulity of her over-forward and bouncing Secretary; but it is no strange thing to see honest Masters abused by the knavery of their fawning, glavering Servants.

However, if this Figure should be true [which is very uncertain and dubious] it is far fetcht, and at the best given in a general term, *about Noon*, which no man ought to rely on without Corection, by as many Accidents as the Case requires, or can be gotten; and to affirm this his true Nativity, without such Reasons and Authority, especially in such a Case as this is, where it is made a principal Pillar to support so great a Structure, as he here endeavours to build upon it, is to me a great Argument, either of the mans Weakness, or his Confidence, believing his *ipse dixit* is over and above sufficient to stem the Torrent of all other Authority; and therefore I will bring it to the Touchstone, as the real test of its truth or falshood; and in that trial I shall rest my self very well satisfied of either, without troubling you with many Arguments, which at the best serves but to spoil Paper, and tire your Patience. Yet, let me tell you, this is as notorious a piece of Falshood and Imposition, as any he hath brought to this purpose and proof.

But before I begin to examine the Figure in general, it will be very necessary to settle the Figure to some particular degree on the Midheaven and Ascendant; for [as I said before] if we allow 2 degrees of ♑ on the Tenth, there will be but 4 degrees of ♈ on the Ascendant; and if we should allow 1 degrees of ♈ ascending, there

there will be about 5 degrees 30 minutes of ♑ on the Tenth: And because I will give him all the fair play imaginable, I will take that which stands fairest for his advantage; [tho he did not serve me so when I was in *Holland*.] and I think that is 11 degrees of ♈ on the Ascendant; for I do suppose out of the *Abundance* of his *Ignorance*, he doth conclude the Ascendant to the ☍ of the ☉ was the Direction upon which this Native did expire; now, if so, I would fain be resolved, whether the Ascendant to the ☍ of the ☉, is likely to give the *Gout* and *Dropsy*; which Diseases he fathers on ♄ in his *Doctrine of Nativities*, p. 122. And tells us there also, That the ☉ gives *Swbonings*, *Inflamations* of the *Eyes*, *Palpitation* of the *Heart*, and *Wringings* at the *Stomack*; which Diseases are not the usual Attendants of *Dropsies* and *Gouts*.

I cannot find any other Direction he can pretend to, that may be allowed to give Death; but that of the Ascendant to the ☍ of ☉; for the ☽ by Direction, is at that time in their way come to the ninth degree of ♑, having past the Body of the ☉, and her own ✶; and not come to the Body of ☿, and ☍ of ♃, Lord of the 8th House, that pernicious part of Heaven; and the ☉ is at that age in 2 degrees of ♓ by Direction, being come to the place of his own ✶, and within Rays of the ☽'s △, which is the next Direction, and therefore we must conclude [seeing none of these can be lug'd in to do the business] that the ☍ of the ☉ to the Ascendant, was the fatal Point that kill'd him, notwithstanding the △ of the ☽ was very near after. Thus you see a sorry shift is better than none; and for ought we know, had not this unlucky Direction fell in so untowardly, he might have lived till this time; unless ♃, Lord of the 8th, had happened to have birded him off; for ♂ being Lord of the Ascendant, would without doubt not hurt his own; and ♄ durst as well have eat his Fingers, being under the power of ♂ in his Triplicity, [and besides very weak in his detriment] as molest or kill him; such a pretty sort of Astrology he pretends to be Master of.

In this Nativity we find both the ☉ and ☽ in Aphetical Places; and it is certain one of them must be *Hileg*, or Giver of Life; and yet the Ascendant to the ☍ of the ☉ kill'd the Native; which if so, I am sure it can do it always, and that with much more ease and certainty, when the Ascendant is Giver of Life. But let us have recourse to his Collection of Genitures, and there you will find abundance of Nativities, where the Ascendant to the □

and

and ☍ of the ☉ did not kill, as in Pope *Paul* V. *p.* 80. Dr. *Morton*, p. 92. Bishop *Usher*, p. 96. Mr. *Cataker*, p. 102. Mr. *Childrey*, p. 114. Mr. *Vaughan*, p. 171. who had his ☉ in the Eighth in direct ☍ to the ☽; and yet the Ascendant to the Body of the one, and ☍ of the other did not kill: what think you now, are these partial Stars or not? Sir *Robert Holburn*, p. 124. Sir *Frech. Hilles*, p. 159. that was to live some Decades of years, he also out-lived the ☍ of the ☉. Major-General *Lambert*, p. 166. *Vincent Wing*, p. 182. an even half-score that out-liv'd the Ascendant to the ☍ of the ☉; and some of them underwent its Influence at a considerable Age too. And I could furnish you with more likewise under his own hand, only I think these sufficient to prove that Direction false and fictitious as to his Death, and the Cause of it; and to shew this Learned Artist's Skill, is as little as his Modesty and good Nature.

But besides all this, there are several Nativities in being, in which our Nativity-maker allows the Midheaven to the Bodies or Oppositions of ♄ and ♂ to kill; sometimes by violence, and sometimes other ways, and this done only by a single Direction of either, as in the Case of *Charles Gustavus*, and *William Laud*, the Midheaven to the Body of ♄ in the one, and to the Body of ♂ in the other; but in this Nativity the ☉, who is Giver of Life, and the Midheaven, were both at once directed to the Body of ♀, and ☍ of ♃, Lord of the 8th in the 4th; and then to the ☍ of ♄ and ♂ from the 4th likewise; all which had not power enough to kill him till the Ascendant came to the ☍ of the ☉; *Ha, ha, ha*, a pretty sort of Stars, and as prettily managed by those that pretend an acquaintance with them. Indeed I cannot blame People, when I hear them cry out against the Fooleries and Cheats of Astrology; for according to this kind of Doctrine, no man would trouble his Head with the Study of a thing so contradictory and uncertain, that could find any thing else to exercise his Thoughts and Meditations in. I know the Answer some of them will make me, and say, *The Midheaven never kills but in violent Deaths*, Collect. Genitur. Aph. 92. To that I answer, They know nothing of the Cause of a violent Death, till it is over and past; and therefore that is but a sham, and a silly one too; for if it hath power to kill at one time, it hath at another; and tho a man may not dye by an Ax, or a Halter, yet he may dye violently in his Bed, or some other way, for the Stars are not bound to a particular way

and

and method. And I do assert it for truth, that if it did ever kill, it must do so always [without Rules of Exception] and I know no reason [nor he neither] why all those Directions to the *Sun* and *Midheaven* should not have kill'd this Native. And besides, he talks without knowledge about the violence of Nativities; for what violent Positions are there more in *Gustavus Adolphus*'s Nativity, than in this of *Nostradamus*? And also, what is there of violence more in *Charles Gustavus*, than in the Duke of *Albemarle's* Collect. Genit. p. 70. and yet two of them died violent Deaths, and the other two Natural ones; but besides, before the People are dead, he knows not a word which is a violent one for Death, and which not; but when they are dead, and that by violence, he can presently find the Cause. What Nativity in his Collection carries more violence with it, than that of *Charles Tortenson* the *Swedish* General, where the ☉ and ♂ are in ☌ in ♑ in the Ascendant, and both in □ to ♄ in his own Dignities; the ☽ is in ☌ with ♃, Lord of the 12th in ♋, with violent Stars, in direct □ to ♄, and in ☍ to ♂. and the ☉ Lord of the 8th, and also to ♀, who hath Dignities there likewise. Now, is it not strange, that this Native under so violent a Position should dye a quiet Natural Death, when those two Kings of *Sweden*, especially *Gustavus Adolphus*, under a very moderate Position should dye violently? Which things Mr. *John* would very much oblige the World with, to let us know the Reasons of them, and to acquaint us with those curious *Nostrum's*, by which we may be able to understand these [hitherto improbable] Nativities as well as he.

To conclude, This Nativity was about Noon, that is, a little before 11 a Clock, at which time he will not have ♈ ascending, but the latter part of ♒, and the Sign ♐ on the Tenth. And under this Position and its Effects, he will at the time of his Death labour under the Influence of the ☉, Giver of Life, to the Mundane Parallel of ♂ and ♄, Direct and Convers; which are proper Directions to give the *Gout* and *Dropsy*. And therefore, if Mr *John* doth not think this a reason sufficient, I would desire one from him more Authentick.

The next he brings to exercise his Talent in, is that of *Gregory Lopez*, a *Spanish* Hermit, one of his own Religion, and therefore he ought to know the exact time when he was brought into the World. The Figure follows.

Gregory

Opus Reformatum.

Gregory Lopez.

Natus die 4 Juliis hor. 11. min. 30. Mane 1542.

Latitud. 41. Madrid.

	Latitud Planetar.		
♄	2	35	No
♃	1	13	No
♂	2	0	So
♀	2	57	So
☿	1	21	No
☽	3	15	No

I wonder Mr *Gad* should have so much confidence on his Reputation, as to think to be believed in this, and such like Cases, when he says the thing is so; seeing we have found him tardy so often in his befriending Mankind with such Curiosities as these are. Nativities I mean, and not one in forty of them true, as may be justified by his Learned Collection, and the Opinion of every one about that Book; for it is not only my self, but divers others also, that are of the same Persuasion with me about the Falsities, and visible Contradictions so openly justified and asserted by the Author in that Treatise, and not only there, but in most of those Books he hath published, to inform the unlearned World. Do you think it is reasonable to believe, that he should obtain the true time of this man's Birth, who was born at so great a distance, as *Madrid* in *Spain*, and perhaps unknown to all his Friends and Acquaintance [and probably himself too] till after his Death? When we may be certain he could not give us the true Nativities of those born at home in our own Nation, and near him, and had the opportunity of their

S   Acquain-

Acquaintance besides, as Sir *Frech. Holles*, *Nic Culpepper*. Mr. *Lilly*. Nay, he hath given us *his own* false, and printed it three or four times over, besides those of *Oliver Cromwell*, Two Kings of *Sweden*, Judge *Hales*, and abundance more, too many here to relate. I say for those very reasons he ought [since he hath crackt his Credit so] to endeavour always to prove those Nativities he gives us, that when they shall happen to be questioned by any in mine, or other mens Company, we may have something to say in his Vindication, which now we have not, relying only upon his *Say-so*.

To give us an old *Lowsy Popish Hermit*, born 150 years ago, to prove an Innovation of his own, that stands in need of better Authority and Security than he is able to produce. A Fellow born in *Spain*, and not a Soul living now that ever knew him, which at the best tells us, it can be known no otherways, but by report and hear-say, and for ought we know [or he either] it may be some days, but I am sure some hours distance from this time, or else the Rules of Astrology that I am Master off, are not true. I admire he hath not made a Nativity for Pope *Joan*, his Brother *Judas Iscariot*, St. *Patrick*, Monsieur St. *Ruth*, and the *Golden Farmer*; for without doubt, they had all of them Cardinal Signs on their Angles, and would mightily conduce to the Probation of that Aphorism, if he would but take the pains to let us know them according to his best and most approved Rules of Nativity-making.

Do but consider how many People he hath told us died on the Midheaven and *Sun* to the Square of *Saturn* and *Mars*; how many he tells us died on the Ascendant to the Square of the *Sun*, Body of *Saturn*, and Body of *Mars*; how many he hath affirmed went to the silent Shades on the *Moon* to the Square of the *Sun*, the Opposition of *Saturn*, the Opposition of *Mars*, the Midheaven and *Sun* to the Antiscions of *Mars* and *Saturn*, all which have passed over in this Nativity, and none of them had power to kill. Neither do I know when he died, yet am partly sure they went off without Death, because *Gadbury* says, he was about Twenty one years of Age before he grew thus Religious; and he must continue some years in this method of Piety, or else he would not have obtained so great an Esteem and Reputation to be counted a Hermit. But these Directions came up, some at Twenty, others at Four or Five and twenty, some at Thirty; and they that came up latest,

latest, were at Thirty six or seven by this Position; and yet I am of opinion he out-lived that Age, if ever there were such a man, and that he did not starve himself to be counted Holy.

Besides all this, I see no reason why a Conjunction of *Mars* and *Saturn* in *Scorpio*, the Square of the *Moon* and *Sun*, and *Moon* and *Mercury*, the Square of *Jupiter* and *Venus*, and also the Mundane Parallel of *Jupiter*, *Saturn*, and *Mars*, should make a man so extreamly Pious and Religious, as our Friend *J. Gad.* tells us he was. I have heard him often say, it was a very hard thing for him to be good and honest, who had a Conjunction of *Saturn* and *Mars* at the time of his Birth; and if so, I am sure 'tis the worse for being in *Scorpio*. I do really judge, if this Figure is nearly true, or within an hour and a half of it, he did not turn Hermit for the sake of Religion, but for the loss of a Mistress, or else a Disobligation by some Debauchery of hers. For at the Age of twenty years, he had his *Sun* to the *Sextile* of *Venus*, and Square of *Mars* by Direction, which is very likely to give such an Effect; and if so, he only grew surly and sour on that Affront; by the continuance of which, and his own forgetfulness, it became a custom to be thus Religious; to signify which, he labour'd under the *Moon* to the Opposition of *Saturn* with and without Latitude, about four years together, from Twenty three or Twenty four forwards.

And tho' I have not so good a proof for the falsity of this Figure, as I have of several of the former, yet I am partly sure it is false, because he out-lived the *Sun*, who is *Hileg* to the Square of *Saturn* and *Mars*. And so I come to his Ninth Example of Truth in the Case of Cardinal Signs on the Angles. The Figure follows; set *Ptolomaically*,

Opus Reformatum.

Sir *Theodore Mayerne.*

Natus die 28. Septembris, Hor. 5. Min. 25. Mane, 1573.

Latitude 46.

♄	1	49	North
♃	1	22	South
♂	0	30	North
♀	0	36	North
☿	2	56	South
☽	3	55	North

I am certain [seeing my good Friend *J.G* makes *William Laud*, and Sir *Theodore Mayerne*, to have almost the same Positions, or with very little difference, scarce considerable] that they cannot be both true; if either of them be so; for we see here, that they have both 4 degrees of ♎ ascending, and ♀ Lady of the Ascendant in ♏ in both Nativities; and the ☉ in both their Ascendants, and ♃ in △ to the degree ascending exactly, the ☽ in a Watery-sign in both also. Hence, seeing they are so much alike in their Births, why should not their Bodies and Constitutions also have been somewhat proportional in reference to their Statures, Corpulency, Passions, general Fate in Fortunes and Misfortunes; in all which, these two men were nothing alike; the Bishop being a little man, Spare bodied, Rash and Furious; the Doctor a full-grown, large Body, extream Corpulent, with a gentle, easy Temper. The Bishop had the latter part of his Life full of Trouble, Disquiet, and Confusion, and in conclusion attended with a violent Death. The Doctor had the latter part of his Life Quiet, Easy, and Composed, and at *Chelsy* where he lived, died of good old Age. And the

difference

difference in their Births is not any ways remarkable; what is, you may observe in the places of the ☽ and ♀. In the Doctors, the ☽ is in the beginning of ♏ in ☌ with ♀, and both going to the ✶ of ♂. In the Bishop's, the ☽ is in ♓ in □ to ♃ and ☍ to ♂, applying to both. But why these should cause such vast difference and disproportion in their Bodies, I confess, I know not, nor do I believe my Friend is able to reconcile the one to the other, or either of them to his Stars. Indeed I will allow the Bishops Intellectuals to be wholly different from the Doctors, as his ☽ in □ to ♃, (the Patron of Religion) in ☍ to ♂, ♀ with ♄ in ♏, and ☿ Retrograde with the *Virgins Spike*, do very well shew. And I could tell you, what they promise in such Positions too, if I thought I might escape the severe Censure of being maliciously inclin'd; but this I do say, the Positions are naturally like the man, as to his Temperature and Humour, in the way and order of Nature.

As to the Soul, that Divine and Eternal part of Man, I can by no means allow to be affected, governed, or swayed by the power of the Stars, any further than it is informed, or misled by its Natural Organs, the Senses I mean; for without doubt, by how much the more bruitish a man is, the more vicious and depraved is his Mind and Thoughts, those Preliminaries to the Soul, by which medium it is always conversant with, and exalted to those glorious Mansions above, or confusedly hurried among those Corruptions of Nature, which are not only a Clog to the volatile Soul, but a Sink of Ruin and Destruction, in which [it is to be feared] too many have perished, both Body and Soul.

But to return to our Starry-business again; There are many more things to prove these two Nativities do not agree in, besides these mentioned. The Bishop he lived all his days single or unmarried. The Doctor had both Wife and Children, [one of which married to a *French* Marquess] and the Lord of the Seventh the same Star, and in the same place in both the Figures; and I hope my Friend *John* will not make the ☽ in ☍ to ♂, an Argument of a single Life; that Position, I confess, is often judged to be a wanton one, but never forbids Marriage. Nor I cannot believe he will lay any weight or stress on the ☽'s Separation from the □ of ♄, they being now at 7 degrees distance, and the ☽ in Aspect both to ♃ and ♂ applying in the Zodiack, and to a Mundane Aspect of ♀ also. Well, but how shall we reduce all this into a way for Practice, and to be serviceable another time, when we meet with such

crabbed

crabbed stuff again? Why, really I cannot tell you which way to begin that work; it is beyond all the Rules of Astrology that I have learn'd and read, and do think it will prove a knotty, puzling piece of Work; for which reason we must be forced to intreat our worthy good Friend, to favour us with this Information, and let the World know, why Sir *Theodore Mayerne* should marry, and why *William Laud* should not, and indeed he is the only man able to do it, being furnished with all the curious, delicate, fine-spun Notions, and those lofty *Nostrums*, the Quintessence of the whole Art, lodged only in his capacious Head, that mighty Magazine, or rather Kittle-drum of Astrology.

But besides this, it will not be improper to consider the Directions in this Figure and Nativity; for it is certain, that Planet which was *Anareta* in the Bishop's, must of necessity do the same Office in the Doctor's, because the Figures are both the same, and the same *Hyleg* also; and the Planets of a Malefick Influence are in the same parts of Heaven, and Lords of the same Houses in the one Figure, as well as in the other; and if the Lords of the 8th and 4th had power to Imprison and Kill in the Bishop's Nativity, I know no reason to the contrary, why they should be debarred of that force and ability in the Doctor's, pursuant to their Dominion in those two fatal Houses beforementioned, which my Friend lays a mighty weight upon. For if their Dominion is so considerable by being Lords of those Houses, as our Friend *John*, and some other Authors tells us it is, then, beyond all doubt, we may rationally judge that the Malign Influence that Authors say is lodged in ♄ and ♂, which renders them perfect Enemies to our Nature and Being, and also Authors of Death and Sickness, must mightily add to their Power and Ability in point of Death, especially in the Doctor's Nativity: And yet our Learned Author kills the Bishop on the Ascendant to the Body of ♄; and lets the Doctor live ten years beyond that Direction, and dye on the Ascendant to the □ of ♂, and ☌ of ♃. which to me seems a mighty Mystery, that ♄ should have power to kill, and yet not have power to kill; when I am sure there is no reason to be assigned, that can reconcile the Contradiction to any rational man. But if Mr. *J. G.* can shew me, or any one, by what Direction, Configuration, or Position, &c. ♄ is more enabled to kill in the Bishop's, than he is in the Doctor's, or by what way or means he is disabled in his power of killing in the Doctor's Figure more than in the Bishop's, I will cease my further Inquiry into the rest

of

of his Errors, and not only acknowledg my Ignorance, but do him right in Print; nay, *Erit mihi Magnus Apollo.* For he tells us in plain terms, That the Bishop was taken up and imprisoned on the Mid-heaven to the Body of ♂, where he continued about four years, and was then Beheaded on the Ascendant to the Body of ♄; and yet the Doctor had both these Directions, and neither of them kill'd him, tho at that time he was very Infirm and extreamly Corpulent; therefore, if these things should be true, or believed so to be, how shall we reconcile this Doctrine to his 92d Aphorism, where he says, *The Directions of the Midheaven never kills, but where a violent Death is threatned.* Which Aphorism was made from the King of *Sweden*'s, to serve a turn at that time. In which Nativity, how shall we believe that his *M. C.* to the Body of ♄ did kill him, when we see plainly these two Gentlemen out-lived their *M. C.* to the Body of ♂, and *John* himself his *M. C.* to the Body of ♄.

But besides all this, my Friend hath mightily discovered his Ignorance in the Direction assigned for the Doctor's death, which tells us plainly, That tho he doth make a noise with *Ptolomy*'s Name, yet he doth not understand one word of *Ptolomy*'s Matter and Doctrine. For he says [*Collect. Gen. p.* 126.] that he died on the Ascendant directed to the □ of ♂ near the *Antares.* Now, if you please but to observe, ♃ is 5 degr. 20 m. in ♊, and ♂ is 5 degr 27 m. in ♍, which is a very small difference in ♐, where the Opposition of the one falls on the Square of the other exactly, and both Directions must be allowed to come up at the same time, and this in the House and Terms of ♃. Therefore, if he or any one else please but to look into the 14th Chapter of the Third Book of *Ptolomy*'s *Quadripartite*, they may find these words, he there discoursing of those things that do prevent Death in dangerous and killing Directions; his words are these, *Impediuntur enim, cum in fines beneficarum Incurrunt, aut cum benefica adspexerit quadrato Aspectu, aut Trigono, aut opposito gradu Interfectorem.* The Mortal Effects [says he] is hindred, when the Direction happens in the Terms of the Beneficks, or when a Benefick beholds the Interfector by a Quadrate, Trine, or opposite Degree. So, that by *Ptolomy*'s own Rule, this Direction of the Ascendant to the □ of ♂ could not kill, because ♃ beholds his Radical Place, and the place of Direction to a minute, and because the *Opposition* is a more perfect *Aspect* than the *Square*, it must without doubt have over-powered it, taken away the Sting of its Nature, and prevented the Mortal Effect, had this Learned Physician's Na-

tivity

tivity been true and exact. Nay, you see *Ptolomy* makes two distinct Rules of them; the *Rays of Jupiter*, and the *Terms of Jupiter*, which are, I dare be confident, sufficiently able to over ballance both the □ of ♂, and the *Antares*. And therefore I shall rest my self satisfied [till that worthy Gentleman shall better inform my Judgment] that seeing Sir *Theodore Mayerne* did out-live the Midheaven to the Body of ♂, and the Ascendant to the Body of ♄, when there was not any thing to support, assist, or save him; it is highly improbable this supposed Direction [for indeed it is no more] of the Ascendant to the □ of ♂ near the *Antares*, should send him to his Grave, when it was so much over-swayed by a Benefick Ray, and in the Terms of ♃ besides: All which considered, speaks aloud in my Ears, that the pretended Nativity of this Learned Physician is most notoriously false, and either ignorantly or knavishly obtruded upon us, to prove one of his supposed Mysteries, as vain as his new Religion he was so fond of in the year 1687. &c. which now he seems to be asham'd of; for he denies that ever he was a Papist; but, *Oportet mendacem esse memorem.*

And yet to be more plain with my Reader, in pursuing the Rules of Astrology in the track of Truth, give me leave to make these further Observations on the falsity of his Figure in improving little false Notions and Directions with a great deal of flourish, and passing by those of more weight and moment in perfect silence, as if they were not worth noting, or fit to be observed by the studious Reader. And the first is, The *Sun* in the Ascendant, which is allowed by all Artists [nay, our Author too] to be *Hileg*, or giver of Life; and for to chuse a giver of Life, and never intend any further use of it, is but to give a man or thing a Nick-name to cause it to be admired without any peculiar use or Advantage, unless it is by chance to serve a turn, and then its Power and Virtue is proclaimed in words at large; as in *James* I. King of *Great Britain*, in Dr. *Le Neve's*, p. 119. in the Duke of *Glocester*, p. 17 *Collect. Gent.* and also in that of *Oliver Cromwell*, where our Author makes use of that Term to inforce his Argument with the greater power and probability of Death. And to be plain with you, I know no reason we have to observe a *Hileg*, if we do not make it the only and principal point in Directions of Life and Death: and I am sure *Ptolomy* would not have given so many curious Rules for the more exact finding of the Giver of Life, had it not been of more than ordinary use in Nativities, and especially in those Predictions of Life and

Death.

Death. Nay, the word it self bespeaks its Power and Office, which by the *Latin* Authors is rendred, *Prorogator Vitæ, a verbo prorogare*, which is to prolong or continue; and nothing can do that, but what hath the full and sole Power and Command of it. And pray observe, That all the five Hylegiack points, are not called Prorogators at the same time, but that Point or Star only, that is Giver of Life. By the *Greeks*, it is called, κύριος τῆς ζωῆς, aut Ἀφέτης, that is, the Lord of Life, or a Messenger sent out on a particular Business; and it is derived from the Verb, Ἀφίημι Demitto. But by the *Arabs* or *Chaldees*, who seem to be the first Authors of the word, it is called *Hileg* or *Hilech*, derived from the Radical *Hebrew* word, הלך, *Ambulavit*; which signifies one that walks forward, as in a Journey, making a regular Progress from the *à quo* to the *ad quem*; and besides, a very Eminent Author tells us it is, *Planeta vel Locus Cœli, ex cujus digressione seu directione de statu vitæ Judicant Astrologi*.

Now, if this should happen to be true, That from this Point, and from this only, we ought to judge of the length of Life, and also the time of Death by the dangerous and mortal Directions; let us see what use our profound Author makes of the *Hileg* in this Nativity; as well as in that of the Bishop, in both which the *Sun* is certainly Giver of Life, by the Rules given by *Origanus*, *Pezelius*, and *Ptolomy*; nay, we may add *Argol*, *Campanella*, and the Learned Author, &c. of the *Doctrine of Nativities*, p. 90. all which agree, That the *Sun* in the Ascendant [the *Moon* being under the Earth] is certainly Giver of Life, as in the Nativity of this Learned Gentleman. Therefore, if you direct the ☉ to the Body of ♄, with and without Latitude, you will find it comes up at or near the Age of 51. *cum Lat.* and at the Age of almost 53. *sine Lat.* and this in ♏, the Dignities of ♂, Lord of the 8th House, and not far from his Square, what the Effect of this Direction was, I know not, but this you may be certain, that he did not dye of it. The next is the Direction of the ☉ to the □ of ♂, near the *Scorpions Heart*, with the 8 of ♃, Lord of the 6th; at or about the Age of 66 years, an Age that generally brings Death; but especially when the Giver of Life is directed to the Malefick Rays of ♂, *Dominus domus Mortis*, and to the beams of ♃ Lord of the 6th, and these among violent fixed Stars of both their Natures; and yet this surly old Man would not dye upon these neither, but lives, expecting further orders for his remove. What! not dye on the Giver of Life, being directed to ♂, Lord of the 8th House, their true and only *Anareta*? This is a wonder with a witness; *Tace, tace*, it is so;

and

and too true to make a Jest of it; he did out-live that Direction, or else the Nativity my honest old Friend hath printed for his Birth, is false, and indeed I would advise Mr. *John* to knock under, and say it is false, or else he breaks two of the main Hinges of Astrology at once, *i. e.* the Power of *Hileg*, and their *Anareta*. Well, well; but what needs all this triumph and noise about a thing of nothing, or nothing worth at least? For tho the *Sun* to the Lord of the 8th House did not kill him, yet the Ascendant did his business [and verified the true Rules of Art, every whit as well as the *Sun*] upon its Direction to the *Square* of *Mars*, which you will find came up at 81 years of Age, *aut circum circa*; and therefore the *Anareta* is not to be blamed. And for your *Hileg*, it may be all nonsence for ought I know, neither am I bound to believe a pack of old musty Authors; and I know no reason to the contrary, but the Horoscope ought to be a standing *Hileg* in all Nativities, and at all times of the day.

Soft and fair my good Friend, not so hot and passionate, I pray; methinks you talk a little out of the way, when you would have the Ascendant to be a standing *Hileg*, which you will not suffer to be so; but you dance it backwards and forwards, as they do the Puppets in the Shows, and make it serve any turn, and do any service you have occasion for, as Marriage, Death, Preferment, Death of a Wife or Husband, Sickness, Sorrow, Change of Religion, Loss of Estate, Getting of Riches and Children; and twenty things more of this nature, you make the Direction of the Ascendant signify in your Correction of Nativities. And I doubt not, but if you could dance the *Sun* and *Moon* too and fro, from one Degree or Sign to another, as you do the Ascendant, there would be nothing difficult in the Art of Astrology, but there would be a plain reason for every thing, and also a forcible Direction for every Accident. Oh, the wonderful Horoscope, and the excellent use of it! But my design and desire is, that this Ingenious Author would be so kind to us, as to let us know when the ill Directions to the *Hileg* will not kill, and when the Directions to the Horoscope shall do it, that the young Students and Practitioners may not be cheated and deluded with expectations of a thing that will never succeed the Operations. And indeed, the Direction he here builds upon, of the Ascendant to the *Square of Mars* for his Death, was over almost twenty years before his Death; so that in truth there could be no Cause assigned for it, but the *Opposition* of *Jupiter*, and the *Scorpions Heart* to the Ascendant. And tho I have here not mentioned the Bishop's Nativity,

tivity, yet the same Errors here alledged in the Doctor's, do most of them also claim the same Remarks in the Bishop's, which for brevity's sake, I here omit; having already observed several things there, that are not mentioned here, which I would advise you to compare in the reading, and then consider, whether these Nativities are true or false, and what credit and repute they can bring to *Cardinal Signs* on *Angles*, according as he hath stated the matter. I having already granted, that Planets in *Cardinal Signs* on *Angles*, do and will give Glorious Effects and Eminent Men; and so will the Planets in *Cardinal Signs* out of the *Angles*, or in their own Dignities in *Angles*, tho not in *Cardinal Signs*. And so I conclude this Examen of his Ten Genitures, with the Errors observed.

But yet, before I conclude with my old worthy Friend, I will shew you a visible Demonstration of his Ignorance and ⸺ ; and also what Credit is to be given to his Calculations Astronomical, as well as Astrological. He having a great Opinion of his own Abilities in Astronomy, and of his being capable to Judge between the truth of the *Caroline Tables*, and the rest Extant, took an occasion in *Trigg's* Almanack [which is written by him] to fall foul upon those Tables, and those that use them also, in the year 1691. upon the occasion of the ☉'s entring into ♈; and the better to facilitate his design, and make it plain and clear to his Reader, that the *Carol. Tables* are false, he Calculates the ☉'s place [or at leastwise says so] by the *Astronomia Anglicana* written by Mr. *Nicholas Greenwood*; by which Operation Mr. *J. G.* tells us, That the ☉ enters the first point of ♈ on *March* 10. at 53 min. past 6 a Clock in the Morning, according to which time he ought to make 0 degr. of ♉ ascending in the Vernal Figure, but he makes 2 degr. of ♉; yet that mistake I will allow him, tho 'tis false. And then he begins to blutter, and tell us, how some *Almanack-makers* lov'd to be singular, to oppose manifest verity; that they are in love with falshood, and believe lies: Oh, brave *John!* *Num nulla mendacia fide fuerunt in novâ tuâ?* But at last he is very Civil, and tells them, they may hug their own Conceits, and ride their own Hobby-horses, and welcome. Now, after all this impudent sort of dating, let any impartial Man but look into Mr. *Greenwood*'s Almanack for that year, and the Calculation of the ☉'s entrance into ♈ done from his own Tables, by which *J. G.* also pretends to do his; and you will there find, that the ☉ enters ♈ on *March* 10. at 51 min. past 7 a Clock in the Morning; differing from the Learned Mr. *J. G.* 58 min.

58 min. near an hour. In which Case we must certainly allow Mr. *Greenwood* to understand his own Tables well; and therefore the other must be in the Error, and not he; which if so, then what need *J. G.* make such a noise about the truth and exactness of any Tables, when he thus deals in Error by Whole-sale, to tell us, that the *Caroline Tables* are false; when for ought he knows, it is nothing else but his weakness and inability in the Operation. For here 'tis plain, That he hath made an Error of 58 min. and this done too in a Controversy for the truth, as he says; a very pretty way to support and build the Structure of Truth upon Pillars of Error; just as the Priests of his Religion have done, plunged the People into so many Errors, and there keep them, that now they themselves know not one step in the way to truth. Thus I have fairly given my Reader an Account of the Errors in those Nativities printed in the *Cardines Cæli*, and that they have not *Cardinal Signs* on *Angles*, as he pretends; nor are there any of his Calculations to be credited, especially in Nativities, most of them being made to serve a turn, and not founded on the true Basis. And if the Reader will read with care, the Examination of the Errors in this Book about Genitures, he may soon discover which point he ought to Steer, to come up with Truth, or at leastways in sight of her; a prospect always giving some hopes of the fruition of what they pursue. And so I take my leave of *John* at this time, and promise my Reader to present him with my *Defectio Geniturarum*, in which I shall examine the Nativities in *Gadbury*'s Collection; in *Argol*'s *De Diebus Criticis*, and in *Morinus*'s *Astrologia Gallica*; it being already in a good forwardness.

In the former part of this Treatise, I promised to shew you, That there was never any Eminent and Famous Prediction made of any ones Death, but when the Astrologers made use of the *Hileg* in Direction, and did direct that to some of the Malefick Rays of ♄ and ♂, &c. And you may see throughout this Book, that my Doctrine there delivered is wholly pursuant to this Principle, for I allow no Promittor to any Significator to kill; but to the Giver of Life only; and how to take or elect that, I refer you to Book III. Chap. 13. of *Ptolomy*'s *Quardripartite*.

And the first Example we have (that occurs to my Memory) is that of *Don John of Austria* in *Sixtus ab Heminga*, p. 49. whose Death the said *Heminga* predicted seven years before, and that almost to a day, from the Direction of the ☽ to the ☍ of ♄; for the ☽ was in

the

Opus Reformatum.

the 7th, and beyond all doubt Giver of Life. And we find there, that the Ascendant to the ☍ of the ☽, Lady of the 8th House did not kill, nor did that to the ☐ of the ☉ and ♀ effect it; nor could the ☉ to the ☐ of ♄ kill, tho the Direction fell in the 4th House, that fatal part of Heaven, as some esteem it, and the reason of this was, because none of those Significators were Givers of Life, but the ☽ only; and therefore, when she was directed to the ☍ of ♄, this Princely Native was made a Sacrifice to Death; as you may see by his Nativity, printed in the beforementioned Treatise. And here give me leave to observe one thing; it is plain from *Heminga*'s own words, That this was done by chance too, he not knowing the reason of the thing, nor could he ever do so again, and therefore brings this Example in to refute Astrology, and tells us at last, *Unica hirundo non efficit ver*; and it is indeed no wonder, that he could not do so again, when he did not know the true reason why this had such an effect as it had; which is the fault of too many beside *Heminga*, who could never arrive yet at a true Rule, to judge of the Effects of Directions in Death and Sickness.

The second Example, is that of *Lucius Bellantius*, in the Nativity of *Picus Mirandula*, where you may observe, that the ☽ to the ☐ of the ☉ did not kill, nor the M.C. to the ☍ of ♄, nor the Ascendant to the ☐ of ♃ in the 4th; but the Ascendant, who is the true *Hileg*, or Giver of Life, to the Square of ♄, and Body of ♂ did do it effectually; so that it is plain, the Giver of Life is to be principally and only taken notice of in Directions of Death.

The third Example, is that of *Edward* VI. King of *England*, who died *July* 16. Anno 1553: being almost Sixteen years of Age; and as it is reported, it was predicted before by *Cardan*, altho he had his Nativity imperfect, as to the exact time, yet did say, That the Ascendant to the Body of ♄ would kill him, and indeed so it proved; and that because the Ascendant was Giver of Life by *Ptolomy*'s Rule; a *Conjunction* preceding, and both the Luminaries, and part of Fortune under the Earth; and neither ♃ nor ♀, who are in Aphetical Places, do behold the Points of Heaven that are mentioned by him in the like case after an *Opposition*, and therefore I do affirm, That the Ascendant was the real and true *Hileg*, and the Effect confirms it to be so.

The fourth Example; is that of the Nativity of *Vincent Wing*, where we shall find upon inquiry, that neither the Ascendant to the ☍ of the ☉, nor the ☽ to the ☐ of the ☉, was able to kill this

- Native.

Native; no, nor the Midheaven to the □ of ♄ neither, that fatal Direction (as some think) to Life. But the ☉ to the Body of ♄ kill'd him with the Mundane Square of ♂; and the reason was, because the ☉ is certainly Giver of Life, and this beyond all dispute; so that you still see the *Hileg* is always concern'd, and but seldom misseth, and when it doth, there are (as indeed there ought) very good Reasons to be given for it, by any that understand Directions in their true Motion; and from those that do not understand them, it is not expected.

The fifth Example, is from the Nativity and Death of *Charles* II. which was predicted by a certain Person some years before it happened; and it is well-known too, to several in and about the City of *London*, to be true, what I here say, and that Person to my knowledg made use of no other Significator, but the true Giver of Life; and in that Nativity you may observe two or three things that are very remarkable. 1*st*, The Ascendant to the Body of ♄ did not kill him, neither did the Midheaven to the □ of ♄ kill him, nor the ☽ to the Body of the ☉; nay, and what is more, the ☉ *Hileg* to the □ of ♄, did not kill neither; which admits of a question, and that a very rational one too. But why did it not kill him? Because ♄ was not Lord of the 8th; is not that a very good reason; Ha, ha, ha! Or else, because he was strong, and like a noble Enemy, scorn'd to hurt him, by which Rule the Stars are always, either too strong, or too weak, according as Mr. Astrologer pleaseth to turn the Scales with his Finger; or perhaps the Direction falling in the House of Hope, a fortunate Corner of Heaven, and to it could not kill him; or else, because the ☽, who disposeth of the place of Direction is in Trine to the Ascendant, which for ought we know might save; and if not singly, yet certainly, altogher may be allowed to do it, notwithstanding the place of Direction was in *pitted and deep degrees*; a plaguy kind of an unhappiness to a man under an ill fate! But to tell you the plain truth of the matter, these are all Shams and Fooleries. And as a Learned Divine once said of the Pictures in Church-windows, That *they serve only to keep out the Light*, and so do these in their places. And for the true Reason why it did not kill, you have it in Book III. Chap. 14. of *Ptolomy's Quadripartite*, where you may find it if you please. And so I come to tell you, That when the ☉ came to be about 9 or 10 degrees in ♌ by Direction, he met there with seven Malefick Directions, without any assistance to relieve

lieve or save the Native, which I say, *Modo Astrologico*, was the real and true Cause of his Death. Thus I have performed, what I promised in Page 20. and I think spoke enough to the purpose I intended it for; but if any think it not sufficient, or at least-wise useless, they have the liberty, either to improve it, or reject it.

A Supplement *serviceable to the former Work.*

BY way of Supplement, I will add a few Nativities, to shew further how we ought to proceed in the discovery of truth, the only thing I intend by publishing this and other Treatises, that shall come forth in their due time; and also how mistakes do arise in the Astrologick Practice in Nativities, which being printed and obtruded on the World, they are received as truths by the younger Students, because not detected by those of more Years and Experience. And this I shall endeavour to prove from some Nativities already printed, that the mistakes of some People have been as a Hinge to the present Errors that we labour under at this time; those Errors I mean, that this Age is so in love with; and I believe it will be a very hard matter to separate the one from the other. However I will do my part, and let the Multitude believe, and the lesser Number act as they see convenient. Neither shall I be angry with any man, that will not believe he is in an Error; but as he hath lived hitherto, so let him go on and proceed to the end.

I have had a Nativity of a young Man in my hand these Dozen or Thirteen years, and I hear he is dead of a *Consumption*, at the Age of Nineteen years and a half, or thereabouts. It was given to me for a remarkable and prodigious Birth; one that was to be of long Life, great Repute and Fame, and also Rich; and this was, because all the Planets were in their own Dignities, and no ill Directions in a long time. The Figure is as followeth, set to the estimate Time of his Birth, as it was given me without any Correction at that time, or since, till now.

R. 352.

Opus Reformatum.

R. 35 2. 39. a.

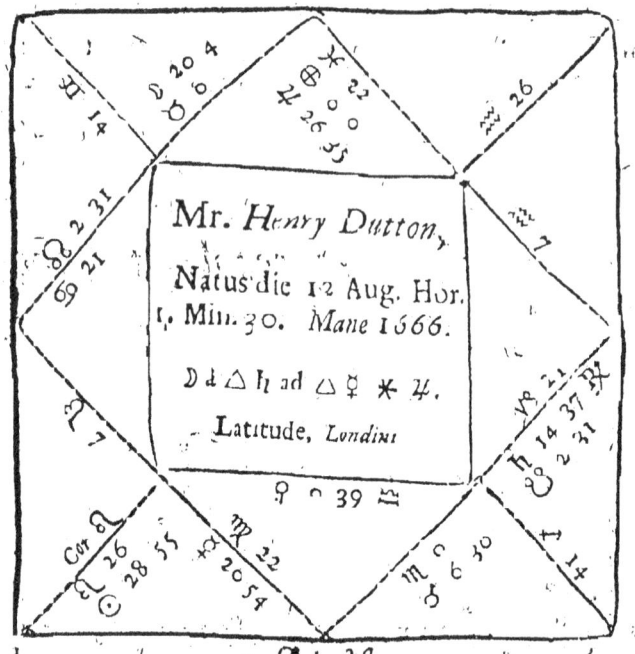

	Latitud.	Planet.
♄	0	7 North
♃	1	33 South
♂	0	47 South
♀	c	47 North
☿	0	5 South
☽	3	34 South

Mr. *Henry Dutton*,

Natus die 12 Aug. Hor.
1, Min. 30. Mane 1666.

☽ d △ ♄ ad △ ☿ ✱ ♃.

Latitude, *Londini*.

This is the estimate Time of this Gentleman's Birth, and he died of a *Consumption* at almost Twenty years of Age. Now, the main thing to inquire, is, what was the Direction that kill'd this Man, and why it should be a *Consumption*? I have told you already, That the *Hileg*, or Giver of Life must be directed for Death, for if all the other points are afflicted by Direction, and the *Hileg* free and befriended by a good Ray, the Native shall not dye at that time; therefore we must first endeavour to find out who is Giver of Life, before I proceed to determine the Cause and Time of his Death. First then, The ☉ cannot be *Hileg*, because in the third House; nor can the ☽, because she is not in an Aphetical Place, unless we should alter the Figure, and make it later about Nine or Ten Minutes in time; but if she had been *Apheta*, she could come to no violent Direction before the □ of ♀ in *Zodiaco* at about Twenty nine years; and *Sesquiquadrate* of ♂ in *Mundo* at Thirty six, or thereabouts; the Mundane Parallel of the *Sun* excepted, which comes up sooner or later, according as you alter the Figure in the 10th and 1st Houses.

Therefore

Opus Reformatum.

Therefore that Dominion will fall on *Jupiter*, or the part of Fortune in the Tenth House; if we accept of this Figure, being the estimate Time of Birth; or if we make it sooner, as it is most generally. The part of Fortune cannot, because *Jupiter* is strong in the Tenth, in *Sextile* to the *Moon*, Light of the Time; and besides there are no Directions to that Point, nor near it, that are very considerable; neither can *Jupiter* be singly Giver of Life, because the part of Fortune is in the Tenth: Therefore I will alter the time given about 11 minutes later, and make 25 degrees of *Pisces* on the Tenth House, at which time the *Moon* will be *Hileg*, and yet *Jupiter* bear a share also in the Natives Death, as you shall see by the Directions following: The R. A. of the M C. to that time, is 355 d. 25 m. and the distance of the *Moon* from that point of Heaven, is 53 d. 6 m. her Oblique Ascention under her own Pole of Position, is 39 d. 46 m. and her Temp. Hor. 18 d. 5 m. from whence you have the Directions following wrought.

	D.	M.		Y.	M.
☽ ad △ ☿ in mundo dd	11	28		12	7 1679
☽ ad Parallelum ☉ in mundo dd	12	15		13	3 1679
☽ ad □ ☉ in mundo dd	12	15		13	3 1679
☽ ad Aldebaran, cum Latitudine	14	33		16	1 1682
♃ ad □ ♄ in Zodiaco sine Latitudine	15	58	gives	17	6 1684
♃ ad □ ♄ in Zodiaco cum Latitudine	16	35		18	2 1684
☽ ad Parallelum ☉ in mundo dc.	17	43		19	5 1686
☽ ad ☍ ♂ motu Convers.	19	5		20	11 1687
☽ ad Parallelum ♀ motu rapto	21	20		22	3 1688
☽ ad □ ☿ in Zodiaco sine Latitudine	25	26		28	0 1694
☽ ad Parallelum ♄ in Zodiaco	26	19		28	10 1695

Thus you see here are Eleven Directions, and Nine of them to the *Moon*, who is Giver of Life, the other two to *Jupiter*. I have not deviated far from the estimate Time, because it should not be objected to me, that I had made a Figure for my own purpose, and yet I dare not swear this to be true; but I am sure it is as likely to be true, as any time that can be selected within an hour or two of the estimate. I confess, I did not know the Gentleman, and therefore I do leave the Directions here wrought, to be applied, and judged by those that did know him. But as to his last six years, I will give my Opinion on the Directions; about the Age of Thirteen years, he had two dangerous Directions, after which I judge he was never perfectly healthy; nor do I believe

U he

he appeared Consumptive till about his Eighteenth year; and for his Death, he had the *Moon* Convers to the Parallel of the *Sun*, and also to the *Opposition* of *Mars*; and these followed by three other Directions that were violent. As for allowing the Directions of *Jupiter* to the *Square* of *Saturn*, I do not bring that in as an Argument of Death, but a Consumption; An Observation that I have made in divers Nativities of those that died Consumptive. And tho I do but just mention it here, and so leave it to the Censure of the Candid or Sceptical Reader, to give his Opinion as he thinks fit; yet I shall endeavour to prove it when, I print those Nativities I have promised, among which you will find several of *Consumptions*. But besides, if there is such a thing as the Planets governing particular Parts of the Body [which I believe they do] then why should not those Planets directed to the Malefick Beams of *Saturn*, *Mars*, &c give a weakness and debility to those Parts they govern? For I suppose we all own bad Directions to be an Affliction; and all Authors do give the principal Parts of the Body to *Jupiter*'s Government: *Ptolomy* allows him the *Lungs*, *Arteries*, and *Seed*; and *Cardan* the *Lungs*, *Blood*, *Liver*, and *Flesh*; so that, take which you will, 'tis plain, they allow him to govern those very Parts of the Body, that always suffer in *Consumptions*; and tho these Directions do give such Diseases; yet, as above, I do not allow them to kill, but when they are followed with violent Directions to the Giver of Life. Therefore you see some People fall into a *Consumption*, and dye of it, and all in the space of six Months, and yet others linger under it Ten or a Dozen years before they dye, and yet fall by that single Disease at last, with those Attendants that always bear it company. Therefore, I say, 'tis my Opinion, he fell into that Consumptive habit of Body under that Direction of *Jupiter* to the *Square* of *Saturn*, and had no Balsamick and Healing Direction came up afterward to repair that Breach, till the *Hileg* came to those Violent and Malefick Beams, that proved his *Atropos*; as you may see above.

But I partly foresee what the *Capricio*'s may object to this Correction, and Directions, and tell you, that they can give a good substantial Reason for his Death, without this trouble and labour, and that is the Ascendant to the *Square* of *Mars*, which comes up exactly by this very Figure that I give for his true one. To this I answer, The Direction which they call the *Square* of *Mars*, doth come up then certainly by their Measure of Time. Now, if that Direction [which is but a single one] can kill, when the *Sun* or *Moon* is Gi-

Giver of Life, then I am sure it will kill at any time: For if that single Direction can kill when the Ascendant is not *Hileg*, it must certainly do it when it is; and if so, then, why did it not kill in *Nostradamus*'s Nativity, when both ♄ and ♂ was in ☉; and in Sir *Frech. Hiller*'s Case, *Collect. Genit. p.* 159. and in *Don John of Austria, p.* 65. and in that also of the Earl of *Essex, Ejusdem Libri, p.* 45.

Perhaps, likewise, I may be questioned, why the *Moon*, *Hileg* to the Square and Parallel of the *Sun in Mundo*, did not kill him at the Age of Thirteen or Fourteen years, as well as the Convers Parallel at Nineteen? To that I answer, He had then with those Directions, the *Moon* to the Mundane *Trine* of *Mercury*, who was in Parallel with *Jupiter*; *Trine* with the *Moon* and *Saturn* also in his *Radix*; and besides, that Mundane Square was not indeed a Square in the Zodiack, for the *Moon* was then by Direction in 9 degrees of *Gemini*, with Latitude.

Thus I have endeavoured to give an Account of the Cause of this Gentleman's death, by the best of that little skill I have in Astrology; but if it should happen not to be true in some mens Judgment or Opinion, I shall take it as a great Favour to be corrected by any man that doth really understand it, and will allow his own Rules to be General, and not confined to one Nativity only, as most of their Rules and Aphorisms are; and I shall be so far from taking it ill, or being angry at it, that I do invite any one, and will thank him for his pains, that truth may receive the advantage so many of us talk of, and pretend to. And one thing I shall desire of my Antagonist, whosoever he is, that shall undertake to correct me; That if he shall assign any other Cause for this Native's death, than what I have done, I do intreat him to tell the World why it should be a *Consumption*; and especially, if any man thinks fit to rely on the Ascendant to the *Square* of *Mars* for his Death, that they would be pleased to give us a Rule or two, how we shall know before-hand when that Direction gives a Fever, when a *Consumption*, and when a *Dysentery*, *Madness*, *Small-pox*, &c. For of all the Authors I have ever yet read, I have not yet met with any one so bold, as to assert that Direction to give *Consumptions*; nor indeed is there any reason it should be thought to do it; for the Nature of the Direction is rapid and furious, and kills *Citatim*; but this disease, *Lento pede*, makes no such haste, but kills *Gradatim*.

Opus Reformatum.

The Second Nativity is that of my old Friend Mr. *J. B*'s Son, who died of the *Stone, Fever*, and other Illness, at the Age of Seven years, and a little more; and the estimate time of his Birth was almost three quarters of an hour after Ten at Night, *Dec.* 14. 1673. And so it was given to me by his Father above Ten or Eleven years since.

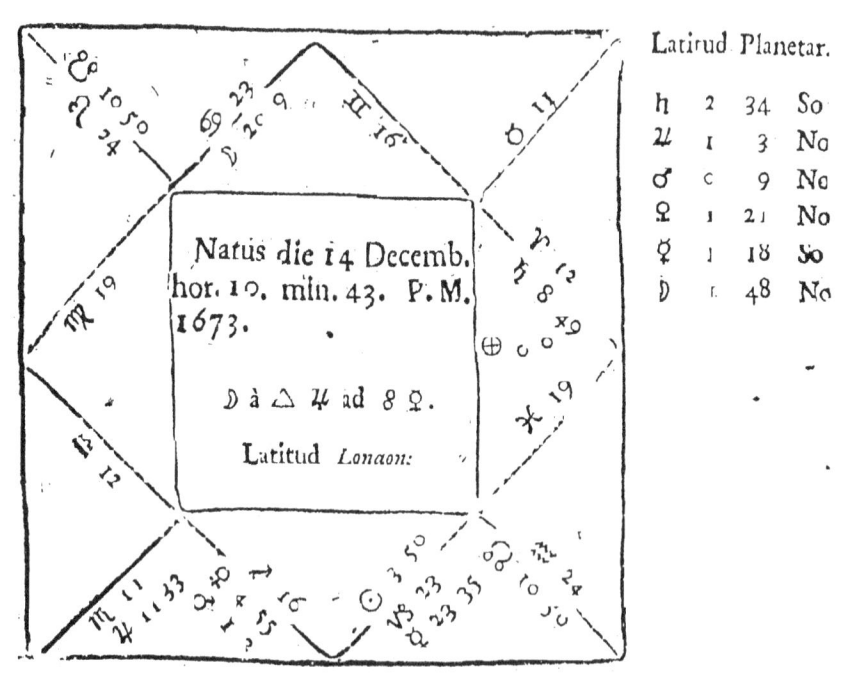

Latitud Planetar.

♄	2	34	So
♃	1	3	No
♂	0	9	No
♀	1	21	No
☿	1	18	So
☽	1	48	No

Natus die 14 Decemb. hor. 10. min. 43. P.M. 1673.

☽ à △ ♃ ad ☍ ♀.

Latitud *London*:

This Figure, as I told you before, is set to the estimate Time first given; but upon strict enquiry of his Father, he did confess it might be allowed a quarter later in the Evening, and I shall strain it about 7 or 8 minutes later than that time he allows, and so make it come to 5 or 6 minutes after 11 P.M. To which time the M C. is almost 22 degrees of *Gemini*, whose R. A. is 80 d. 47 m. and the Ascendant is 23 degrees and a half in *Virgo*, the O. A. of it 170 d. 47 m. And from this Figure, I shall endeavour to give a Rational Account of the Diseases and Death of this Child, he having lain under that tormenting disease of the *Stone* about two years before his Death. And I hope I may be excused for my altering the Ascendant three degrees from the estimate Time, and the Midheaven almost six; and especially by those that alter their correct time so many hours from the estimate.

And

And the first thing I shall fall upon by way of Enquiry, is, why this Child should be of so short a Life, seeing the *Moon*, who is *Hileg*, was in *Trine* to *Jupiter*, in her own House, and Angular? Why, truly this is no very strange thing, if rightly considered; for tho she hath been in *Trine* to *Jupiter*, yet she is in direct Opposition to *Mercury* applying, and in a Mundane Square to *Saturn*, and all this from Cardinal Signs; to which we may add likewise, that she was very near the Sesquiquadrate of *Mars in Mundo*, and no less than three of the Hylegiack Points afflicted by Directions near at hand, as I shall presently make appear, and those of the *Moon* in the Terms of an Infortune; which Positions of themselves [had the Giver of Life been free from the ill Rays of the Infortunes] were sufficient to have given great Weakness and Distempers to the Body, not only with danger, but continuance too; and therefore it need not remain a wonder, that he should live no longer, nor be more healthy while he lived.

Secondly, Why the Stone? I shall not enter into a long Discourse about the Opinion of Authors concerning the Stone, and its generation; Whether it proceeds from a Lapidifick spirit, according to the Opinion of *Riverius*; or a stony Disposition, according to *Fernelius*: or whether a petrifying Ferment be the original and efficient Cause, as it is defined by *Helmont*; but I shall consider it Astrologically, which perhaps may be allowed to take its beginning before their Causes, and likewise be no stranger to the reconciling them in peace. For I look upon the Stony Spirit, the Calculous Disposition, and petrifying Ferment, to be but the effect of a precedent Cause; and though they differ in their Terms, yet they all do design the same thing; and therefore that which is the cause of them, is certainly the cause of the Disease: And I do not understand that the Child had it from its birth, and therefore it had a time to begin.

I have generally observed in many Nativities, that where-ever the Stone was produced and caused in the Bladder, both *Saturn* and *Mars* had a finger in it both by position and Direction; as if *Saturn* afforded matter for the Terrene ferment, and *Mars* for the petrification; so likewise in this Nativity we shall find them both concerned in the Cause and quality of his Death, as you may observe by the Directions following.

	D	M	Y	M
☽ ad ☌ ☿ cum Latitudine	4	40	4	00 1677
☉ ad □ ♄ in Zodiaco	5	30	4	09 1678
☽ ad Sesquiquadratum ♂ in mundo	5	38	4	10 1678
⊕ ad Corpus ♄	6	44	5	8 1679
☽ ad Parallelum ♂ in mundo ad.	7	46	6	9 1680
☉ ad □ ♄ in mundo ad.	8	56	7	11 1681

To which we may add the *Sun* secondary to the Square of *Saturn* at 5 years, and the *Moon* by secondary motion to the Opposition of *Saturn* and Square of the *Sun* at six years of age, which did not a little add to the Effects of the other Directions, and on the day of his last Revolution, *Saturn* was to a degree on the Radical place of the *Moon*, and *Mars* on the Radical Ascendant.

Hence I conclude these Directions to have been the natural Cause of this Child's Disease, and Death: Especially, if compared with the Radical Positions of the *Moon* in Square to *Saturn in mundo*, and within Rays of the Parallel and Sesquiquadrate of *Mars* So that I judge this Disease begun at, or about 5 years of Age, on the *Sun ad □ ♄ in Zodiaco*, and the *Moon ad Sesquiquadratum Martis in Mundo*, and that the part of Fortune to the Body of *Saturn*, the *Moon* to the Parallel of *Mars*, and the *Sun* to the Square of *Saturn in Mundo*, wore out his Life by a continued succession of pain. And let no man object, that the Rays of *Venus* succeed the Parallel of *Mars*, which according to *Ptolomy's* Doctrine ought to save and support Life: I confess it is his Doctrine, and my Rule; but in this Case, where three of the Hilegiack Points are afflicted by direction, and the fourth very near it, the Rays of *Venus* could by no means save: She might indeed protract, and perhaps specificate the Disease; and therefore she might add near his Expiration some flux of the Bowels, distemper of the Liver, and by accident, as being in conjunction with *Mars*, a Fever, or injury by Physick.

The next is of a Child that died within the year at the age of six Months, or before it, and was given me by an accident; he that gave it, and they that sent it, designing a Trick upon me, which proved in the conclusion one upon themselves: The Figure of the Estimate is as followeth, and brought to me just after its death.

It

Opus Reformatum.

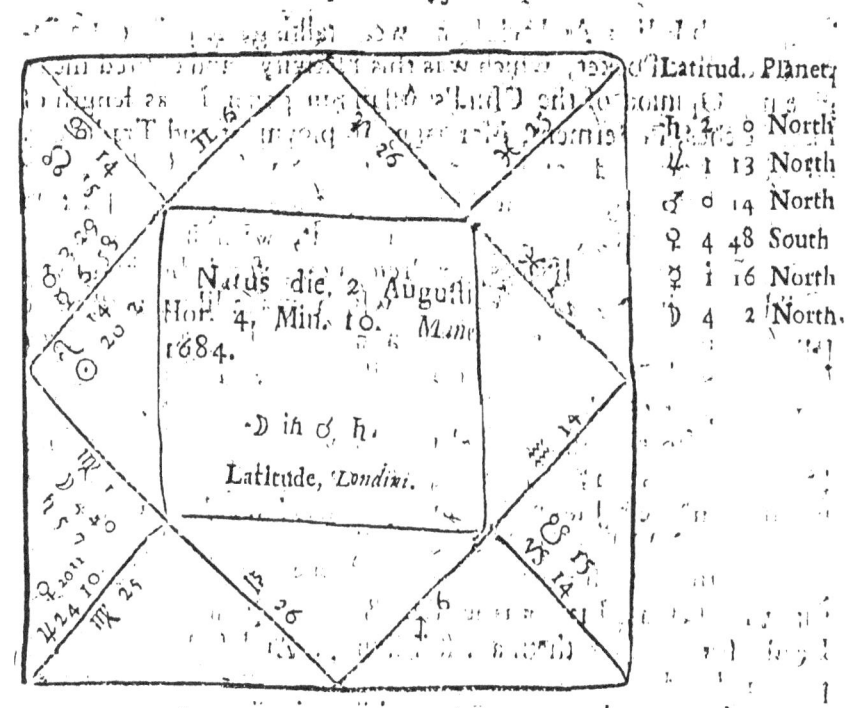

		Latitud.	Planet
♄	4	0	North
♃	1	13	North
♂	0	14	North
♀	4	48	South
☿	1	16	North
☽	4	2	North

Natus die 2 Augusti
Hor. 4. Min. 10. Mane
1684.

☽ in ☌ ♄.

Latitude, *Londini.*

It is no great matter for the exact time of this Nativity [though I do indeed believe it was a few minutes sooner] because those that dye within the year, do for the most part dye by position; as you may see Book the Third, *Quadripart.* chap. 9. seldom by direction, and so did this Child: the Positions of themselves being sufficiently able to kill it, if well considered.

But before I proceed, it may not be amiss to tell you the Story I hinted at above, and it was this. About the middle of *January* 1684/5, one that kept a Coffee-house, and was a Pretender to Astrology, call'd on me one Afternoon, and told me I was desired to come to his House the *Thursday* following in the Evening to meet four or five very great Astrologers that had a mind to spend an hour or two with me, and also told me their Names; so I promised to be there [*Deo permittente*] at his hour, and did accordingly perform my Promise, but what the matter was, I know not, he nor his Company were not there; and when I had staid about two hours, and was preparing to be gone, in comes he, and excused the matter as well as he could, telling me he was very sorry the Company had disappointed me, but desired me to stay and smoak a Pipe with him,

him, which I did: And while we were talking he pulls out a Paper out of his Pocket, which was this Nativity, and defired me to give my Opinion of the Child's Affairs in general: as length of Life, Riches, Preferment, Marriage, Imployment and Trade, &c. all which he named, and more likewife. So after I had feriouſly confidered the Figure [without asking him any queftion] I told him I ſhould make a ſhort Judgment on it, without the confideration of Marriage, Riches, or Preferment, for I did judge the Child was either *dead*, or *dying*, which he readily confeſt to be true, that it was dead, and died about a month before; and defired I would tell him my Reaſons for it, which I refufed. For, ſays he, Mr. C. ſaid it would live till 60 years of age; and Mr. S. ſaid it would live to 58, and a third told him it would live till all his Friends were weary of him. So that after they ſaw themſelves befool'd in their Judgment, in hopes that I would have made a ſtumble alſo, defired my Opinion that I might have taken my place on the ſame form with them. And I doubt not, but if any thing here afferted is not true, I ſhall hear of it on both ſides my Head, for ſome of them are ſtill living: And ſo I come to the point in hand.

The Reaſons therefore of this Child's death were, the *Sun in Leo* in parallel with *Mars* and *Mercury* in Conjunction in the Twelf Houſe, and the *Sun* Hileg. the *Sun* is with the *Lyons Heart*, and the *Moon* in Conjunction with *Saturn in Virgo* both peregrin, for although the *Moon* is not *Aphæta*, yet every Affliction of an Aphetical place adds to the weakneſs of the Body; and every Diſeaſe or Weakneſs helps death in at the door; therefore this affliction of the *Moon* is no ſmall cauſe in the Child's death, but I allow the other to be the *cauſa ſine qua non*. Again, the *Sun*, *Mars* and *Mercury* are all in a violent Zodiacal Parallel, and ought to be conſidered in particular, becauſe the part of Heaven, where they are ſcituate, doth much influence their good or ill Effects: And Laſtly, The *Moon* is applying to the Zodiacal Parallel of *Saturn*, and neither of the Fortunes helped nor hindred in all this Affair; neither can *Jupiter* or *Venus* kill by direction, let them govern what Houſes they will. Theſe, I ſay, are the true Reaſons of this Child's death according to the Doctrine here delivered in this Treatiſe of Nativities, and ſhall in all Caſes hold, whether there are Directions or not; as in many Nativities you will find no directions for Childrens dying within the year. And beſides, if a Direction is able to kill four

months

months after birth, that Position certainly affects the Child all the time of its Life, for the Child's Life is but a continued effect of such a Position or Direction, if you have one: And therefore I will sum up all with that Text of *Ptolomy*, *Vivet Natus tanto spacio quantus est numerus graduum inter prorogatorem & proximam maleficam, tot videlicet menses, dies, vel horas pro modo & viribus Causarum nocentium;* and here you see the Child died when the *Sun* came to the Square of *Saturn*, and there is sixteen degrees almost between their two Bodies, and that lived so many weeks; make the best use you can of this Instruction. These three Nativities have been all printed in *English* already.

The next is that of *Johannes Baptista Cardanus*, the Son of the Great *Cardan*, which hath been printed by his Father already, by *Sixtus ab Heminga*, who brings it as an Argument against Astrology, because there was no reason given by him, nor *Naibod*, nor *Maginus* (who had the surveying of it, and were, I really believe, three of the greatest Men, and Masters of Astrology, that have appeared in the last Century) for his violent death: And it is also brought against us to confute and confound the Art, and its Professors, by *Alexand. de Angelis*, pag 301. in his Treatise against Astrology.

The Story is thus: This *Baptista Cardanus* was the eldest Son of his Father, brought up to Learning, and imployed himself in the study of Physick, which afterward he profest and lived by: But in the 24th year of his age, he [without the Advice of his Father or other Friends] married a Wife with a small Fortune, and less Modesty; and being incumbred, and overcharged with her Relations, and his Practice being small, they fell into necessity, and thence into difference, which difference being aggravated by Discontent on the one side, and increased by greater Provocations on the other, they at last came to down-right hate of each other; and under this Perturbation of Mind he contrived how to destroy her; and the method he pitch'd upon, was Poyson. This Poyson he put into a Cake, and sent it to her by a Servant, she being then in Child-bed; and in a small time after she had eat it, dyed. The next day he was taken up by the Officers of Justice, and examined; but was so far from denying the Fact, that he confessed he had been two months contriving how to do it; and in that time had made two Attempts at it, but mist of his design. For this Crime he was Beheaded [which is the common way of Execution in those parts, of those guilty of Blood] on *April* 7. *Anno* 1560. being almost Twenty-six years of Age; and this without any Account of its Cause Astrologically; which made *Heminga* and *Alex. de Angelis* laugh at us, and all those also, that pretend to Astrology. I have therefore made use of this opportunity to let the World know my Opinion, as well as that Learned Monk's, who hath already discoursed of it. The Figure I shall give is the same with his Father's; the estimate Time of Birth, for I am sure it cannot be far from truth, because his Father was so Ingenious a Man, and I presume careful in taking the time of it. The Figure follows, with the Planets places calculated from the *Caroline Tables*, both in Longitude and Latitude.

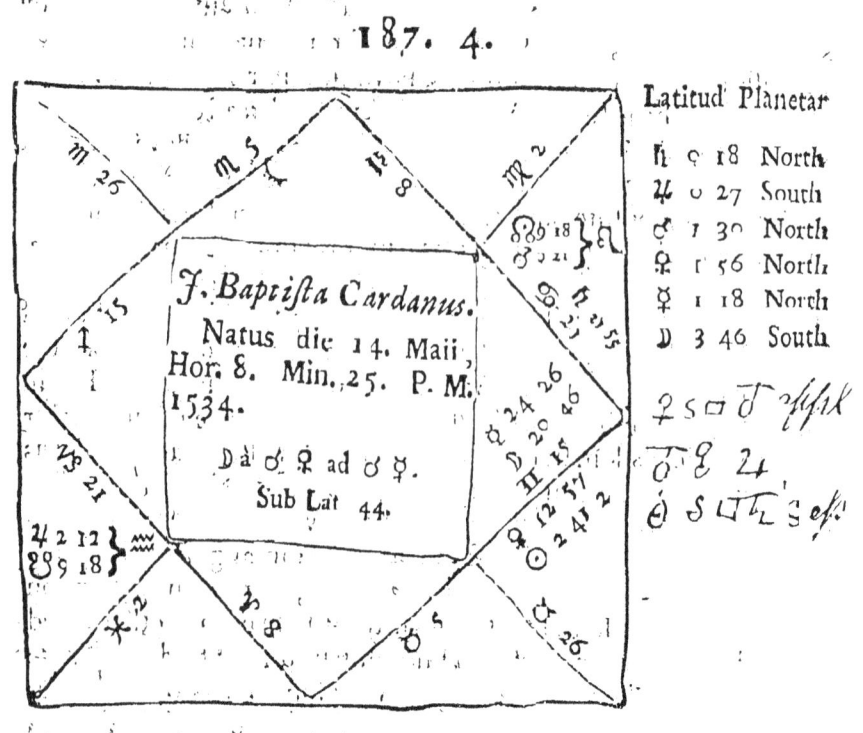

187. 4.

J. Baptista Cardanus.
Natus die 14. Maii,
Hor. 8. Min. 25. P. M.
1534.

D à ♂ ♀ ad ♂ ☿.
Sub Lat. 44.

Latitud Planetar

♄ 0 18 North
♃ 0 27 South
♂ 1 30 North
♀ 1 56 North
☿ 1 18 North
☽ 3 46 South

The *Moon* is beyond all doubt Giver of Life in this Nativity. and must be directed for Death, and therefore without altering or straining any thing in the Figure, we shall find Cause sufficient at that time it did, to put a period to his Life, and the principal Direction, which destroyed it, was the *Moon*, *Hileg* to the Zodiacal Parallel of

the

Opus Reformatum.

the *Sun*, which she meets in 14 degrees of *Cancer*, whose Ark of Direction is 26 d. 26 m. which gives in time 25 years and 10 months, at which time he fell into that unhappy misfortune, as you have before heard; and that was attended with four other Directions, which helped to compleat that fatal and dreadful Sentence, as you may see by the following Table.

	D.	M.	Y.	M.	A.C.
☉ ad Parallelum ♂ mundo dd	19	24	18	10	1553
☽ ad Parallelum ♄ mundo dc.	22	14	11	8	1556
☽ ad Parallelum ☉ in Zodiaco	16	26	15	10	1560
☽ ad Parallelum ♂ mundo dc.	29	1	18	5	1562
☽ ad Parallelum ♃ in Zodiaco	10	56	30	4	1564
☽ ad Corpus ♄	34	14	33	8	1568

And altho these are sufficient to kill in any Nativity, yet you may observe in the Revolution from that year, *i.e. May* 14. 1559. that *Saturn* was in *Conjunction* with the *Sun*, *Mars* in direct *Opposition* to the *Moon's* Radical place, and *Jupiter* in *Square* to it; and to add to all, the *Moon* was in *Virgo*, and there separating from the *Square* of the *Sun* and *Saturn*, and going to the *Square* of *Mars*, and her own Radical place, and *Saturn* in the end of *Taurus* in the same Parallel of Declination with them all in the *Radix*, and the *Sun* not far from the *Opposition* of *Mars* applying. I say, these considered with the Directions, are *in modo naturali*, more than probably able to give Death.

But perhaps it may be asked, Why a violent Death? And why by the hand of Justice? *First*, The Direction falls in *Cancer*, and there too where the Parallels of the *Sun*, *Moon*, *Saturn*, *Mars*, and *Jupiter*, do all Center, and in the Terms of *Mercury* also; the *Sun* and *Moon* are with violent fixed Stars; and the *Moon* at Birth afflicted by the Parallels of the *Sun*, and the Infortunes, who are likewise Promittors in Death. And these very Rules you may (if you please) find drawn out for your use, by *Ptolomy*, in that Chapter, where he discourseth about natural and violent Deaths; as in these words, *Erunt autem mortes violentæ, & insignes, quando aut ambo Malifioi Dominantur loco Interfectori, sive Conjuncti, seu ex quadrato se aspicientes aut oppositi secundum Longitudinem*, &c. Now, it is your work to inquire how they govern in the Anaretick Point, and how they behold one another. And I dare assure you, it is worth your while, if you are a Lover of Astrology.

Secondly,

Secondly, It is as plain by the hand of Justice too; if you will observe *Ptolomy*'s Rules, which in these very words he expresseth it. *Et cum Jupiter adspicit martem adflictus, erunt neces Insigniores ex Judiciis aut ira ducum aut Regum.* And now examine the Figure, and see whether *Jupiter* is not afflicted, and whether he doth not behold *Mars*, or not; and lastly, whether his Rays are not intermixed with the Maleficks in the Cause of Death; and when you have done that, read the Paragraph that next follows, which I quoted before.

These things, I confess, are out of the common Road, and for that Reason I expect to be censured for an Innovator; but God be thanked, there are no Penal Laws in the Case. I expect also to be censured for a Heretick, for you know that the greater Number are always in the right; but right or wrong they will be so. And therefore, if I should happen in this my humble offer to the World, to be out of the way, or misled by an Opinion without Authority, that *J. G.* or some other, as Great, Good, and Charitable, as himself, would do me and all Mankind the service, to put me into the right way, and pick out those Nativities that our Enemies have mocked at, give substantial Reasons for their Deaths, &c. such Reasons as may be all of a piece, and not only serve once and no more, but in all others where the like Positions happen, for I intend mine shall be such. And the sooner they take this course, the sooner they will stop my Pen; for I intend to call most of their Authors to the Bar, and see what Defence they can make for thrusting so many Errors upon us, and deluding the People from the Truth, which hath been a Trade too long used. But before I conclude this Nativity, give me leave for a word or two more.

What I have here done, is by the Figure of the estimate Time, without any Correction, and the Directions agree very well; nay, to a Miracle; but if it were to be corrected, and the Figure set to the true Time, which would be about 10 minutes sooner than the time here used, then should we have all the Directions fall exact; as the *Sun ad par Mars mundo dd.* the *Moon ad par Saturn mundo Mot. Con:* and with these the Midheaven to the *Trine* of *Venus* for his Marriage at almost Twenty four years of Age, with divers other things that might be observed; but I will leave that to the ingenious Reader to exercise his Thoughts on, when he thinks it convenient.

The next I shall consider, is that of *Lewis* King of *Bohemia* and *Hungary*, which I perceive *Heminga* hath taken from *Leovitius*, and printed

printed that very Figure, which he makes to be half an hour before Noon; and for that Reason, *Heminga* says, it cannot be true; because the Chronicles of his Life say he was born at Noon; but that Alteration I could have excused, had they with it rendred a good and sufficient Reason for his Death; but that on the one side, and the Objection on the other, are much alike; neither of them becoming such Learned Men as they two were, for *Leovitius* [as says *Heminga*] tells us, it was the *Moon* to the *Square* of *Mars* that kill'd him. A very unlikely story.

The History of him is thus; he was born the 30th of *June* at Noon, in the year 1506. and in the Month of *August*, in the year 1526. he was put to Flight in a Battel against the *Turks*, and by the weight of his Armour, passing a River, he was drowned; but others say, That his Horse threw him [in the Flight] in a wet, muddy Place, where he was suffocated; and this when he was but Twenty Years and a Month old. *Comminiscetur* [says *Heminga*] *Astrologus accidentis hujus Causam, Directionem Corporis Lunaris ad sinistrum quadratum Martis.* But if any Astrologer should imagine such a Cause of this Accident, in my Opinion he would shew himself but a very weak man in his Profession, because the *Moon* is not Giver of Life, neither did that Direction kill in those two preceding Genitures of Sir *Theodore Mayerne*, and Mr. *Hobbs*; yet I will not disown, but that this Direction of the *Moon* to the *Square* of *Mars*, might add to the Violence of the other, but in no wise kill without them.

As to the time of his Birth, which *Heminga* lays so much stress on, and quarrels because it was not kept to exactly, tho he himself doth not assert the time to be exactly at Noon, but useth these words, *Sub Meridiem*, about Noon; I hope then, if I make a little Alteration from the exact time of Twelve, I may be pardoned by the Candid, if not by the Sceptical Readers; and I assure you, whoever keeps so near to his estimate Time as I do here, shall never be blamed by me, for I have alter'd the Figure but 12 minutes from Noon, the Time he asserts; and do believe I can give a better Account of his Death, then the *Moon* to the *Square* of *Mars*, which *Heminga* smiles at; and well he might. The Figure follows.

R. 113. O. A.

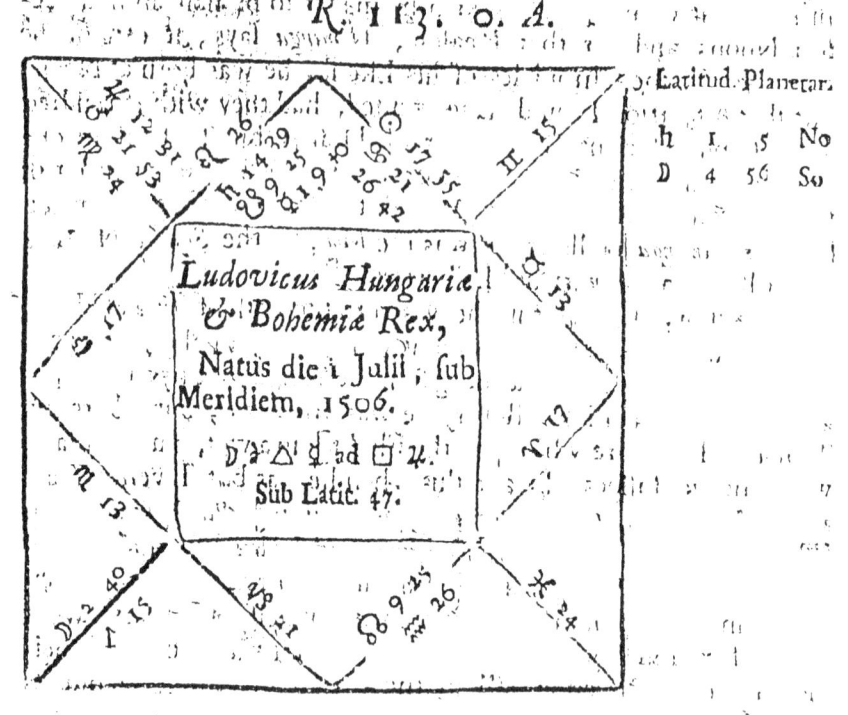

Ludovicus Hungariæ & Bohemiæ Rex,
Natus die 1 Julii, sub
Meridiem, 1506.

☽ △ ☿ ad □ ♃.
Sub Latit: 47.

	Latitud. Planetar.
♄	1. 5 No
☽	4. 56 So

I have given you the Planets places according to *Heminga* in all, except *Saturn* and the *Sun*, which are wrought from the *Caroline Tables*; and I do really believe, if the Estimate were true in the general, this of the correct Time is very exact; and this the rather, because the Directions are so naturally proper to give Death by such means and ways, as he died.

The *Sun* is certainly *Hileg*, being so near the Cusp of the 10th House, and *Saturn* is *Anareta*, tho' he is not Lord of the 8th House, but perhaps you will say of one as bad, that is, the 4th; and indeed, you may believe it if you please, it being the common Opinion now in practice. And he died on the *Sun* to the Mundane Parallel of *Saturn dd.* with four others, as you may see.

	D	M	Y	M. A.C.
☽ ad Quadratum ♂ sine Latitudine	20	2	19	10 15 26
☉ ad Parallelum ♄ Mundo dd	20	27	20	3 15 26
☽ ad Quadratum ♂ Zodiaco cum Latitudine	21	52	21	8 15 28
☉ ad Parallelum ♄ in mundo ic.	22	24	22	3 15 28
☉ ad Parallelum ♄ in Zodiaco	24	16	24	1 15 30
☉ ad Corpus ♄	27	38	27	6 15 34

Thus

Opus Reformatum.

Thus you see the *Sun* was directed to the Parallel of *Saturn* by direct Direction at Twenty years of Age; and at the same time by the Convers Motion, the *Sun* was also put into the Parallel of him *&c.* and these attended with two other violent Directions to the *Sun* likewise, and all in *Cancer*, a Watery-sign, and no Benefick Beams to assist and support Life. Now, what think you? Are not these Directions of *Saturn* to the *Sun* more proper to kill, than that of the *Moon* to the *Square* of *Mars* under the Earth? Which I dare undertake to prove, never yet kill'd any man since the Art of Astrology was known, but often serves for a Sham, when nothing else is to be found to do it. Now, if any Gentleman, *&c.* shall think these Directions assigned in this Case, either to be no Directions, or not to have the force that I allow them, [for such I expect to meet with] that they will be pleased to give any other Reasons, that seems to them more proper than these, and also print them, as I do, for the benefit of our Brethren; and not only in these, but to take others already printed, or some of their own collecting, and be so kind also to print the estimate Time of each of their own, and by that means they will excite others to try their Skill, and make Observations.

But pray observe, Altho *Venus* is Lady of the Eigthh House, that pernicious place; yet we do not find, that the Ascendant to her Square had power to kill, nor do we find the *Sun* in *Square* to the Radical Horoscope could do it either; and tho the *Square* of *Mercury* in the Zodiack came up then to the Ascendant, yet it added nothing to the time nor manner of his Death.

The next is the Nativity of *Gemma Frisius*, which is inserted by *Heminga*, [from whom I take it] with a great many pretty Comments, Objections, and Observations thereon; the chiefest of which I will Answer, and make use of the Planets places as he hath printed them.

This Native, *Gemma Frisius*, was born the 8th of *December*; at 10 h. 53 m. P. M. 1508. he was a Learned, Ingenious Man, and both an able Physicain and Mathematician; well skilled in Musick, and divers other curious Studies; but in the year 1555. May 25. he died of the *Stone*, being then compleatly Forty six years and Five months old. The Elevation of his place of Birth, *Heminga* hath not told us; but I judg by the setting of the Figure, is is about 54 degrees, or near it; and so I have set the following Scheme.

R. 70.

Opus Reformatum.

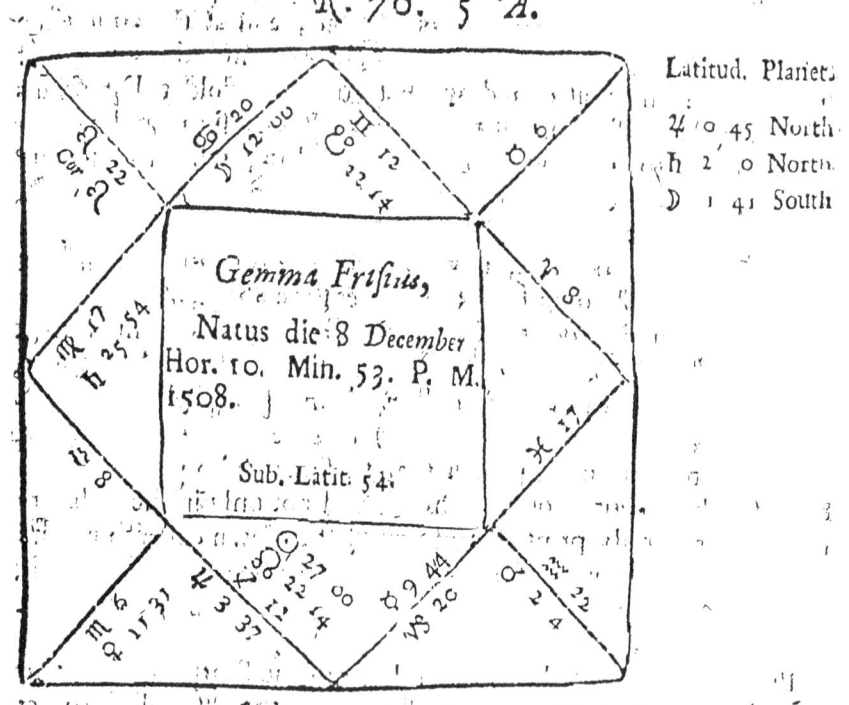

R. 70. 5 A.

Latitud.	Planet.
♃ 0 45	North
♄ 2 0	North
☽ 1 41	South

Gemma Frisius,
Natus die 8 December
Hor. 10. Min. 53. P. M.
1508.

Sub. Latit. 54.

    I have ventured to alter the Figure about 3 degrees in the Midheaven, and two in the Ascendant, which amounts to about 15 minutes in time, sooner than *Heminga*'s Figure was, which is no great cause of difference in the method *Heminga* used; and for his Death, he could find nothing that he thought the Astrologers would alledg, but the *Moon* to the *Lyons Heart*, which he doth a little laugh at, and so do I; but with this difference, I will tell you the reason, why I do very little esteem that Direction, and he doth not: The *Moon* passeth that Star with 4 degrees and 30 minutes of *South-Latitude*; and the Star it self hath half a degree of *North*, so that their distance is at least 5 degrees when she passeth the Star, and for that reason can have very little Effect in point of Death; and indeed that Direction came up Five years before his Death, as you may see by the following Table. The *Moon* is here certainly *Hileg*, or Giver of Life, and was directed to the Parallel of the *Sun in Mundo*, Direct and Convers at the Time of Death, the *Moon* having before passed the *Lyons Heart*, and Parallel of *Mars in Mundo motu rapto.*

☽ ad

Opus Reformatum.

	D.	M.	Y.	M.	A.	C.
☽ ad Cor Leonis	45	15	41	8		1550
☽ ad Parallelum ☉ mundo Asc.	49	5	45	6		1553
☽ ad △ ☉ in Zodiaco	49	37	46	0		1554
☽ ad Parallelum ☉ mundo dd	50	5	46	5		1555
Ascendens ad □ ♂	53	26	49	9		1557
☽ ad Parallelum ♄ Zodiaco Sequit						

These Directions I judge more proper and natural to give Death, than the *Lyons Heart*; but as to its Quality and Morbifick Cause, that takes its Origination from other Principles, as well as Directions, as the *Moon* in *Leo* in *Opposition* to the *Sun*, and both in *Square* to *Saturn*, in an Earthly Sign in the Ascendant. But, perhaps I may be questioned, why I bring the Direction of the *Moon* to the *Trine* of the *Sun*, as an Argument of Death, which was ever judged otherways. I do not say, The *Moon* to the *Trine* of the *Sun* kills; but I do affirm, That to be a Concurrent Cause of Death; and is so far from saving, that it strengthens the Violence of the other Directions, as I can shew in divers Examples by me, in observed and carefully taken Nativities. But besides, that *Trine* was indeed a *Sesquiquadrate*, if you consider it well, and hath naturally Violence with it. But I lay no stress thereon to inforce the Argument of Death.

But *Heminga* is pleased to ask two Learned Questions: The first is, why the *Moon ad oppositum Martis*, did not kill? And 2*dly*, Why the *Sun* afterward to the Body of *Mars* did not kill? 'Tis strange, a man of his Reading in that undertaking should ask two such sorry, silly Questions. The first could not kill according to *Ptolomy*'s Rule in that Case; because the *Trine* of *Jupiter* followed within a degree and a half; nay, it could scarce give any Sickness. Nor the latter could not kill, because the *Sun* was not giver of Life, it might give Trouble and Sickness, but by no means Death. With these and some more idle Objections doth *Heminga* shew the Excellence of his Parts in bantring an Art and Study that he never understood; and after he hath magnified the non-effect of these two Directions [because the Native did not dye upon them] he gravely tells us, the whole Art is a Lye and Deceit; his words are these, *Arguit itaque seipsam hæc Doctrina falsitatis & mendacii*. But indeed it was his Ignorance, not the Art that was accusable.

Another Nativity I have taken from *Heminga*, which to me seems the most plain of any that ever I have judged or seen, and yet he raiseth many Doubts and Objections, that do indeed either shew him

Y

Opus Reformatum,

to be very Capricious, or else very Ignorant in Astrology; yet some of his Objections are rational enough; as you shall see anon. I have chosen this Geniture, because he was *Heminga's* Acquaintance and Neighbour in *Westfriesland*, and Governour of *Lewardin*, for which reason, I suppose the estimate Time was true, and the Direction of the Ascendant to the *Opposition* of *Mars* was also true for his Death; and yet many Doubts remain, that *Heminga* hath not offered at. The Figure is as followeth, with the Planets places as he hath given them; but I have altered the Time 24 minutes later than his; and yet we both agree upon the same Direction for Death; we only differ in our Measure of Time, which is the cause of our difference in the Figure.

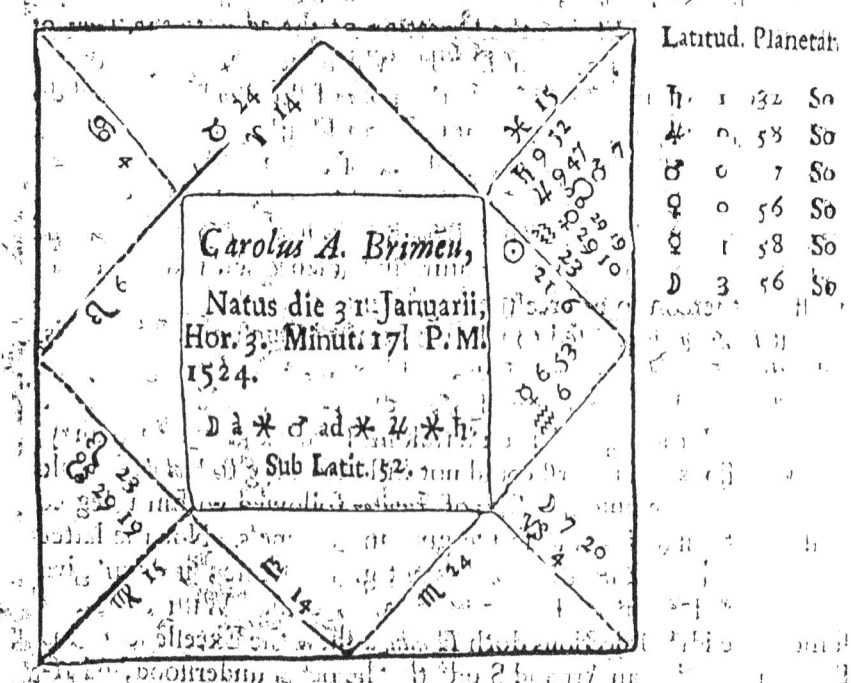

Latitud. Planetar.

♄	1	32	So
♃	0	58	So
♂	0	7	So
♀	0	56	So
☿	1	58	So
☽	3	56	So

Carolus A. Brimeu,
Natus die 31 Januarii,
Hor. 3. Minut. 17 P.M.
1524.
☽ à ✶ ♂ ad ✶ ♃ ✶ ♄
Sub Latit. 52.

This Gentleman died of an *Apoplexy* on the 7th of *January* 1572, being then almost Forty eight years of Age. Having drunk plentifully the Night before, which was *Twelfday*, and the Direction which gave it, was the Ascendant to the *Opposition* of *Mars*, Ark 44 d. 25 m. which turned into Time, gives Forty seven years, and about Eleven months. And tho *Heminga* allows this Direction, yet he asketh, why he did not dye on the Ascendant to the *Opposition* of the *Sun*, and after that, to the *Dragon's Taile?* And why the *Sun* in his younger years

years to the Bodies of *Mars* and *Saturn* did not kill, *Saturn* being Lord of the 8th, and in it, which in the old way hath a mighty sway. I will give you an Answer to these things, before we leave them. 1st, The Ascendant to the *Opposition* of the *Sun* could not kill, because the *Opposition* of *Venus* did so soon succeed it; and for the *Dragoons Taile*, I know no reason why that should kill, nor cannot be perswaded that it ever kill'd any one yet, or ever will, for it is an empty void place in the Heavens, being but the Intersections of two Imaginary Circles, and can have no Influence of its own, because it is no body, nor is it visible, and therefore very improbable to give any Effect, especially Death. And for the *Sun* to the Body of *Mars* and *Saturn*, could not kill, because the *Sun* is not Giver of Life; but I judge the first of those might give the *Small-pox*; and the second, some little kind of Illness, but neither of them any thing very Remarkable or Eminent, as to the Native's Health.

But it might be very rationally asked, why the Ascendant to the *Opposition* of *Mars* should give an *Apoplexy*? Which *Heminga* takes no notice of in his Objections, and is far more proper to be asked in my Opinion, than all those things that he enquires after. In this Case we are to take the Time of Death from *Mars* and his Direction, but not the Quality of it; for that is taken from the other Directions that do operate with, and are next succeeding in directional Motion to the Giver of Life. And in this Case, *Jupiter* doth govern the place of Death, both by Dignity and Presence; and for that reason specificates it, who you find in *Conjunction* with *Saturn*, and in *Sextile* to the *Moon*; and the *Moon* in the Terms of *Jupiter*; and both *Mars*, *Jupiter*, and *Saturn* in the Terms of *Venus*, all which add to the Diseases of Redundance, and Repletion of Humours; and besides, *Jupiter* doth naturally give an *Apoplexy*, and Diseases of the Stomack, by such a Position as this is; as you may see, if you consider that Chapter in *Ptolomy's De Genere Mortis*. But by the common and general Opinion of Directions, this of *Mars* should rather have given a *Flux* of the Bowels, a *Fever*, or some Disease that is attended with Inflamation or Heat, continual or intermitting.

2dly, If the Eighth House is the House of Death, and that every Planet according to his Dominion must do his Office; why did not the Ascendant to the *Opposition* of *Venus* kill, she being afflicted, and assisted by the Beams of the *Sun* and *Mars*, and Lady of the so-fam'd fatal Fourth House.

3dly, These things considered, may help to inform their understanding better, who believe that the *Sun* ought to be always Giver of Life; but especially when he is above the Earth in any part of Heaven; when they observe, that the *Sun* to the Body of *Mars*, and Body of *Jupiter* and *Saturn*, did not kill; but the Ascendant to those Rays did do it, and that because it was *Hileg*, or Giver of Life.

Lastly, That the *Sun* should not kill, is plain from the old Notion, he being Lord of the Ascendant, and will by no means hurt his own. A most absurd Opinion! but, why *Mars* by that Rule should kill, I wonder, he being Lord of no ill House; and yet he turns Murderer; which must certainly proceed from his falling into bad Company there; he happening to associate himself with the Lords of the Eighth, and by that means grew as barbarous as they. *Ut socius sic homo.*

Thus I have given you four Nativities out of *Heninga*, that he brings to affront and ridicule Astrology with, which you see are not guilty of what he alledgeth, nor is Astrology blamable in those things he obtrudes upon the World. He was, I confess, a very Learned Man, and indeed a far better Gramarian than an Astrologer; for in this he was Master of no more than what was common to all. I could, I confess, have given you divers Nativities more of his in the same Treatise; but I am fearful of medling with bad Tools; divers of his Nativities there mentioned, being to my knowledge false, and yet serves him to make a noise about that which he was but little acquainted with, as to its Truth and Operation. He tells us, *Henry* VIII. was born the 28th of *June*; and yet *Stow* says, he was born the 22d of that Month. *Mary*, Queen of *England* [he says] was born the 8th of *September*, *Anno* 1515. but *Stow* tells us, it was the 11th of *February*, 1516. and *J. G.* asserts it to be the 17th of *February*, *eodem Anno*. And tho he is right in the day of Queen *Elizabeth*'s Birth; yet he is out in the Time, if *Stow* may be believed. From whence I conclude, that most of his far-fetch'd Nativities are false; if so, then it is no wonder, that they failed his expectation of Effects; and pray, who can believe his mighty Objections raised from false Nativities? Or, what can be expected besides wrangling, where falshood is made the Foundation? And so I take my leave of him.

I have this year 1692, seen a Nativity printed in an Almanack, and brought as a proof of a particular Direction there alledged

Opus Reformatum. 165

to give the *Small-pox* at almoſt Five years of Age; and *all the Pretenders to Aſtrology in this Nation, are challenged* to produce any other Direction, proper to give that Sickneſs at that Age, beſides the Earth directed to the Heliocentrick place of *Mars*. And I being one of thoſe Pretenders, think my ſelf concerned to offer ſomething of my thoughts in that Matter, and humbly caſt in my Mite to that Treaſury of Truth, that this curious new Invention is thought to increaſe. It is without doubt a thing moſt ingenious, and worthy of every curious man's Remark and Notice; and if it will hold in all Nativities to the end and purpoſe it is here made uſe of, it will be of admirable Service in the further diſcovery of Celeſtial Truths, and give its Inventor that Repute, which the Worm of Time ſhall never deface, nor the endeavour of Enemies deſtroy, but raiſe to his Fame an Everlaſting Pillar of Honour, that all who come after ſhall pay a Gratitude to his Memory. The Figure follows, ſet according to my way, and his time.

R. 326. 41. A.

	Latitud.	Planet. &c.
♄	1 12 No	17 55
♃	1 00 No	18 12
♂	2 29 No	7 23
♀	1 45 No	10 14
☿	6 23 No	1 57
☽	4 22 So	18 9
☉	0 00	4 30

P. P.
Nata die 23 Martii,
Hor. 9. Mane, 1683.
☽ △ ✶ ☉ ✶ ♃ ad ✶ ♄.
Sub. Latit. *Lond.*

The

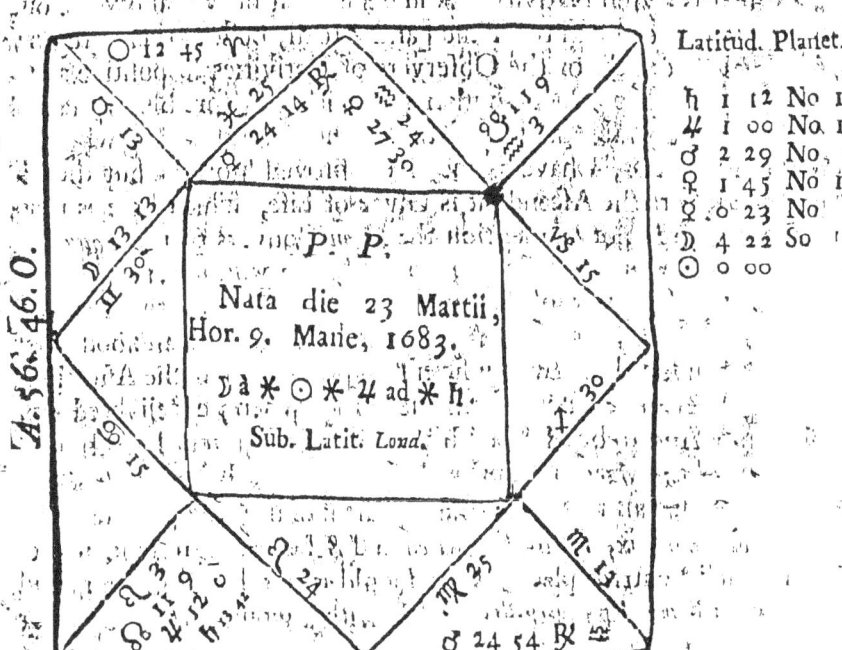

The Disease you have heard, was the *Small-pox* at Four years and Ten months old; and the Direction that gave that Disease [*ut dicit*] was the Earth to the Heliocentrick place of *Mars*; and he is *morally sure*, no man can give, nor assign any other Direction proper to that Case, at that time to operate; which if true, then that must be allow'd to be the Cause of it, which will better appear upon the further enquiry into the matter it self.

I wonder, That a Man of his vast Parts and Abilities, should so confidently affirm, That there was no other Direction to be found at that time suitable to the Effect, but the Earth to the Heliocentrick place of *Mars*. When any man that understands the directional Motion, may almost by Inspection see, that the *Sun* to the Zodiacal Parallel of *Mars* comes up at the same time, whose Ark is 4 d. 14 m. and gives in time Four years and Eight months; and this by his own Figure, not altering it a minute. And therefore I suppose, when *Mars* came to the place of Driection about the middle of *January*, 1683. then the Fermentaion began that gave the Disease. Now, this is no false, but a real Motion, and a Direction of that force, that it often times kills; but in this case, I judg it could not, because it is a vital Nativity. And besides, if he will allow me but 5 minutes of error in the Time [and I really believe there are very few Dials so exact, or the Observers of Nativities so positive as to deny it] I will produce another Direction [as forcible as this is] of *Mars* to the Ascendant, and that is the *Sesquiquadrate*, which in divers Nativities, I have by me, hath proved Mortal, but then it must be where the Ascendant is Giver of Life, which here is not; and therefore, not to mention the *Moon* Convers to the *Square* of *Saturn in Mundo*, the Ascendant to the *Square* of *Venus*; the *Moon* to the Zodiacal Square of *Mercury cum Latitudine*; to the Zodiacal Square of *Mercury sine Latitudine*, &c. which came up all about that time. I judge these two sufficient to prove, That the Assertion, or the Assertor departed from the Truth when he delivered that Notion. And to be plain with you, It was that very Direction of the *Sun ad par. Mars*, that proved the *Atropos* to King *Charles* II.

But besides all this, Why should the Earth to the place of *Mars* give the *Small-pox*, seeing the *Moon* and *Saturn* are so near in Aspect to his Heliocentrick place? Why should it not have been a putrid continual *Fever, Epileptick-fits*, a *Fall*, with a wound attending it, or such like, rather than that it was?

Again,

Again, Why should not the *Sun* directed to the Heliocentrick Opposition of *Mars*, be every way as effectual as the Earth to the Body of *Mars* [for the Directions of each are equal in every thing, only opposite Points] which if it be, then he had two Directions at the same time; which are doubtless of more force than one. Now, if these things are allowed, then we must direct to the Heliocentrick Sextiles, Squares, and Trines of all the Planets; to do which, we must have a new Theory of Directions; which would be of excellent use to those that are studious in that way; and I am sure it would puzzle me untowardly to find a way to direct the *Sun*, *Ascendant*, and *Midheaven*, to the Heliocentrick Bodies and Squares of some, or all the Planets, and at the same time reconcile it to my Reason and Senses; for if I should direct the Midheaven to the Body of *Mars* Heliocentrical and Geocentrical, and believe it too, I must give my Eye the lye, because I see it passeth the Meridian point but once. And to believe the other, is next to *Transubstantiation*; yet I believe, if any man would go into the *Sun* with his Telescope at his Back, I doubt not, but he might see *Mars* in 17 degrees of *Libra*, when we see him in 25 degrees of the same Sign, &c. And I am sure it will require a larger Faith than mine, to believe [in this Figure for Example] that the Heliocentrick place of *Venus* in *Scorpio* should any ways affect, or be taken notice of by us Geocentrick Bodies. Nor can it concern us, than as we being Subjects of *England*, are obliged to keep the Laws of *Constantinople*; for tho there are such Laws, yet they have no force upon us in *England*, nor take no notice of us.

Many more things might be alledged in this Case, to inform the Ignorant World about this Mystery, as when it is *Hileg*, and what Parts of Heaven are most proper for that Power and Dominion; Let us suppose the *Moon* in the Tenth, the *Sun* in the Ascendant, then the Earth must be in the Seventh. Now the Query is, which of these three must be allowed to be Giver of Life, seeing they are all in Aphetical places. Again, how we shall know when the Directions of the Earth have power to kill, and when not; and whether the Earth to the Heliocentrick place of *Mars* doth always give a *Fever*, or the *Small-pox*. For if it hath not always an adequate Effect, or Rules laid down to shew when it will, and when it will not do it, I am sure no Man of reason will believe that, nor many other things in Astrology.

Lastly,

Lastly, The Earth directed to any Bodies or Aspects, doth destroy the Principles of directional Motion, that is, it renders that Motion useless, by which all Directions are made, and therefore must set up a new one of its own; and whosoever asserts the Directions of the Earth distinct from those of the *Sun* in opposite points, I am certain they understand not the Motion by which all Directions are made; for they are all made by one Motion, both Direct and Convers. And what I have else to say in this Case, I shall reserve till the next time I see occasion to use it.

Perhaps this may give some People a disgust, and provoke them to an ill Opinion of our self, and think we have done this out of a capricious Humour; but we do assure them it is no such thing, and that it was only two things engaged our Thoughts in this matter. *First*, The Challenge, we our self being one of the Number there included, and have done this purely in Vindication of our self; leaving all other Pretenders to act or say what they think convenient, or find themselves able to do in the Vindication of their selves. *Secondly*, Our respect to Truth, concerning which we have no mean thought, but a very mean and low Opinion of our own Parts and Abilities; and therefore desire humbly to lay our poor weak Endeavours before every ingenious Artist, desiring our self may be candidly read and understood, and we are morally sure, that no ingenious Man will deny his Concession to this our Request. So wishing all the true Sons of Science, a success answerable to their Endeavours and Wishes, We shall take our leave of them at this time.

Omnis ab assiduo nimirum ars nascitur usu.

Palinge, *Lib.* 5.

FINIS.